Just Briefs

Aspen Coursebook Series

Just Briefs

Preparing for Practice

Fourth Edition

Laurel Currie Oates
Professor of Law
Seattle University School of Law

Anne Enquist
Professor Emeritus
Seattle University School of Law

Jeremy Francis
Clinical Professor of Law
Writing Specialist
Michigan State University College of Law

Wolters Kluwer

Published by Wolters Kluwer in New York.

Wolters Kluwer Legal & Regulatory U.S. serves customers worldwide with CCH, Aspen Publishers, and Kluwer Law International products. (www.WKLegaledu.com)

Cover image: iStock.com/ftwitty.

To contact Customer Service, e-mail customer.service@wolterskluwer.com, call 1-800-234-1660, fax 1-800-901-9075, or mail correspondence to:

Wolters Kluwer
Attn: Order Department
PO Box 990
Frederick, MD 21705

Printed in the United States of America.

1 2 3 4 5 6 7 8 9 0

ISBN 978-1-5438-1563-4

Library of Congress Cataloging-in-Publication Data

Names: Oates, Laurel Currie, 1951- author. | Enquist, Anne, 1950- author. |
    Francis, Jeremy (Law teacher) author.
Title: Just briefs : preparing for practice / Laurel Currie Oates,
    Professor of Law, Seattle University School of Law; Anne Enquist,
    Professor Emeritus, Seattle University School of Law; Jeremy Francis,
    Associate Clinical Professor of Law, Writing Specialist, Michigan State
    University College of Law.
Description: Fourth edition. | New York : Wolters Kluwer, [2021] | Series:
    Aspen coursebook series | Includes bibliographical references and index.
    | Summary: "Introductory book on writing briefs"— Provided by publisher.
Identifiers: LCCN 2020016923 (print) | LCCN 2020016924 (ebook) | ISBN
    9781543815634 (paperback) | ISBN 9781543821062 (ebook)
Subjects: LCSH: Legal briefs—United States.
Classification: LCC KF251 .O18 2021 (print) | LCC KF251 (ebook) | DDC
    347.73/8—dc23
LC record available at https://lccn.loc.gov/2020016923
LC ebook record available at https://lccn.loc.gov/2020016924

To my daughter, Julia Fishler, and her family, Michael, Milla, and Braxton Fishler; to my son, Michael Oates, and to his family, Emily and Logan Oates; and to my partner, Tom Deal. Thank you for everything.

Laurel Currie Oates

To my family, Steve, Matt, Mary, Natalie, Zach, Jeff, Ilana, Theo, and Sophia Anne, for their love and support.

Anne Enquist

To my family, Andrea, Leighton, and Alex Francis. Your love and support mean the world to me.

Jeremy Francis

Summary of Contents

Contents.. xi
Preface... xix
Acknowledgments.. xxi

Part I   The Art (and Science) of Advocacy................................. 1
Chapter 1   Introduction to Rhetoric and Bias............................... 3

Part II   Motion Briefs.. 15
Chapter 2   Motion Briefs.. 17
Chapter 3   Beginning the Motion Brief: Theory of the Case, Caption,
             and Preliminary Statement.................................... 21
Chapter 4   Statement of Facts... 25
Chapter 5   Issue Statements and Ordering the Issues and
             Arguments.. 39
Chapter 6   Argumentative Headings and the Arguments.................... 47
Chapter 7   Finishing the Motion Brief: The Prayer for Relief and
             Signing the Brief... 71
Chapter 8   Sample Briefs... 73

Part III   Appellate Briefs... 119
Chapter 9   Practicing Before an Appellate Court......................... 121
Chapter 10   Audience, Purpose, and Conventions.......................... 127
Chapter 11   First Steps: Getting the Case and Preparing to Write the
             Brief.. 135
Chapter 12   Planning the Brief.. 147
Chapter 13   Beginning the Appellate Brief: The Cover, Tables,
             Jurisdictional Statement, and the Statement of Issues...... 157
Chapter 14   Statement of the Case.. 167
Chapter 15   Drafting the Summary of the Argument and
             Argumentative Headings...................................... 189
Chapter 16   Drafting the Arguments....................................... 201
Chapter 17   Finishing the Appellate Brief: Drafting the Final Sections
             and Revising, Editing, and Proofreading..................... 231
Chapter 18   Sample Briefs... 235

Part IV   Oral Advocacy.. 285
Chapter 19   Preparing and Presenting an Effective Oral Argument..... 287

Glossary of Terms... 305
Index... 313

Contents

Preface.. xix
Acknowledgments.. xxi

Part I   The Art (and Science) of Advocacy.......................... 1

Chapter 1   Introduction to Rhetoric and Bias....................... 3

§1.1   Rhetoric.. 3
    §1.1.1   The Greeks (425 BCE to 225 BCE)....................... 4
        a.   Syllogism...................................... 5
        b.   Enthymeme..................................... 5
        c.   Antithesis..................................... 5
        d.   Anadiplosis.................................... 6
        e.   Anaphora....................................... 6
        f.   Antistrophe.................................... 6
    §1.1.2   The Romans (35 CE to 410 CE)......................... 7
    §1.1.3   The Middle Ages (426 CE to 1320 CE).................. 7
    §1.1.4   The Renaissance (1426 CE to 1623 CE)................ 8
§1.2   Using Rhetoric Today.. 8
    §1.2.1   Storytelling/Narrative............................. 8
    §1.2.2   Priming.. 9
    §1.2.3   Negativity Bias.................................... 9
    §1.2.4   Confirmation Bias.................................. 10
    §1.2.5   Racial and Gender Bias............................. 11
§1.3   Ethics of Using Implicit Biases to Support Your Position.......... 12

Part II   Motion Briefs... 15

Chapter 2   Motion Briefs.. 17

§2.1   Audience.. 17
§2.2   Purpose... 18
§2.3   Conventions.. 18
§2.4   *State v. Patterson*.. 18

Chapter 3   Beginning the Motion Brief: Theory of the Case, Caption, and Preliminary Statement.......................... 21

§3.1   Theory of the Case... 21
§3.2   The Caption.. 23
§3.3   Introductory Paragraph/Preliminary Statement............. 23

Chapter 4   Statement of Facts.. 25

§4.1   Select the Facts.. 26
    §4.1.1   Background Facts.. 26
    §4.1.2   Legally Significant Facts...................................... 26
    §4.1.3   Emotionally Significant Facts............................... 26
§4.2   Select an Organizational Scheme...................................... 27
§4.3   Present the Facts in a Light Favorable to Your Client............. 27
    §4.3.1   Prime the Judge to Rule in Your Client's Favor........ 28
    §4.3.2   Create a Favorable Context.................................. 28
    §4.3.3   Tell the Story from the Client's Point of View.......... 29
    §4.3.4   Emphasize the Facts That Support Your Theory of the
             Case, and De-emphasize Those That Do Not........... 30
             a.   Airtime.. 30
             b.   Detail.. 31
             c.   Positions of Emphasis................................ 32
             d.   Sentence Length....................................... 33
             e.   Active and Passive Voice............................. 34
             f.   Dependent and Main Clauses....................... 34
    §4.3.5   Select Words Both for Their Denotation and Their
             Connotation.. 35
§4.4   Checklist for Critiquing the Statement of Facts.................... 36

**Chapter 5   Issue Statements and Ordering the Issues and
           Arguments**.. 39

§5.1   Issue Statements... 39
    §5.1.1   Select the Lens... 39
    §5.1.2   Select a Format.. 40
    §5.1.3   Make Your Issue Statement Subtly Persuasive......... 41
    §5.1.4   Checklist for Critiquing the Issue Statement........... 43
§5.2   Ordering the Issues and Arguments.................................... 44
    §5.2.1   Present the Issues and Arguments in a Logical
             Order.. 44
    §5.2.2   Decide Which Issues and Arguments Should Be
             Presented First.. 45

Chapter 6   Argumentative Headings and the Arguments................ 47

§6.1   Argumentative Headings... 47
    §6.1.1   Use Your Argumentative Headings to Define the
             Structure of the Argument.................................... 47
    §6.1.2   Use Your Argumentative Headings to Persuade....... 49
    §6.1.3   Make Your Headings Readable............................. 50
    §6.1.4   Follow the Conventions: Number, Placement, and
             Typefaces.. 51
§6.2   Checklist for Critiquing the Argumentative Headings............. 52
§6.3   The Arguments... 53

§6.3.1   Identify Your Assertions and Your Support for Those
Assertions.. 54
a.   Setting Out Your Assertion........................... 54
b.   Supporting Your Assertion........................... 54
§6.3.2   Select an Organizational Scheme........................ 56
§6.3.3   Present the Rules in the Light Most Favorable to Your
Client... 60
§6.3.4   Present the Cases in the Light Most Favorable to Your
Client... 64
§6.3.5   Present the Arguments in the Light Most Favorable to
Your Client... 66
a.   Present Your Own Arguments First.................. 66
b.   Give the Most Airtime to Your Own Arguments... 67
c.   Use Language That Strengthens Your Arguments
and Undermines the Other Side's Arguments.... 68
d.   Use the Same Persuasive Techniques You Used
in Setting Out the Facts, Issues, Rules, and
Analogous Cases..................................... 68
§6.4   Checklist for Critiquing the Argument................................. 69

**Chapter 7   Finishing the Motion Brief: The Prayer for Relief and
Signing the Brief**.. 71

§7.1   The Prayer for Relief... 71
§7.2   Signing the Brief... 72

Chapter 8   Sample Briefs... 73

§8.1   Briefs from the *Patterson* Case.................................. 75
§8.2   Briefs from a Civil Case Seeking Motion for Summary
Judgment... 98

Part III   Appellate Briefs.. 119

Chapter 9   Practicing Before an Appellate Court............................ 121

§9.1   Types of Appellate Review.. 122
§9.2   Time Limits for Filing the Notice of Appeal or Petition for
Discretionary Review.. 123
§9.3   The Notice of Appeal or Notice for Discretionary Review........ 123
§9.4   Scope of Review.. 124
§9.5   The Record on Appeal.. 124
§9.6   Types of Briefs.. 125

Chapter 10   Audience, Purpose, and Conventions........................... 127

§10.1   Audience.. 127
§10.2   Purpose... 128

§10.3   Conventions.. 129

Chapter 11   First Steps: Getting the Case and Preparing to Write the Brief.. 135

§11.1   Getting the Case.. 135
§11.2   Preparing to Write the Brief.................................. 138
        §11.2.1   Reviewing the Record for Error.................. 138
        §11.2.2   Selecting the Issues on Appeal.................. 139
                  a.   Was There an Error?....................... 140
                  b.   Was the Error Preserved?................. 140
                  c.   What Is the Standard of Review?........ 141
                  d.   Was the Error Harmless?................. 143
        §11.2.3   Preparing an Abstract of the Record......... 144
        §11.2.4   Preparing the Record on Appeal.............. 145
        §11.2.5   Researching the Issues on Appeal............ 146

Chapter 12   Planning the Brief................................... 147

§12.1   Analyzing the Facts and the Law............................ 147
§12.2   Developing a Theory of the Case............................ 150
        §12.2.1   Exercise: Developing a Theory of a Case...... 151
§12.3   Selecting an Organizational Scheme....................... 153
        §12.3.1   Deciding on the Number of Issues and Headings..... 153
        §12.3.2   Ordering the Issues and Arguments......... 154

Chapter 13   Beginning the Appellate Brief: The Cover, Tables, and Jurisdictional Statement, and the Statement of Issues... 157

§13.1   The Cover, Tables, and Jurisdictional Statement........ 157
        §13.1.1   Preparing the Cover............................. 157
        §13.1.2   Preparing the Table of Contents............. 157
        §13.1.3   Preparing the Table of Authorities.......... 158
        §13.1.4   Drafting the Jurisdictional Statement....... 158
§13.2   Statement of Issues Presented for Review................ 159
        §13.2.1   Drafting the Statement of Issues Presented for Review... 159
        §13.2.2   Select a Format................................. 160
        §13.2.3   Make the Issue Statement Subtly Persuasive........... 161
                  a.   State the Question So That It Suggests the Conclusion You Want the Court to Reach.......... 161
                  b.   Emphasize the Facts That Support Your Theory of the Case.................................. 163
                  c.   Emphasize or De-emphasize the Burden of Proof and Standard of Review................... 164
        §13.2.4   Make Sure the Issue Statement Is Readable............ 165

Chapter 14   Statement of the Case.. 167

§14.1   Check the Rules.. 167
§14.2   Draft the Statement of the Case... 168
§14.3   Draft the Statement of Facts.. 169
    §14.3.1   Select the Facts... 169
        a.   Legally Significant Facts.............................. 169
        b.   Emotionally Significant Facts........................ 169
        c.   Background Facts... 170
    §14.3.2   Select an Organizational Scheme.......................... 170
    §14.3.3   Present the Facts in the Light Most Favorable to the Client.. 171
        a.   Prime the Judges to Rule in Your Client's Favor... 171
        b.   Create a Favorable Context............................ 171
        c.   Tell the Story from Your Client's Point of View... 174
        d.   Emphasize Those Facts That Support Your Theory of the Case and De-emphasize Those That Do Not... 176
            1.   Airtime.. 176
            2.   Detail.. 177
            3.   Positions of Emphasis.......................... 179
            4.   Sentence and Paragraph Length.............. 181
            5.   Sentence Construction.......................... 182
            6.   Active and Passive Voice....................... 183
        e.   Choose Words Carefully............................... 184
        f.   Be Subtly Persuasive................................... 185
§14.4   Identifying Persuasive Techniques: Exercise....................... 186

Chapter 15   Drafting the Summary of the Argument and Argumentative Headings... 189

§15.1   Drafting the Summary of the Argument............................... 189
§15.2   Drafting the Argumentative Headings................................. 191
    §15.2.1   Use the Argumentative Headings to Outline the Argument for the Court....................................... 191
    §15.2.2   Use the Argumentative Headings to Persuade......... 191
        a.   Make a Positive Assertion............................. 192
        b.   Provide Support for Your Assertions................ 194
        c.   Make Sure That Your Headings Are Neither Too Specific Nor Too General................................ 195
        d.   Make Your Headings Readable........................ 196
        e.   Use the Same Persuasive Techniques You Used in Drafting the Issue Statements and Statement of Facts.. 197
    §15.2.3   Use Conventional Formats for Headings................. 198

Chapter 16   Drafting the Arguments................................... 201

§16.1   Knowing What You Need, and Want, to Argue..................... 202
§16.2   Selecting an Organizational Scheme..................................... 202
§16.3   Presenting the Rules, Descriptions of Analogous Cases, and
         Arguments in the Light Most Favorable to Your Client........... 207
         §16.3.1   Presenting the Rules... 207
         §16.3.2   Presenting the Cases.. 210
         §16.3.3   Constructing and Presenting the Arguments........... 217
         §16.3.4   Using Quotations.. 220
         §16.3.5   Responding to the Other Side's Arguments............. 222
         §16.3.6   Avoiding the Common Problem of Neglecting to
                    Make Explicit Connections................................... 225
         §16.3.7   Avoiding the Common Problem of Not Dealing with
                    Weaknesses.. 227
         §16.3.8   Avoiding the Mistake of Overlooking Good
                    Arguments.. 228

**Chapter 17   Finishing the Appellate Brief: Drafting the Final
                Sections and Revising, Editing, and Proofreading**........ 231

§17.1   Drafting the Final Sections of the Brief................................. 231
         §17.1.1   Conclusion or Prayer for Relief............................. 231
         §17.1.2   Preparing the Signature Block.............................. 232
         §17.1.3   Preparing the Appendix...................................... 232
§17.2   Revising, Editing, and Proofreading..................................... 233

Chapter 18   Sample Briefs... 235

§18.1   Appellant's Brief... 236
§18.2   Appellee's Brief.. 264

Part IV   Oral Advocacy.. 285

Chapter 19   Preparing and Presenting an Effective Oral Argument... 287

§19.1   Audience.. 287
§19.2   Purpose.. 288
§19.3   Preparing for Oral Argument.. 288
         §19.3.1   Deciding What to Argue...................................... 288
         §19.3.2   Preparing an Outline.. 289
         §19.3.3   Practicing the Argument...................................... 289
         §19.3.4   Reviewing the Facts and the Law.......................... 289
         §19.3.5   Organizing Your Materials................................... 290
                    a.   Notes or Outline... 290
                    b.   The Briefs... 290
                    c.   The Record... 290
                    d.   The Law... 290

§19.4   Courtroom Procedures and Etiquette...................................290
    §19.4.1   Seating..290
    §19.4.2   Before the Case Is Called.....................................291
    §19.4.3   Courtroom Etiquette...291
    §19.4.4   Appropriate Dress...291
§19.5   Making the Argument..291
    §19.5.1   Introductions...292
    §19.5.2   Opening...292
    §19.5.3   Statement of the Issues..293
        a.   The Moving Party...293
        b.   The Responding Party.....................................293
    §19.5.4   Summary of the Facts...293
        a.   The Moving Party...293
        b.   The Responding Party.....................................294
    §19.5.5   The Argument...294
    §19.5.6   Answering Questions...295
    §19.5.7   The Closing..296
    §19.5.8   Rebuttal..297
§19.6   Delivering the Argument..297
    §19.6.1   Breathe...297
    §19.6.2   Do Not Read Your Argument..............................297
    §19.6.3   Maintain Eye Contact...298
    §19.6.4   Do Not Slouch, Rock, or Put Your Hands in Your
            Pockets..298
    §19.6.5   Limit Your Gestures and Avoid Distracting
            Mannerisms..298
    §19.6.6   Speak So That You Can Be Easily Understood..........298
§19.7   Making Your Argument Persuasive.....................................299
§19.8   Handling the Problems...299
    §19.8.1   Counsel Has Misstated Facts or Law.....................299
    §19.8.2   You Make a Mistake...300
    §19.8.3   You Do Not Have Enough Time............................300
    §19.8.4   You Have Too Much Time.....................................300
    §19.8.5   You Do Not Know the Answer to a Question...........300
    §19.8.6   You Do Not Understand a Question.......................301
    §19.8.7   You Become Flustered or Draw a Blank.................301
    §19.8.8   You Are Asked to Concede a Point........................301
§19.9   A Final Note...302
§19.10   Checklist for Critiquing the Oral Argument..........................302

Glossary of Terms..305
Index...313

Preface

The title of this book and its double meaning might be a bit of a misnomer. The book is about "just" briefs in the sense that we intend it to remind you that your briefs to the court should work toward a just result; however, it is not a book just about briefs because it includes more than brief writing. *Just Briefs* is really a book about the larger topic of effective advocacy as it plays out in trial and appellate briefs, oral argument, and the thinking process that informs both.

"Effective advocacy" might not make a jazzy title, but we find the topic of effective advocacy tremendously engaging. Admittedly, the process of researching, analyzing, and writing a brief that is effective advocacy can be arduous and time-consuming. But it is also deeply rewarding. When lawyers write a persuasive brief or make a compelling argument, they make a difference. They protect the rights of their clients, they help enforce or change the law, and they make sure that the legal system works as it was intended to work.

Thus, as you work through the chapters in this book, keep your eye on the larger goal of becoming an effective advocate. Instead of focusing primarily on getting an A on your brief or oral argument, focus on learning to be the best advocate that you can be. Learn how to develop a theory of the case that will appeal to both the judge's head and heart, learn how to tell your client's story, and learn how to construct persuasive arguments. In addition, work on developing your writing skills. Learn how to make your points clearly, precisely, concisely, even eloquently. Finally, think about the role you need and want to play as an advocate. As you think through how zealous you want to be when representing your client, remember that your own reputation as an attorney affects your ability to persuade. Your reputation and your credibility might ultimately be your most effective tools as an advocate.

Acknowledgments

One of the pleasures of writing a derivative work is that it allows the authors to think about all of the people who have helped them along the way. In our case, the preparation of this work has reminded us of all of the people who helped us as we wrote the first through seventh editions of *The Legal Writing Handbook* and the first through fourth editions of *Just Briefs*.

We would like to begin by thanking our students and colleagues who, in the eighties, provided the inspiration and insights that led to the writing of *The Legal Writing Handbook*. We would, however, also like to thank our most recent students and colleagues whose suggestions and corrections made each edition better than the earlier one. In particular, we would like to thank Denis Stearns, who developed the problem that forms the basis of the two sample summary judgments briefs that are set out at the end of Chapter 1, and to our students Michael Oates and Rosemary East, whose briefs we used as the starting point for the sample briefs. We would also like to thank Michigan State students Elizabeth "Biz" Chirco, Glynis Gilio, and Carette-Lynn "Carlye" Reynolds for their hard work and contributions to this book. Finally, we would like to thank our law school deans who have supported us in this endeavor: Annette Clark, Dean of the Seattle University School of Law, and Lawrence Ponoroff and Melanie Jacobs, Deans of the Michigan State University College of Law.

Finally, we would like to thank the editors at Wolters Kluwer for their support and advice.

Laurel Oates
Anne Enquist
Jeremy Francis

April 2020

The Art (and Science) of Advocacy

We have all had arguments. As teenagers we argued with our parents about what we could and could not do, as college students we argued with our roommates about noise and about whose turn it was to do the dishes, and today we argue with family and friends about current events.

Having an argument is not, though, the same as making an argument. As a lawyer, it is not enough to say what you think, believe, or feel. Instead, you must set out legal arguments, and those legal arguments must be set out clearly, concisely, and persuasively.

In this book, we show you how to write two types of persuasive documents: a motion brief and an appellate brief. Much like the process of writing legal memoranda, writing a brief requires you to research, outline, draft, revise, edit, and proofread. However, writing a brief requires even more. In writing a brief, you must complete these tasks in such a way that you persuade the judge or judges to side with your client. For that reason, it is essential that you learn the rules and conventions governing the brief that you are writing and that you learn to use a range of persuasive techniques.

In this part of the book, Part I, we provide you with a short history of the study of rhetoric. Then, in Part II, we show you how to write a motion brief and, in Part III, how to write an appellate brief. In the final part, Part IV, we introduce the art of making an effective oral argument.

Introduction to Rhetoric and Bias

In this chapter we do two things. First, we set out a short history of the study of rhetoric. In doing so, we have tried to place the techniques that we describe in later chapters into a larger context. Second, we look at the work of some of today's psychologists and rhetoricians. Because space is limited, we describe just a handful of relevant studies, and we touch just briefly on bias and the choices that attorneys must make in deciding how to use the research on bias.

§ 1.1 Rhetoric

Rhetoric is the art of persuasion. As the ancient rhetorician Gorgias states in Plato's dialogue by the same name, rhetoric is the art of persuading the people about matters of justice and injustice in the public places of the state.

Today, rhetoric has two faces. One is positive. Because there are times when we cannot know the "truth," rhetoric is the art of establishing the probable. For example, lawyers might use rhetoric to persuade the judge that it is more probable that the legislature wanted the statute in question to be interpreted broadly (or narrowly) or that it is more probable that their client's version of the facts is the "true" version of what occurred.

The second is pejorative. Some believe that rhetoric allows individuals to hide or manipulate the truth. The lawyer knows that his or her client committed the crime or is at fault but uses rhetorical techniques to trick or deceive the judge and jury.

Note: By necessity, the following descriptions are broad and do not reflect all the contributions and nuances associated with each era.[1]

§ 1.1.1 The Greeks (425 BCE to 225 BCE)

Because the Athenian version of democracy gave all "males of ability" the opportunity to participate in the governance of the state, there was a demand for individuals who could teach young males how to construct and present a persuasive argument. The Sophists filled this need. As itinerant professional teachers and intellectuals, the Sophists frequented Athens and other Greek cities, and for a price, taught young men how to make an argument. Protagoras, one of the more famous Sophists, is said to have boasted that he taught his students to turn a weak argument into a strong one through the manipulation of language, patterns of emphasis, and metaphors.

Two of the chief critics of the Sophists were Plato and Aristotle. Plato condemned sophistry, arguing that the Sophists were more interested in the impression the orator made than on the truth of his words. Aristotle, in *The Art of Rhetoric*, noted that the Sophists "chiefly devote their attention to matters outside the subject, for the arousing of prejudice, compassion, anger, and similar emotions . . . ." While Aristotle favored using reason to persuade, he acknowledged that at times an audience would not be sophisticated enough to follow arguments based solely on logical and scientific principles. In those instances, he believed that it was necessary to use persuasive language and techniques to help the audience perceive the truth. Moreover, Aristotle noted that sometimes it was necessary to use persuasive techniques and language to refute demagogues and those who used rhetoric for evil purposes. According to Aristotle, it was sometimes necessary to fight fire with fire.

Aristotle identified three "modes for persuasion" or "rhetorical appeals."

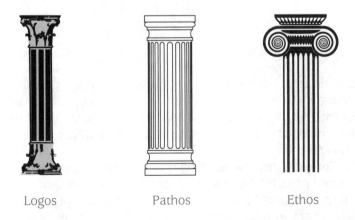

Logos   Pathos   Ethos

---

[1] For a more detailed discussion, see James Boyd White, *Law as Rhetoric, Rhetoric as Law: The Arts of Cultural and Communal Life,* 52 U. Chi. L. Rev. 684 (1985).

Logos is an appeal to logic, pathos an appeal to emotion, and ethos an appeal to the reputation or character of the speaker or writer. Both the Sophists and Aristotle refer to a related mode of persuasion: kairos. Kairos was central to the Sophists, who stressed the importance of timing: Some moments are more propitious than others. Aristotle uses kairos to refer to making an argument at an opportune time.

The Greeks are given credit for naming many of the types of arguments and persuasive techniques that we use today. Because the list is long, we set out only a representative few.

a. Syllogism

A *syllogism* is a logical deduction from two premises. The classic example goes like this:

All men are mortal.
Socrates is a man.
Therefore, Socrates is mortal.

b. Enthymeme

An *enthymeme* is a type of *syllogism*. However, in an enthymeme, one of the premises is not stated.

Socrates is a man.
Therefore, Socrates is mortal.

or

All men are mortal.
Therefore, Socrates is mortal.

c. Antithesis

Antithesis is a persuasive technique used to emphasize a concept, idea, or conclusion by contrasting two or more items. Note that the parts use parallel grammatical structures.

[A]sk not what your country can do for you, ask what you can do for your country.
—John F. Kennedy, inaugural address, January 20, 1961

Injustice anywhere is a threat to justice everywhere.
—Martin Luther King, Letter from a Birmingham Jail,
April 16, 1963

Daniel Klein was loyal to his parents, loyal to his wife, loyal to his friends, but disloyal to the company that had employed him for thirty years.

d. Anadiplosis

Anadiplosis is repeating a word at the end of the first sentence at the beginning of the next sentence. Note that anadiplosis is a form of dovetailing.[2]

> *Fear is the path to the dark side. Fear leads to anger. Anger leads to hate. Hate leads to suffering.*
> > —*Yoda, Star Wars: Episode I – The Phantom Menace, 1999*

> *I am Sam; Sam I am.*
> > —*Dr. Seuss, Green Eggs and Ham, August 12, 1960*

e. Anaphora

Unlike anadiplosis, in which you repeat a word that was at the end of the first sentence or clause, with *anaphora* you repeat the first word of a sentence.

> *Let us not wallow in the valley of despair. I say to you today, my friends, that in spite of the difficulties and frustrations of the moment,* **I still have a dream**. *It is a dream deeply rooted in the American dream.*
> **I have a dream** *that one day this nation will rise up and live out the true meaning of its creed: "We hold these truths to be self-evident: that all men are created equal."*
> **I have a dream** *that one day on the red hills of Georgia the sons of former slaves and the sons of former slave owners will be able to sit down together at a table of brotherhood.*
> **I have a dream** *that one day even the state of Mississippi, a state, sweltering with the heat of injustice, sweltering with the heat of oppression, will be transformed into an oasis of freedom and justice.*
> **I have a dream** *that my four little children will one day live in a nation where they will not be judged by the color of their skin but by the content of their character.*
> **I have a dream** *today.*
> > —*Dr. Martin Luther King Jr., speech delivered at the Lincoln Memorial, August 28, 1963*

f. Antistrophe

Unlike anaphora, in which you repeat a word or phrase at the beginning of a sentence or clause, *antistrophe* involves repeating a word or phrase at the end.

> *I swear to tell the* **truth**, *the whole* **truth**, *and nothing but the* **truth**.
> > —*Oath by witness in court of law*

---

[2] For a discussion of dovetailing, see section 4.3.1 in *Just Writing, Fifth Edition.*

*Government of **the people**, by **the people**, for **the people***
—Abraham Lincoln

*I say to them tonight, there's not a liberal **America** and a conservative **America**, **there's the United States of America**. There's not a black **America** and white **America** and Latino **America** and Asian **America**; **there's the United States of America**.*
—then Illinois State Senator Barack Obama, keynote address,
2004 Democratic National Convention

For a more in-depth explanation of the persuasive techniques named by the Greeks, see Craig D. Tindall, *Rhetorical Style*, Fed. Law. 24 (2003).

§ 1.1.2 The Romans (35 CE to 410 CE)

While the early Romans talked very little about rhetoric, the study and practice of rhetoric began to flourish after the Romans conquered the Greeks. While the Romans incorporated many of the rhetorical techniques named by the Greeks, Roman rhetoric relied less on logical reasoning and more on stylistic flourishes.

The most often cited Roman contribution to rhetoric is the *Five Canons of Rhetoric*, described by both Cicero and Quintilian, two Roman philosophers and teachers. The Five Canons, which apply to arguments presented orally, are as follows:

1. **Invention:** The process of identifying, developing, and refining the argument
2. **Arrangement:** The process of organizing the argument for the maximum impact
3. **Style:** The process of determining how to present the argument using rhetorical techniques
4. **Memory:** The process of learning and memorizing the speech
5. **Delivery:** The process of practicing the delivery of the speech using gestures, tone of voice, etc.

§ 1.1.3 The Middle Ages (426 CE to 1320 CE)

While the study of rhetoric did not disappear during the Middle Ages, the focus shifted from using rhetoric as a tool to shape political decisions to using it as a tool that could save souls. For example, St. Augustine talks about how religious leaders could use the "pagan art of rhetoric" to spread the gospel to the unconverted and to preach to believers.

During the latter part of the Middle Ages, universities were established in England, France, and Italy. While the study of rhetoric was an important part of these universities' curricula, neither the teachers nor their students made any significant contribution to the understanding of rhetoric. Instead, students studied Aristotle and spent hours repeating rote exercises designed to improve their rhetorical skills.

§ 1.1.4 The Renaissance (1426 CE to 1623 CE)

It was during the Renaissance that the study of rhetoric flourished. The classical texts were rediscovered, and printed copies were available throughout Europe. The Humanists—that is, individuals who emphasized the value of human beings, individually and collectively—associated the study of rhetoric with the study of culture. Humanists believed that true eloquence could arise only out of a harmonious union between wisdom and eloquence.

Over time, rhetoric was not studied by just the cultural elite, but became associated with a broader social movement that impacted the study of the humanities. This revival of the study of rhetoric was not limited to Greece and Italy, where it began, but over time it spread to northern, western, and eastern Europe.

§ 1.2 Using Rhetoric Today

For thousands of years, advocates have assumed that the persuasive techniques the Greeks identified do in fact work. While the research is still very limited, during the last few decades a small group of individuals have begun to test these assumptions. What follows are brief summaries of a handful of experiments. As you think about these studies, keep in mind that most of the techniques operate at a subconscious level. Readers or listeners are not likely to be aware of how the use of any given technique is affecting the way they are processing information.

§ 1.2.1 Storytelling/Narrative

From our own experiences, we know that stories are powerful. As David Ball writes:

> Story is the strongest non-violent persuasive method we know. Tell me facts and maybe I will hear a few of them. Tell me an argument and I might consider it. Tell me a story and I am yours. That is why every persuasive enterprise from the Bible to television commercials relies on story.[3]

Today, a growing number of scholars and practitioners are studying something called "applied legal storytelling." Those interested in the subject examine how stories, or narratives, can be used in the practice of law.

---

[3] Brian J. Foley & Ruth Anne Robbins, *Fiction 101: A Primer for Lawyers on How to Use Fiction Writing Techniques to Write Persuasive Facts Sections*, 32 Rutgers L.J. 459, 461 (2001) (quoting David Ball, *Theater Tips and Strategies for Jury Trials* 66-98 (1994)).

For instance, they look at how attorneys can use stories in developing a theory of the case, in setting out the facts, and in framing the issues.[4]

In one of the few studies on the effect of using storytelling techniques in briefs, Professor Kenneth D. Chestek found that judges rated a "story brief"—that is, a brief in which the writer not only set out the law but also created a strong storyline—as more persuasive than a pure "logos brief." In addition, staff attorneys, law clerks, and appellate attorneys found the story brief more persuasive than the logos brief.[5]

§ 1.2.2 Priming

"Priming" is a technique in which the introduction of one piece of information influences how an individual perceives or processes subsequent pieces of information. As Professor Stanchi writes:

> Priming plants a seed in the brain. This "seed" causes us to form an impression that we then use to interpret new information. So, for example, we are more likely to see Pete Rose as a "baseball player" rather than a "gambler" if we had earlier been exposed to words about baseball like bat, strike, or New York Yankees. In this example, the "prime" or stimulus (the words or information about baseball) "excites" an area of the brain that contains information about a particular category (like baseball). Then, when confronted with new information, the person who has been "primed" uses the excited or primed knowledge category to evaluate the new information.[6]

§ 1.2.3 Negativity Bias

Professor Kenneth Chestek has also written about "negativity bias."[7] Studies indicate that our brains are more apt to process, and retain, negative information as opposed to positive information. Professor Chestek quotes one neuropsychologist as saying "[y]our brain is like Velcro for negative experiences and Teflon for positive ones."[8]

For his study, Professor Chestek recruited 163 judges from around the country to read one of nine different introductory paragraphs/preliminary

---

[4] For a bibliography of articles dealing with applied legal storytelling, see J. Christopher Rideout, *Applied Legal Storytelling: A Bibliography*, 12 Legal Commc'n & Rhetoric: JALWD 247 (2015).

[5] Kenneth D. Chestek, *Judging by the Numbers: An Empirical Study of the Power of Story*, 7 J. Ass'n Legal Writing Directors 1 (2010).

[6] Kathryn M. Stanchi, *The Power of Priming in Legal Advocacy: Using the Science of First Impressions to Persuade the Reader*, 89 Or. L. Rev. 305, 307-08 (2010).

[7] Kenneth D. Chestek, *Fear and Loathing in Persuasive Writing: An Empirical Study of the Effects of the Negativity Bias*, 14 Legal Commc'n & Rhetoric: JALWD 1, 26 (2017).

[8] Kenneth D. Chestek, *Of Reptiles and Velcro: The Brain's Negativity Bias and Persuasion*, 15 Nev. L.J. 605, 606 (2015).

statements, each of which had either a positive, a negative, or a neutral theme, and then an identical statement of stipulated facts. Based on his data, Professor Chestek offers the following advice:

- Priming matters! Whatever theme you choose (positive or negative), be sure it is expressed in some fashion in the Introduction or Preliminary Statement.
- If you want the court to focus on the facts of your case, choose a negative theme.
- Always state policy arguments in terms of avoiding negative outcomes.
- If you represent a more powerful party against a relatively weaker party, going negative may backfire.[9]

§ 1.2.4 Confirmation Bias

Confirmation bias, which is the tendency to process information by looking for information that reinforces one's existing beliefs, has become a hot topic. Members of one political party read only that information that is consistent with their beliefs, while members of another political party read only that information that is consistent with theirs.

Confirmation bias also exists in the law. In some instances, a police officer who believes that an individual has committed a crime will interpret ambiguous facts in such a way that the evidence supports a conclusion that the defendant is guilty.[10] Likewise, a juror may decide, early on, that the defendant is liable for a tort and interpret all subsequent evidence in such a way that it supports the juror's early conclusion.

Judges are not immune. For instance, in one study, Professor Christine Venter examined the questions that three Seventh Circuit judges asked during oral argument.[11] On the basis of her analysis, Professor Venter concluded that confirmation bias could be one of the factors that affected the judges' questioning. All three judges asked more questions of the losing party, and the tone of those questions was more negative. It seems that the judges were using the questions to confirm their preliminary decision in the case.

---

[9] For a more detailed discussion of the study, see Kenneth D. Chestek, *Fear and Loathing in Persuasive Writing: An Empirical Study of the Effects of the Negativity Bias*, 14 Legal Commc'n & Rhetoric: JALWD 1, 25 (2017).

[10] *See* Moa Lidén, Minna Gräns & Peter Juslin, *The Presumption of Guilt in Suspect Interrogations: Apprehension as a Trigger of Confirmation Bias and Debiasing Techniques*, 42 Law & Hum. Behav. 336, 352 (2018).

[11] Christine M. Venter, *The Case Against Oral Argument: The Effects of Confirmation Bias on the Outcome of Selected Cases in the Seventh Circuit Court of Appeals*, 14 Legal Commc'n & Rhetoric: JALWD 45, 80 (2017).

§ 1.2.5 Racial and Gender Bias

There is good news and bad news regarding racial and gender bias. The bad news is that almost every American has some type of explicit or implicit bias. The good news is that there are studies showing that many judges can set aside those biases.

Explicit bias is the type of bias that an individual knows he or she has and openly embraces. In contrast, implicit bias is a type of bias based on stereotypical associations that an individual might not know affect his or her relationships and decisions. Researchers have found that most people, even those who embrace nondiscrimination norms, hold implicit biases that might lead them to treat black Americans in discriminatory ways.

As Professor Jason Nance has written:

> [S]cholars observe that the association between African Americans and crime and violence is so strong and common that it is essentially bidirectional. That is, thoughts of crime and violence unconsciously trigger thoughts of African Americans, and thoughts of African Americans unconsciously trigger thoughts of crime and violence. Critically, empirical research also confirms that once implicit racial biases are triggered, they influence human judgment, decisions, and actions in measurable ways. Furthermore, empirical research demonstrates that racial cues, such as skin color or even names that are associated with certain racial groups, activate implicit racial biases and affect decision-making.[12]

The most commonly used instrument for testing for implicit bias is the Implicit Association Test or IAT, an instrument that purports to measure the strength of associations between social categories and positive and negative attributes.[13] The racial version of the IAT (black-white) requires subjects to quickly associate images of black and white individuals with positive or negative descriptors. The theory is that because participants must make associations very quickly, the instrument reveals hidden or unconscious biases. The test, which has now been taken by millions of individuals, shows that perhaps 90 to 95 percent of white Americans are racially biased in some way.[14]

The question then is whether judges' decisions are biased. A study by Professor Jeffrey Rachlinski and his colleagues says yes and no. In his article, he sets out three conclusions.[15] First, judges, like the rest of us, carry implicit

---

[12] Jason P. Nance, *Implicit Racial Bias and Students' Fourth Amendment Rights*, 94 Ind. L.J. 47, 60 (2019).

[13] Some individuals believe that the test is flawed because it does not produce consistent results (the same individual may get different results on different days) and because it does not predict biased behavior. https://www.chronicle.com/article/Can-We-Really-Measure-Implicit/238807.

[14] *See* Christian B. Sundquist, *Uncovering Juror Racial Bias*, 96 Denv. L. Rev. 309, 342-43 (2019).

[15] Jeffrey J. Rachlinski et al., *Does Unconscious Racial Bias Affect Trial Judges?*, 84 Notre Dame L. Rev. 1195, 1221 (2009).

biases concerning race. Second, these implicit biases can affect judges' judgment, at least in contexts where judges are unaware of a need to monitor their decisions for racial bias. Third, and conversely, when judges are aware of a need to monitor their own responses for the influence of implicit racial biases, and are motivated to suppress that bias, they appear able to do so.

§ 1.3 Ethics of Using Implicit Biases to Support Your Position

The research on bias gives rise to a number of questions. In our quest to be effective and ethical advocates, how should we use that research? For example, if the defendant is black, should prosecutors reference that fact in their briefs under the assumption that, like most white Americans, a white judge harbors some form of implicit bias?

In deciding what to say and how to say it, the first step is to look at what is and is not constitutional. In the two decades following the Civil Rights Movement, federal courts began to rule that describing the defendant in derogatory racial terms violated the Due Process and Equal Protection Clauses of the Fifth and Fourteenth Amendments to the U.S. Constitution. "Drawing upon the holdings in cases decided by the various Circuit Courts of Appeal, the Supreme Court stated in 1987: 'The Constitution prohibits racially biased prosecutorial arguments.'"[16] Consequently, prosecutors cannot use their preemptory challenges to exclude blacks from the jury panel,[17] and, if a juror states that he or she relied on racial stereotypes or animus to convict a criminal defendant, a trial court may consider the evidence of the juror's statement and any resulting denial of the Sixth Amendment right to jury trial.[18]

The second step is to look at the rules of professional responsibility. The preamble to the Model Rules of Professional Responsibility states that, as advocates, lawyers should zealously assert their client's position under the rules of advocacy:

> [1] A lawyer, as a member of the legal profession, is a representative of clients, an officer of the legal system and a public citizen having special responsibility for the quality of justice.
>
> [2] As a representative of clients, a lawyer performs various functions. As advisor, a lawyer provides a client with an informed understanding of the client's legal rights and obligations and explains their practical implications. **As advocate, a lawyer**

---

[16] Ryan Patrick Alford, *Appellate Review of Racist Summations: Redeeming the Promise of Searching Analysis*, 11 Mich. J. Race & L. 325, 332 (2006).

[17] *Batson v. Kentucky*, 476 U.S. 79, 79, 106 S. Ct. 1712, 1713, 90 L. Ed. 2d 69 (1986).

[18] *Peña-Rodriguez v. Colorado*, 580 U.S. ___, 137 S. Ct. 855, 869, 197 L. Ed. 2d 107 (2017). *See also McCleskey v. Kemp*, 481 U.S. 279, 310, 107 S. Ct. 1756, 1777, 95 L. Ed. 2d 262 (1987) ("This Court has repeatedly stated that prosecutorial discretion cannot be exercised on the basis of race.").

zealously asserts the client's position under the rules of the adversary system. As negotiator, a lawyer seeks a result advantageous to the client but consistent with requirements of honest dealings with others. As an evaluator, a lawyer acts by examining a client's legal affairs and reporting about them to the client or to others. [Emphasis added.]

* * *

However, Model Rule of Professional Responsibility 3.4(e) limits, at least a little, what an advocate can do. An advocate cannot

(e) in trial, **allude to any matter that the lawyer does not reasonably believe is relevant** or that will not be supported by admissible evidence, assert personal knowledge of facts in issue except when testifying as a witness, or state a personal opinion as to the justness of a cause, the credibility of a witness, the culpability of a civil litigant or the guilt or innocence of an accused[.]
[Emphasis added.]

There have been attempts to limit discrimination. For example, in 1994, the ABA Standing Committee on Ethics and Professional Responsibility proposed an amendment that would have prohibited a lawyer from manifesting "by words or conduct, in the course of representing a client, bias or prejudice based upon race, sex, religion, national origin, disability, age, sexual orientation or socio-economic status." While the committee later withdrew the proposed amendment, the ABA added the following comment to Rule 8.4:

[3] A lawyer who, in the course of representing a client, knowingly manifests by words or conduct, bias or prejudice based upon race, sex, religion, national origin, disability, age, sexual orientation or socioeconomic status, violates paragraph (d) when such actions are prejudicial to the administration of justice. Legitimate advocacy respecting the foregoing factors does not violate paragraph (d). A trial judge's finding that peremptory challenges were exercised on a discriminatory basis does not alone establish a violation of this rule.

Some states have gone further. For instance, Florida Rule 8.4(d) states that a lawyer may not

(d) engage in conduct in connection with the practice of law that is prejudicial to the administration of justice, including to knowingly, or through callous indifference, disparage, humiliate, or discriminate against litigants, jurors, witnesses, court personnel, or other lawyers on any basis, including, but not limited to, on account of race, ethnicity, gender, religion, national origin, disability, marital status, sexual orientation, age, socioeconomic status, employment, or physical characteristic[.]

And the Washington State Rule of Professional Conduct 8.4(h) states

> (h) in representing a client, [an attorney cannot] engage in conduct that is prejudicial to the administration of justice toward judges, lawyers, or LLLTs, other parties, witnesses, jurors, or court personnel or officers, that a reasonable person would interpret as manifesting prejudice or bias on the basis of sex, race, age, creed, religion, color, national origin, disability, sexual orientation, honorably discharged veteran or military status, or marital status. This Rule does not restrict a lawyer from representing a client by advancing material factual or legal issues or arguments.

Unfortunately, the cases and rules do not provide all the answers. For example, may an attorney who represents a person with a disability play to a judge's or juror's biases related to individuals with disabilities? More specifically, may a lawyer create a narrative that presents her client as a victim or a person who is less able? The answer is, we are not sure. It is not yet clear how attorneys can or should use the research on bias.

In our opinion, there are some easy cases. First, we believe that attorneys can use the persuasive techniques that we describe in Parts II and III. For instance, attorneys may use priming, and they may emphasize favorable facts and de-emphasize unfavorable ones. In addition, they may use storytelling techniques and select words for both their denotation and their connotation. Second, we believe that attorneys should not use a person's race, gender, sexual orientation, and so on with the intent to paint an opposing party in a negative light.

For the harder cases, we suggest that, as attorneys, we consider the following:

1. **Our role.** In criminal cases, does it make a difference which side we represent? Will our decision depend on whether we are a prosecutor representing the interests of the State or defense counsel representing a client charged with a crime? In civil cases, does it make a difference who our client is?
2. **Client's opinion.** If we are thinking about playing to an implicit bias that may help our client, is that strategy one with which our client is comfortable? For example, if our client is seeking damages for injuries sustained in a car accident, is the client okay with being portrayed as a victim, for example, someone who has "suffered" injuries or who is "confined" to a wheelchair?
3. **Type of bias.** Does the type of bias matter? For example, should we think differently about different types of bias? Are some types of bias worse than others?

Discussions about how attorneys should use the new research on bias are just beginning. Consequently, we hope that you will view this section as we do, as a work in progress.

Motion Briefs

In this part the focus is on motion briefs, which play an ever-increasing role in motions practice. Given their caseloads, most judges want—and need—well-written briefs that identify the questions on which the motion turns and set out the law and the party's arguments clearly and concisely.

In the chapters that follow, we walk through the process of writing a brief in support of a motion to suppress. You will meet Mr. Patterson, who has been charged with assaulting a young woman, and then you will watch as Mr. Patterson's attorney and the prosecutor craft the introductory paragraph/preliminary statement, the statement of facts, and the issue statement and then the argument section and prayer for relief.

At the end of this part, there are two sets of sample briefs: the defendant's and State's briefs in *State v. Patterson,* and the briefs in support and opposition to a motion for summary judgment.

2

Motion Briefs

Much of litigation is motions practice. For example, as a trial attorney, you may file motions for temporary relief, to compel discovery, to suppress evidence, to dismiss, or for summary judgment. Although not all of these motions will be supported by briefs, many will.

> **PRACTICE POINTER** The names of these briefs vary from jurisdiction to jurisdiction. In some jurisdictions, they are called "briefs in support of a motion" or "motion briefs," while in other jurisdictions they are called "memoranda of law," "memoranda of points of authority" or "P and A memos," for short. Check your court rules and with local attorneys to see what these briefs are called in your jurisdiction.

§ 2.1 Audience

In writing a brief in support of or in opposition to a motion, your primary audience is the trial judge.

Sometimes you will know which judge will read your brief. Either the brief has been requested by a specific judge, or you know which judge will hear the motion. At other times, though, you will not know who will read your brief. The brief will be read by whichever judge is hearing motions on the day that your motion is argued.

If you know which judge will read your brief, write your brief for that judge. Learn as much as you can about that judge, and then craft a brief that he or she will find persuasive. If you do not know which judge will read your brief, write a brief that will work for any of the judges who might hear your motion.

In whichever situation you find yourself, keep the judge's schedule in mind. It is not uncommon for a judge hearing civil motions to hear twenty motions in a single day. If in each of these cases each party has filed a twenty-page brief, the judge would have 800 pages to read. Given this work-load, it is not surprising that for most judges the best brief is the short brief. Know what you need and want to argue, make your argument, and then stop.

Also keep in mind the constraints placed on trial judges. Because trial judges must apply mandatory authority, they need to know what the law is, not what you think it should be. Whenever possible, make the easy argument. Set out and apply existing law.

§ 2.2 Purpose

In writing to a trial judge, you have two goals: to educate and to persuade. You are a teacher teaching the judge both the applicable law and the facts of the case. You are not, however, *just* a teacher; you are also an advocate. As you teach, you will be trying to persuade the court to take a particular action.

§ 2.3 Conventions

The format of a particular brief will vary from jurisdiction to jurisdiction and, even within a jurisdiction, from court to court. Consequently, check both the general and the local rules. Is there a rule that prescribes the types of information that should be included in the brief, the order in which that information should be presented, and the particular format? If there is, follow that rule. If there is no rule, check with other attorneys or with the court clerk to see if there is a format that is typically used.

§ 2.4 *State v. Patterson*

In Part II, our example case is *State v. Patterson*, a criminal case in which the defendant has filed a motion to suppress the identifications obtained at a show-up conducted shortly after an assault and at a line-up held one day later. The facts of the case are as follows.

At about 4:00 p.m. on Monday, August 19, 2019, Beatrice Martinez left her apartment and began walking down residential streets to her place of employment, a restaurant located about one mile from her apartment. As she was walking, Ms. Martinez noticed an older silver SUV with a chrome luggage rack as it drove by her. A few minutes later, the same vehicle drove by once again. This time, the driver pulled in front of Ms. Martinez, blocking the sidewalk. The driver then got out of the car; walked toward Ms. Martinez; and when he was about five feet from Ms. Martinez, pulled a gun from his coat pocket and pointed it at her.

At about 4:15 p.m., Chester Clipse was walking home when he saw a man in a silver SUV driving slowly down the street. Because it appeared that the driver was going to pull into Mr. Clipse's private parking spot, Mr. Clipse's attention was drawn to the car. As a result, Mr. Clipse was watching when the driver got out of the car and pulled a gun. As soon as he saw the gun, Mr. Clipse shouted, "Hey!" Startled, the man turned and went back to his car, got in it, and drove away. Crying, Ms. Martinez ran across the street.

Mr. Clipse then took Ms. Martinez, who was visibly shaken, to his land-lady's apartment, where they called the police. While the landlady com-forted Ms. Martinez, Mr. Clipse went back out to the street to wait for the police. While he was waiting, Mr. Clipse saw a parking enforcement officer and told him what had happened and gave him a description of the vehicle.

As the parking enforcement officer was looking for the vehicle, Officer Yuen and Officer Cox arrived at Mr. Clipse's apartment building. Officer Cox interviewed Mr. Clipse. Because he had been down the street when the inci-dent occurred, Mr. Clipse was able to tell Officer Cox only that the individual was a white man in his late thirties or early forties and that he was of aver-age height and weight. While Mr. Clipse was talking to Officer Cox, Officer Cox received a radio message indicating that the parking enforcement offi-cer had located a car that matched the one that Clipse had described. While Officer Cox took Mr. Clipse in his car to see if Mr. Clipse could identify the car, Officer Yuen went inside to interview Ms. Martinez.

Ms. Martinez told Officer Yuen that her assailant was a white male who was about 5'7" tall; that he weighed between 165 and 170 pounds; that he had wavy blondish-brown hair; that he appeared to be in his early forties; and that at the time of the assault, her assailant was wearing a dark jacket and glasses. Neither Mr. Clipse nor Ms. Martinez had been able to give the license plate numbers on the man's vehicle.

After completing the interview, Officer Yuen asked Ms. Martinez if she wanted a ride home or to work. Ms. Martinez accepted the offer of a ride home and got into the back seat of Officer Yuen's vehicle. About four blocks later, Officer Yuen asked Ms. Martinez whether a man who was on the side-walk in front of them looked like her assailant. Because she could not see the man's face, Ms. Martinez did not respond. As the police car drew nearer, Officer Yuen again asked Ms. Martinez whether the man looked like her assailant. This time, Ms. Yuen answered, "Yes, I think so." On hearing this response, Officer Yuen pulled up next to the man, got out of his vehicle, and talked to the man.

As Officer Yuen was questioning the man, Officer Cox drove up with Mr. Clipse. While Martinez and Mr. Clipse watched, Officers Cox and Yuen con-tinued to question the man. Officer Cox then returned to Ms. Martinez and Mr. Clipse and walked them back to Mr. Clipse's apartment. While he did so, Officer Yuen arrested the man, who was identified as Dean E. Patterson, for assault with a deadly weapon. Later that day, the police searched Mr. Patterson's apartment and found a gun issued to Mr. Patterson by his employer. At a line-up held the next day, Ms. Martinez identified Mr. Patterson as the man who assaulted her. Mr. Clipse was not able to make an identification.

In his statement to the police, twenty-two-year-old Dean Patterson stated that, on the day in question, he finished his shift as a security guard at 7:30 a.m. and walked to his apartment. After having breakfast with his wife, Mr. Patterson went to bed and slept until about 1:00 p.m. At about 2:30 p.m., Mr. Patterson's wife received a phone call asking her to cover for a co-worker, a nurse who was ill. At about 3:00 p.m., Mr. Patterson drove his wife the three-quarters of a mile to the hospital.

A half hour later, Mr. Patterson called his wife to find out how long she would have to work. They had plans to go to a movie that evening, and he wanted to know whether he should change those plans. At about 3:50 p.m., Mr. Patterson took a load of laundry to the apartment complex's laundry room. When he returned to his apartment, Mr. Patterson watched part of an old movie. At about 4:20 p.m., Mr. Patterson went back to the laundry room to put the clothes in the dryer. By this time, it was 4:30 p.m., and Mr. Patterson decided to phone his wife again. He arranged to meet her at 5:15 p.m. for her dinner break. Mr. Patterson picked up the laundry and then left the apartment a little before 5:00 p.m. While Mr. Patterson was walking to the hospital, a police car pulled up behind him, and a police officer got out of his car and began questioning him. Patterson was then arrested and charged with assault with a deadly weapon.

Mr. Patterson owns an older model silver SUV with a chrome luggage rack. He has no prior convictions and has volunteered to take a lie detector test.

PRACTICE POINTER	In writing this summary of the facts, we had to decide how we wanted to refer to the individuals we mention in the summary. We had the following options.

1. Use their first and last names the first time we mention the individual and after that use their title, for example, use "Ms.," "Mr.," and "Officer."
2. Use their first and last names the first time we mention the individual and after that use just their last names.
3. Use their first and last names the first time we mention the individual and after that use different formats for different individuals, for example, use "Ms. Martinez" but "Patterson" and "Clipse."

In the end, we decided to go with the first option because we wanted the summary to be as neutral as possible, and one way of doing that is to treat each of the individuals similarly. As we discuss later, in a brief you may want to use a different option.

Beginning the Motion Brief: Theory of the Case, Caption, and Preliminary Statement

§ 3.1 Theory of the Case

While different people use different labels, good advocates understand the importance of having a theory of the case. Unfortunately, though, most advocates have a hard time articulating what they mean by "theory of the case." It is a bit like pornography—they just know it when they see it.

For some, constructing a theory of the case means selecting the lens through which they want the court to view their client's case. In constructing one they think about where they want to focus the judge's attention. Do they want to zoom in and focus on a particular tree or group of trees, or do they want to zoom out, capturing the entire landscape?

For others, constructing a theory of the case means selecting a theme, which might or might not be summed up in a single sentence or phrase. For instance, in the example problem, defense counsel might select the theme, "wrong place, wrong time." Mr. Patterson just happened to be at the wrong place at the wrong time.

For still others, constructing a theory of the case entails deciding what story they want to tell. Who are the characters, what is the conflict, and how can they weave together the law and the facts so that the judge concludes that the conflict should be resolved in their client's favor?

And, for still others, constructing a theory of the case means sweeping away the details and focusing on the case's essence. One way to do this is to try telling your client's story in just six words. Some famous examples of six-word stories include the following:

> For sale: Baby shoes. Never worn.—Ernest Hemingway
> Longed for him. Got him. Shit.—Margaret Atwood
> Born a twin; graduated only child—Author unknown

Whichever approach resonates with you, keep in mind that a good theory of the case must appeal to both the head and the heart of the decision maker: It must contain both an appeal to logos and an appeal to pathos. Most judges want to make decisions that are both legally sound and just.

In our example case, Mr. Patterson states that he did not commit the crime. His legal arguments are that the identifications on which the State relies are the product of an unnecessary and suggestive show-up and that Ms. Martinez's identification is not reliable. Defense counsel does not, though, rely just on arguments designed to appeal to the head. Instead, she also makes an appeal to the judge's and jury's emotions. Why would a happily married man assault a young woman between doing loads of laundry and making calls to his wife?

In contrast, the State's legal arguments are that the police procedures were not suggestive and, even if they were, Ms. Martinez's identifications are, nonetheless, reliable. It is a bit harder for the State to create a theory of the case that appeals to the judge's emotions. It can emphasize that the victim is a young woman who was on her way to work; that the police were doing what the public wants them do to—actively looking for an individual who had just committed a crime; or, perhaps, that there is some reason why Mr. Patterson should not be believed.

Because your theory of the case should permeate all parts of your brief—your introductory paragraph/preliminary statement, "introductory paragraph" to "preliminary statement," your statement of facts, your arguments, and your conclusion—try to construct one before you start drafting. If you are stuck, look at the cases that you have found while researching the issues, identifying what the parties might have had as their theories of the case. There will, however, be times when the theory of the case does not emerge until you are well into drafting the brief. In these instances, take the time to go back through what you have written, where appropriate emphasizing the facts and law that support your theory of the case.

Note, though, that there is not a place in your brief where you will say, "My theory of the case is . . . ." Instead, use your theory of the case to guide the decisions that you make as you write your brief. Use your theory of the case to help decide how to frame the issues, how to tell the story, which arguments to make and how to present those arguments, and how to counter the other side's arguments. Write down your theory of the case on a piece of paper and, periodically, reread it to make sure that the decisions that you make help you give life to that theory.

§ 3.2 The Caption

While in some jurisdictions motion briefs are printed on pleading, or numbered, paper, in other jurisdictions they are printed on regular paper. In addition, the rules about where the caption is placed and what information should be included can vary from jurisdiction to jurisdiction. In the example case, we have used the Washington rules: The caption is set out on the first page beginning on about line 5. The parties' names are set out on the left-hand side, and the case number and the title of the document are set out on the right-hand side.

EXAMPLE **THE SUPERIOR COURT OF KING COUNTY, WASHINGTON**

```
1

2

3    STATE OF WASHINGTON,     )   Case No.: 19-01-2226
                              )
4                 Plaintiff,  )   DEFENDANT'S BRIEF
5                             )   IN SUPPORT OF
                              )   SUPPRESS
6                     v.      )   MOTION TO
                              )
7    DEAN E. PATTERSON,       )
                              )
8                 Defendant.  )
9    _____     )

10

11

12
```

PRACTICE POINTER Many jurisdictions now allow, or even require, that the parties file their pleadings and briefs electronically. Thus, before filing your brief, check your local rules.

§ 3.3 Introductory Paragraph/ Preliminary Statement

In many, but not all, jurisdictions, the first paragraph after the caption is an introductory one. Most of the time, these paragraphs are very "matter of fact." The attorney simply identifies the motion and sets out the relief that he or she is requesting. At other times, the introductory paragraph is used to introduce the theory of the case or to prime the judge to see the law and facts in a light favorable to the client. In deciding which approach to take, consider the conventional practices in your jurisdiction, the nature and importance of your case, and your own personal style.

EXAMPLE 1   **INTRODUCTORY PARAGRAPH FROM DEFENDANT'S BRIEF**

Mr. Patterson asks the Court to suppress Ms. Martinez's show-up and line-up identifications and to prohibit both Ms. Martinez and Mr. Clipse from making in-court identifications. The show-up was impermissibly suggestive and, because she viewed her assailant for only a few seconds, Ms. Martinez's identifications are unreliable. Mr. Patterson was simply at the wrong place at the wrong time.

EXAMPLE 2   **STATE'S INTRODUCTORY PARAGRAPH/ PRAYER FOR RELIEF**

The State asks the Court to deny the defendant's motion to suppress the victim's show-up and line-up identifications and to allow both the victim and the witness to make in-court identifications. The show-up was not suggestive, and even if it was, the victim's and the witness's identifications are reliable.

EXAMPLE 3   **ALTERNATIVE INTRODUCTORY PARAGRAPH**

August 19, 2019, started out as a normal day for Dean Patterson. After finishing his shift as a security guard, he slept, had breakfast with his wife, and then, after his wife left for work, watched a movie and did the laundry. Everything changed, however, when Mr. Patterson decided to walk to the hospital where his wife worked to have dinner with her. As he was walking down the street, a police car pulled up behind him, and while a young woman who had been assaulted watched, a police officer questioned him. Although Mr. Patterson is twenty years younger than the man the victim said had assaulted her, the police arrested Mr. Patterson and charged him with the assault. Because Mr. Patterson's only "crime" was being at the wrong place at the wrong time, Mr. Patterson respectfully requests that the Court grant his motion to suppress.

PRACTICE POINTER   Capitalize "court" when referring to the court to which your brief is addressed or to the United States Supreme Court, or when you are setting out the full name of the court. In all other instances, do not capitalize "court."

4

Statement of Facts

Great lawyers are great storytellers. They know how to grab their reader's attention and how to keep that attention as they weave together the facts and law. Typically, these stories have a cast of characters (the parties plus other actors) and a plot that incorporates the relevant events and builds to a climax (the conflict that is the basis for the lawsuit). In addition, these stories are subtly persuasive. After reading the story, the judge is inclined to resolve the conflict in favor of the storyteller's client.

Some people are, it seems, born storytellers. They just know how to tell a good story. For them, the challenge is to construct a story that is grounded in the evidence and that focuses on the facts that form the basis for the legal claim. Put differently, they need to write a story that is appropriate for their audience (the judge) and that helps them achieve their purpose (educating and persuading the judge).

For the rest of us the task is more difficult. While we may understand our audience and purpose, we don't know how to persuade. Consequently, we need to take a more mechanical approach. We need to start by learning the process that goes into constructing a persuasive statement of the facts and then we need to learn some persuasive techniques. With luck, and with time and practice, we will then be able to see the story and how the facts are part of the legal arguments that we plan to make.

§ 4.1 Select the Facts

In drafting your statement of facts, you will, typically, include three types of facts: background facts, legally significant facts, and emotionally significant facts.

§ 4.1.1 Background Facts

Background facts play a different role in persuasive writing than they do in objective writing. In an objective statement of facts, the writer includes only those background facts that are needed for the story to make sense. In contrast, in drafting a persuasive statement of facts, writers often use the background facts to support their narrative. Consequently, make sure that you get those facts that you need to tell the story into the record so that you can use them in your brief. For instance, if you were representing Mr. Patterson, you might want to have Mr. Patterson testify at the suppression hearing, having him provide information about his job and wife and describing what he did on the day in question. While having a defendant testify can be risky, in Mr. Patterson's case the benefits might outweigh those risks.

§ 4.1.2 Legally Significant Facts

Because most courts require that the statement of facts be "fair," in writing the statement of facts you must include all of the legally significant facts, both favorable and unfavorable. Thus, in the example case, both the State and the defendant must include all of the facts that will be relevant in determining whether the identifications obtained at the show-up and at the line-up should be suppressed and whether Martinez and Clipse should be allowed to make in-court identifications.

§ 4.1.3 Emotionally Significant Facts

While you must include all of the legally significant facts, you do not need to include all of the facts that are emotionally significant. Although as a defensive move you may sometimes include an emotionally significant fact that is unfavorable, recharacterizing it or minimizing its significance, most of the time you will not. It is more common to include only those emotionally significant facts that favor your client.

The harder question is how to handle emotionally significant facts that are unfavorable to the other side. Should you sling mud, or should you take a higher road and omit any reference to those facts? The answer is that it depends. It depends on the case and on the attorney. If the fact's connection to the case is tenuous, most attorneys will not include it. However, if the case is weak, some attorneys will include it, some using it as a sword, others using it much more subtly.

§ 4.2 Select an Organizational Scheme

In selecting an organizational scheme, consider two factors. First, decide which organizational scheme makes the most sense. Does it make more sense to use a chronological organizational scheme, a topical organizational scheme, or a topical organizational scheme with the facts within each topic set out in chronological order? Second, decide which organizational scheme will allow you to set out the facts in such a way that you are able to present your story and your theory of the case most effectively.

In the example case, it makes sense to set out the facts in chronological order. In deciding whether to suppress the evidence, the trial judge will want to know what happened first, second, and third. A chronological organizational scheme will also allow each side to tell its story. The only difference will be that Mr. Patterson will start his story with his activities on the day in question, while the State will start its story where it started for the victim: with the assault.

> **PRACTICE POINTER** If your statement of facts is long or if you are setting out the facts for two unrelated issues, think about adding subheadings. While the argumentative headings should be in the form of positive assertions (see section 6.1.2), the subheadings in the statement of facts can be in the form of labels.

§ 4.3 Present the Facts in a Light Favorable to Your Client

In writing the statement of facts for an objective memo, you set out the facts accurately and objectively. You do not present the facts in the light most favorable to your client.

In writing the statement of facts for a motion brief, you still need to set out the facts accurately. One of the fastest ways to lose a case is to leave out legally significant facts or to misrepresent either the legally significant or emotionally significant facts. (Think ethos.) Being accurate does not mean, however, that you need to set out the facts objectively. You are permitted and, in fact, are expected to present the facts in such a way that they support your theory of the case.

In presenting the facts, attorneys use a number of different techniques. They prime the judge to rule in their client's favor by setting out the favorable facts early in the statement of facts or by creating a favorable context, they will usually tell the story from their client's point of view, they emphasize the facts that support their theory of the case and de-emphasize those that do not, and they select words both for their denotation and their connotation.

**Techniques for Presenting the Facts in a Light
Favorable to Your Client**

1. Prime the judge to rule in your client's favor
2. Create a favorable context
3. Tell the story from your client's point of view
4. Emphasize favorable facts and de-emphasize unfavorable facts
   a. Airtime
   b. Detail
   c. Positions of emphasis
   d. Short sentences
   e. Main and dependent clauses
5. Select words both for their denotation and their connotation

---

§ 4.3.1 Prime the Judge to Rule in Your Client's Favor

As we discussed in section 1.2.2, priming plants a seed in the brain that can color how individuals interpret subsequent information. Consequently, try to start your statement of facts with facts that favor your client.

§ 4.3.2 Create a Favorable Context

One way to create a favorable context is to start the statement of facts with facts that favor your client. Look, for instance, at Example 1 below. Instead of starting the statement of facts with the assault or Patterson's arrest, defense counsel starts it by describing what Patterson was doing on the day of the assault. By starting with these facts, she is able to begin the story with facts that support her theory of the case: Patterson is an innocent pedestrian who happened to be in the wrong place at the wrong time. Note how defense counsel works in the fact that Patterson is married, that he has a job, and that he does nice things—for instance, he takes his wife to work, does the laundry, and arranges to meet his wife during her dinner break.

**EXAMPLE 1   THE FIRST THREE PARAGRAPHS OF THE
DEFENDANT'S STATEMENT OF FACTS**

At 7:30 on Monday morning, August 19, 2019, twenty-two-year-old Dean Patterson finished his shift as a security guard and walked to his apartment. After having breakfast with his wife, Mr. Patterson went to bed and slept until about 1:00 p.m. At about 2:30 p.m., Patterson's wife received a phone call asking her to work at the local hospital, where she is employed as a nurse.

She got ready, and Mr. Patterson dropped her off at the hospital at about 3:10 p.m. At about 3:30 p.m., Mr. Patterson called his wife to find out how long she would have to work. They had plans to go to a movie that evening, and he wanted to know whether he should change those plans. At about 3:50 p.m., Mr. Patterson took a load of laundry to the apartment complex's laundry room. When he returned to his apartment, Mr. Patterson watched part of an old movie. At about 4:20 p.m., Mr. Patterson went back to the laundry room to put the clothes in the dryer.

By this time, it was 4:30 p.m., and Mr. Patterson decided to phone his wife again. He arranged to meet her at 5:15 p.m. for her dinner break. Mr. Patterson picked up the laundry and then left the apartment a little before 5:00 p.m. to meet his wife.

The State also creates a favorable context. However, instead of starting its statement of facts by describing Mr. Patterson's actions, it begins the story where it started for the victim. In the first paragraph of its statement of facts, the State describes the assault and then the show-up and line-up.

EXAMPLE 2   **THE FIRST PARAGRAPH OF THE STATE'S STATEMENT OF FACTS**

On Monday, August 19, 2019, Beatrice Martinez was assaulted with a deadly weapon. At a show-up held thirty to forty minutes after the attack, Ms. Martinez positively identified the defendant, Dean E. Patterson, as her assailant. The next day, Ms. Martinez picked Patterson out of a line-up, once again positively identifying him as her assailant.

---

§ 4.3.3 Tell the Story from the Client's Point of View

One of the most powerful persuasive devices is point of view. In many cases, you will want to tell the story as your client would tell it.

One way of telling the story from your client's point of view is to make your client the "actor" in most of your sentences. Note how in the defendant's statement of facts, the writer has made Mr. Patterson or his wife the subject in most of the main clauses, while in the State's statement of facts, the writer has made Ms. Martinez the subject in most of the main clauses.

In the following examples, the subject of each sentence is in bold.

EXAMPLE 1   **EXCERPT FROM DEFENDANT'S STATEMENT OF FACTS**

At 7:30 on Monday morning, August 19, 2019, twenty-two-year-old **Dean Patterson** finished his shift as a security guard and walked to his apartment. After having breakfast with his wife, **Mr. Patterson** went to bed and slept until about 1:00 p.m. At about 2:30 p.m., **Mr. Patterson's wife** received a phone call asking her to work at the local hospital where she is employed as a nurse. **She** got ready, and **Mr. Patterson** dropped her off at the hospital at about 3:10 p.m. When he returned, **Mr. Patterson** could not find a parking place close to his apartment and had to park several blocks away.

At about 3:30 p.m., **Mr. Patterson** called his wife to find out how long she would have to work. **They** had plans to go to a movie that evening, and **he** wanted to know whether he should change those plans. At about 3:50 p.m., **Mr. Patterson** took a load of laundry to the apartment complex's laundry room. When he returned to his apartment, **Mr. Patterson** watched part of an old movie. At about 4:20 p.m., **Patterson** went back to the laundry room to put the clothes in the dryer. By this time, it was 4:30 p.m., and **Mr. Patterson** decided to phone his wife again. **He** arranged to meet her at 5:15 p.m. for her dinner break. **Mr. Patterson** finished the laundry and then left the apartment a little before 5:00 p.m. to meet his wife.

EXAMPLE 2 **EXCERPT FROM THE STATE'S STATEMENT OF FACTS**

On Monday, August 19, 2019, **Beatrice Martinez** was assaulted with a deadly weapon. At a show-up conducted thirty to forty minutes after the attack, **Ms. Martinez** positively identified the defendant, Dean E. Patterson, as her assailant. The next day, **Ms. Martinez** picked Patterson out of a line-up, once again positively identifying him as her assailant.

---

§ 4.3.4 Emphasize the Facts That Support Your Theory of the Case, and De-emphasize Those That Do Not

In addition to presenting the facts from the client's point of view, good advocates emphasize those facts that support their theory of the case and de-emphasize those that do not. They do this by using one or more of the following techniques.

a. Airtime

Just as listeners remember best the songs that get the most airtime, readers remember best the facts that get the most words. Consequently, favorable facts should be given considerable "airtime," and unfavorable ones should be given little or no "play." In the example case, if Patterson is going to persuade the court that the identifications are unreliable, he needs to de-emphasize the fact that Martinez saw the car twice. Although he cannot omit this fact, he does not need to give this fact very much airtime. In contrast, if the State is going to persuade the court that Martinez's identifications are reliable, it needs to emphasize the fact that she saw the car twice. Thus, the State wants to give this fact as much airtime as possible. In the following examples, the relevant facts are in bold.

EXAMPLE 1   **EXCERPT FROM THE DEFENDANT'S STATEMENT OF FACTS**

Ms. Martinez told the police that she was walking down Belmont **when a car that had driven by earlier** pulled in front of her. The man got out of his car, took one or two steps toward Ms. Martinez, and then pulled a gun from his pocket. As soon as she spotted the gun, Ms. Martinez screamed, looked away, and then, crying, ran across the street. The entire encounter was over in a second or two.

EXAMPLE 2   **EXCERPT FROM THE STATE'S STATEMENT OF FACTS**

As she was walking north on Belmont, Ms. Martinez observed an older model silver SUV with a chrome luggage rack as it passed slowly by her. Moments later, the same car came down the street again. This time, the driver pulled his car in front of Ms. Martinez, stopping his car so that it blocked her path. As Martinez watched, the driver got out of his car and walked toward her. The man then took a gun from his coat pocket and pointed it at Ms. Martinez. Ms. Martinez looked at the gun, looked back up at her assailant, and then, crying, ran across the street.

---

b. Detail

Just as readers tend to remember best those facts that get the most airtime, they also tend to remember best those facts that are described in the most detail. The more detail, the more vivid the picture; the more vivid the picture, the more likely it is that the fact will stick in the reader's mind. Thus, airtime and detail work hand in hand. In contrast, to de-emphasize unfavorable facts, good advocates describe them in general terms.

Look again at the following examples, this time comparing the way in which the defendant and the State describe the assailant's car. By leaving out the description of the car, is the defendant setting out all of the legally significant facts? What inference does the State want the judge to draw from the fact that Martinez provided the police with a detailed description of her assailant's car?

EXAMPLE 1   **EXCERPT FROM THE DEFENDANT'S STATEMENT OF FACTS**

Ms. Martinez told the police that she was walking down Belmont when **a car** that had driven by earlier pulled in front of her. The driver, a man, got out of his car, took one or two steps toward Ms. Martinez, and then pulled a gun from his pocket. As soon as she spotted the gun, Ms. Martinez screamed, looked away, and then, crying, ran across the street. The entire encounter was over in a second or two.

EXAMPLE 2   **EXCERPT FROM THE STATE'S STATEMENT OF FACTS**

As she was walking north on Belmont, Ms. Martinez observed **an older model silver SUV with a chrome luggage rack** as it passed slowly by her. Moments later, the same car came down the street again. This time, the driver, a man, pulled his car in front of Ms. Martinez, stopping his car so that it blocked her path. As Ms. Martinez watched, the man got out of his car and walked toward her. The man then took a gun from his coat pocket and pointed it at Ms. Martinez. Ms. Martinez looked at the gun, looked back up at her assailant, and then, crying, ran across the street.

---

c. Positions of Emphasis

Because readers tend to remember best information that is placed in a position of emphasis (the beginning or end of a section, the beginning or end of a paragraph, and the beginning or end of a sentence), whenever possible, place the facts that you want to emphasize in one of these positions. Conversely, if you want to de-emphasize a fact, bury it in the middle—in the middle of a sentence, in the middle of a paragraph, or in the middle of a section.

In the following examples, the defendant wants to emphasize that while Ms. Martinez told the police her assailant was in his early forties, Mr. Patterson is only twenty-two. As a consequence, defense counsel places those facts near the end of the paragraph. In contrast, because the State wants to de-emphasize the age discrepancy, it places Ms. Martinez's statement that her assailant was in his early forties in a sentence in the middle of a paragraph. It then places Mr. Patterson's actual age in a separate paragraph.

EXAMPLE 1   **EXCERPT FROM THE DEFENDANT'S STATEMENT OF FACTS**

Because she was upset, Ms. Martinez was able to give the police only a general description of her assailant. She described him as being a short, white male with blondish-brown hair who was wearing glasses and a dark jacket. In addition, **she told the police that her assailant was in his early forties. Mr. Patterson is twenty-two.**

| EXAMPLE 2 | EXCERPT FROM THE STATE'S STATEMENT OF FACTS |

Ms. Martinez told the police that her assailant was a white male who was about 5'7" tall; that her assailant had wavy blondish-brown hair; **that her assailant appeared to be in his early forties**; and that, at the time of the assault, her assailant was wearing a dark jacket and glasses.

---

d. Sentence Length

Just as airtime and detail work together, so do positions of emphasis and sentence length. Because readers tend to remember information placed in shorter sentences better than information placed in longer sentences, good advocates place favorable facts in short sentences in a position of emphasis. For instance, in Example 1, not only did defense counsel place the favorable fact in a position of emphasis, but she also put that fact in a short sentence. In Example 2, the State not only buried the unfavorable fact in the middle of the paragraph, but it also placed that fact in the middle of a long sentence.

| EXAMPLE 1 | EXCERPT FROM THE DEFENDANT'S STATEMENT OF FACTS |

Because she was upset, Ms. Martinez was able to give the police only a general description of her assailant. She described him as being a short, white male with blondish-brown hair who was wearing glasses and a dark jacket. In addition, she told police that her assailant was in his early forties. **Mr. Patterson is twenty-two.**

| EXAMPLE 2 | EXCERPT FROM THE STATE'S STATEMENT OF FACTS |

Ms. Martinez told the police that her assailant was a white male who was about 5'7" tall; that her assailant had wavy blondish-brown hair; **that her assailant appeared to be in his early forties**; and that, at the time of the assault, her assailant was wearing a dark jacket and glasses.

PRACTICE POINTER

Another way to emphasize a favorable fact is by highlighting discrepancies. For instance, in Example 1, defense counsel places the fact that the defendant is twenty-two next to fact that Ms. Martinez told police that her assailant appeared to be in his early forties. By juxtaposing these two facts, defense counsel is able to highlight the discrepancies. In contrast, the prosecutor creates space between these two facts by putting the fact that Mr. Patterson is twenty-two in one paragraph and the fact that Ms. Martinez told police that her assailant was in his early forties in a different paragraph.

e. Active and Passive Voice

Good advocates use active voice when they want to emphasize what the actor did and passive voice when they want to draw the reader's attention away from the actor's actions. Consider the following examples.

EXAMPLE 1 **ACTIVE VOICE**

Mr. Patterson assaulted Ms. Martinez.

EXAMPLE 2 **PASSIVE VOICE**

Ms. Martinez was assaulted.

Because the State wants to emphasize that it was Mr. Patterson who assaulted Ms. Martinez, the prosecutor would use the language in Example 1. In contrast, because Mr. Patterson states that he did not assault Ms. Martinez, his attorney would use the language set out in Example 2. For more on active and passive voice, see section 5.1 in *Just Writing, Fifth Edition.*

f. Dependent and Main Clauses

Another technique is to put favorable facts in the main clause and unfavorable facts in a subordinate clause. While the defendant wants to emphasize the fact that the bystander, Clipse, was unable to make an identification and de-emphasize the fact that Martinez was able to make an identification, the State wants to do the opposite. Compare the following examples.

EXAMPLE 1 **EXCERPT FROM THE DEFENDANT'S BRIEF**

Later that day, the police searched Mr. Patterson's car and apartment. In the apartment, the police found the gun issued to Mr. Patterson by his employer. The next day, the police held a line-up at the police station. **Although Ms. Martinez identified Mr. Patterson as the man who had approached her, Mr. Clipse did not pick Mr. Patterson out of the line-up.**

EXAMPLE 2 **EXCERPT FROM THE STATE'S BRIEF**

A line-up was held the next day. **Although Mr. Clipse was unable to identify the man who had assaulted Ms. Martinez, Ms. Martinez identified Mr. Patterson as her assailant.**

---

§ 4.3.5 Select Words Both for Their Denotation and Their Connotation

Words are powerful. Not only do they convey information (denotation), but they also create images (connotation). Consider, for example, the labels that might be used to describe Mr. Patterson.

- Mr. Dean Patterson
- Dean Patterson
- Mr. Patterson
- Patterson
- Dean
- the suspect
- the accused
- the defendant

While defense counsel would probably want to use "Mr. Patterson" or "Dean Patterson" in referring to her client, the prosecutor might use "the defendant." By using his name, defense counsel reminds the judge that her client is a real person. The title "Mr. Patterson" makes Patterson seem less like a person charged with a felony and more like an average, respectable citizen. In contrast, by using the label "the defendant," the State suggests that Patterson is guilty.

> **PRACTICE POINTER** Because legal proceedings are formal proceedings, as a general rule, do not refer to parties or to witnesses by just their first names. The only times that you might want to break this "rule" are when referring to a child (for example, the child in a juvenile case), or when there are two or more individuals with the same last name.

Other word choices can also subtly persuade the court. For instance, in the following paragraph the defendant's attorney wants to set up the argument that Officer Yuen's actions tainted the identifications. Thus, she uses "agreed" to suggest that Ms. Martinez's identification was prompted by Officer Yuen's questions; "questioned" to suggest that the officers' actions would have indicated to Ms. Martinez and Mr. Clipse that Mr. Patterson was guilty; and "watched" to remind the court that Ms. Martinez and Mr. Clipse may have been influenced by the officers' actions.

EXAMPLE 1   **EXCERPT FROM THE DEFENDANT'S STATEMENT OF FACTS**

Even though Ms. Martinez was unable to see the man's face, she **agreed** with the officer that the man looked like her assailant. At this point, Officer Yuen stopped the car, got out, and approached Patterson. As Officer Yuen was **questioning** Patterson, Officer Cox drove up with the witness, Mr. Clipse. While Ms. Martinez and Mr. Clipse **watched**, Officers Cox and Yuen **continued questioning** Patterson. Officer Cox then returned to Ms. Martinez and Mr. Clipse and walked them back to Mr. Clipse's landlady's apartment. While Officer Cox did so, Officer Yuen placed Patterson under arrest.

§ 4.4 Checklist for Critiquing the Statement of Facts

I. *Organization*

- You have set out the facts in a logical order (chronologically or topically or a combination of the two).
- When possible, you have presented the facts in an order that favors your client.

II. *Content*

- You have included all of the legally significant facts.
- You have included the emotionally significant facts that favor your client.
- You have an appropriate number of background facts.

III. *Persuasiveness*

- You have presented the facts in a way that supports your theory of the case.
- You have primed your reader to see your client and his or her arguments in a favorable light.
- When possible, you have created a favorable context.
- If appropriate, you have presented the facts from your client's point of view.
- You have emphasized favorable facts and de-emphasized unfavorable ones.
  - You have given favorable facts airtime and unfavorable facts little airtime.
  - You have described favorable facts in detail and unfavorable facts more generally.
  - You have used the positions of emphasis effectively. When possible, you have placed favorable facts at the beginning or end of the statement of facts, at the beginning or end of a paragraph, or at the beginning or end of a sentence.
  - You have used short sentences and short paragraphs to emphasize favorable facts; you have placed unfavorable facts in longer sentences in longer paragraphs.

- You have used active and passive voices effectively.
- You have emphasized favorable facts by placing them in the main, or independent, clauses and de-emphasized unfavorable facts by placing them in subordinate or dependent clauses.
- You have selected words both for their denotation and their connotation.
- Your writing is grammatically correct, correctly punctuated, and proofread.

5

Issue Statements and Ordering the Issues and Arguments

§ 5.1 Issue Statements

While you may not include an issue statement in all of your briefs, when you do include one, think carefully about how you want to frame the legal question. By asking the right question, you improve your chances of getting the result that your client wants.

§ 5.1.1 Select the Lens

The issue statement is the lens through which the judge views the case. Select the correct lens, and you improve your chances that the court will see the case as you see it and decide the motion in your client's favor. The difficulty, of course, is in selecting that lens. How do you select just the right one? Unfortunately, there is no easy answer. Because selecting the lens is, at least in part, a creative act, there is no foolproof formula.

There are, however, some strategies that you can use. First, think about your theory of the case. Given your theory, how should you frame the issue? Second, look at how the court framed the issues in cases that are similar to yours. In the cases in which the courts suppressed the evidence, how did the court frame the issue? Then look at the cases in which the courts did not suppress the evidence.

Finally, brainstorm. From what other angles can you view the case? What other labels can you attach? Think outside the box.

§ 5.1.2 Select a Format

Most courts do not prescribe a format for an issue statement. Although you should have the same number of issue statements as you have main argumentative headings, you can state the issue using the under-does-when format, the whether format, or the multi-sentence format. See sections 8.2 and 8.3 in *Just Memos, Fifth Edition*. In addition, in some jurisdictions and for some types of briefs, you can just set out the legal or factual question that you want the court to decide.

> **PRACTICE POINTER**
>
> When you use the under-does-when format, you do not need to use "does" as the verb. You can use any verb that works with your sentence. For example, in the following example, the writer uses "should."

EXAMPLE 1   "UNDER-DOES-WHEN" FORMAT

Under the Fourteenth Amendment, should the Court grant Mr. Patterson's motion to suppress Ms. Martinez's show-up, line-up, and in-court identifications and Mr. Patterson's in-court identification when (1) a police officer pointed out Mr. Patterson to Ms. Martinez, repeatedly asking the shaken Ms. Martinez whether Mr. Patterson looked like her assailant; (2) the police questioned Mr. Patterson in front of Ms. Martinez and Mr. Clipse; (3) during the second or two that Ms. Martinez had to view her assailant, her attention was focused on his gun and not his face; and (4) Ms. Martinez told police that her assailant was in his forties, and Mr. Patterson is twenty-two?

EXAMPLE 2   "WHETHER" FORMAT

Whether the Court should grant Mr. Patterson's motion to suppress Ms. Martinez's show-up, line-up, and in-court identifications and Mr. Clipse's in-court identification when (1) a police officer pointed out Mr. Patterson to Ms. Martinez, repeatedly asking the shaken Ms. Martinez whether Mr. Patterson looked like her assailant; (2) the police questioned Mr. Patterson in front of Ms. Martinez and Mr. Clipse; (3) during the second or two that Ms. Martinez had to view her assailant, her attention was focused on his gun and not his face;

and (4) Ms. Martinez told police that her assailant was in his forties, and Mr. Patterson is twenty-two.

EXAMPLE 3   MULTI-SENTENCE FORMAT

On August 19, 2019, a man jumped out of his car, approached Ms. Martinez, and pointed a gun at her. As soon as she saw the gun, Ms. Martinez screamed and, crying, ran across the street. Shortly after the assault, a police officer twice asked Ms. Martinez whether a pedestrian looked like her assailant. Although Ms. Martinez could not see the pedestrian's face, she agreed. The police then questioned the pedestrian, Dean Patterson, while Ms. Martinez and another witness watched. Both Ms. Martinez and the witness told the police that Ms. Martinez's assailant was in his late thirties or early forties. Mr. Patterson is twenty-two. Under these circumstances, should the Court suppress Ms. Martinez's show-up and line-up identifications and prevent Ms. Martinez and Mr. Clipse from making in-court identifications?

EXAMPLE 4   ISSUE STATEMENT THAT JUST SETS OUT THE LEGAL QUESTION

Whether the Court should suppress Ms. Martinez's show-up and line-up identifications and prevent Ms. Martinez and Mr. Clipse from making in-court identifications.

EXAMPLE 5   ISSUE STATEMENT THAT JUST SETS OUT THE LEGAL QUESTION

Should the Court grant Mr. Patterson's motion to suppress?

PRACTICE POINTER Once you select a format, use that format for each of your issue statements. Do not write one issue statement using the under-does-when format, a second issue statement using the whether format, and a third using the multi-sentence format. Also remember that you are not bound by opposing counsel's choices. You do not need to use the same format that he or she used, and you do not need to have the same number of issue statements. Do not let your opponent dictate your strategy.

§ 5.1.3 Make Your Issue Statement Subtly Persuasive

Your issue statement should be subtly persuasive. After reading it, the judge should be inclined to rule in your client's favor.

There are two techniques that you can use to make your issue statements persuasive. First, state the legal question so that it suggests the conclusion you want the court to reach. For example, if you want the court to grant the motion, ask whether the court should grant the motion. In contrast, if you want the court to deny the motion, ask whether the court should deny the motion. Second, when you include facts, present those facts in the light most favorable to your client.

While in our example case, Mr. Patterson wants to state the legal question so that it suggests that the court should grant his motion to suppress, the State wants to frame the question so that it suggests that the court should deny the motion.

EXAMPLE 1   **THE DEFENDANT'S STATEMENT OF THE LEGAL QUESTION**

"Whether the Court should grant the motion to suppress when . . . ."

EXAMPLE 2   **THE STATE'S STATEMENT OF THE LEGAL QUESTION**

"Whether the Court should deny the motion to suppress when . . . ."

The defendant also wants to set out the facts so that they suggest that the police procedures were unnecessarily suggestive and that Ms. Martinez's identifications are unreliable. Accordingly, the defendant wants to set out the facts that establish that the procedure was suggestive. Instead of allowing Ms. Martinez to independently identify Mr. Patterson, a police officer pointed out Mr. Patterson and repeatedly asked the shaken Ms. Martinez whether he looked like her assailant. In addition, the defendant wants to set out facts that establish that Ms. Martinez had a limited opportunity to view her assailant and that her description was inaccurate. Note that in both instances the writers set out the facts related to the first part of the test first and then the facts related to the second part of the test.

EXAMPLE 3   **THE DEFENDANT'S ISSUE STATEMENT**

Under the Fourteenth Amendment, should the Court grant Mr. Patterson's motion to suppress Ms. Martinez's show-up identification (1) when a police officer pointed out Mr. Patterson to Ms. Martinez, repeatedly asking the shaken Ms. Martinez whether Mr. Patterson looked like her assailant; (2) when, during the second or two that Ms. Martinez had to view her assailant, her attention was focused on his gun and not his face; and (3) when Ms. Martinez told the police that her assailant was in his early forties, and Mr. Patterson is only twenty-two years old?

While the defendant wants to set out the facts that indicate that the police procedures were unnecessarily suggestive and that Ms. Martinez's identifications are unreliable, the State wants to downplay the police officer's questions and emphasize instead that Ms. Martinez had a good opportunity to view her assailant.

EXAMPLE 4   THE STATE'S ISSUE STATEMENT

Should the Court deny the defendant's motion to suppress when the police merely asked the victim whether a pedestrian looked like her assailant and when the victim observed her assailant on two occasions in broad daylight?

Thus, writing a persuasive issue statement is a three-step process. You must select the appropriate lens, choose a format, and then craft your issue statement so that it is subtly persuasive.

§ 5.1.4 Checklist for Critiquing the Issue Statement

I. *Format*

- You have the same number of issue statements as you have main argumentative headings. The heading answers the question that you set out in the corresponding issue statement.
- You have used one of the conventional formats: for example, the under-does-when format, the whether format, or the multi-sentence format.
- You have used the same format for all of your issue statements.

II. *Content*

- The issue statement states the legal question and includes references to the legally significant facts. In addition, when appropriate, it also includes a reference to the rule of law.
- You have framed the legal questions so that they support your theory of the case.

III. *Persuasiveness*

- You have framed the legal question so that it suggests an answer favorable to your client.
- You have emphasized favorable facts and de-emphasized unfavorable ones.
- You have selected words for both their denotation and their connotation.

IV. *Writing*

- The judge can understand the issue statement after reading it through once.
- You have used punctuation to divide the issue statement into manageable units of meaning.
- If you set out a list, you have used parallel constructions for each item in the list.
- In both the main and subordinate clauses, you have kept the verb near the subject.
- Your writing is grammatically correct, correctly punctuated, and proofread.

§ 5.2 Ordering the Issues and Arguments

§ 5.2.1 Present the Issues and Arguments in a Logical Order

In many cases, logic dictates the order of both the issues and, under each issue, the arguments. Threshold questions (for example, issues relating to whether the court has jurisdiction or whether the statute of limitations has run) must be discussed before questions relating to the merits of the case. Similarly, the parts of a test must be discussed in the correct order and, when one argument builds on another, the foundation argument must be presented first.

Although in the example case there is only one issue—whether the court should grant the defendant's motion to suppress—under that issue are several subissues. The court must decide (1) whether to suppress Ms. Martinez's show-up identification, (2) whether to suppress Ms. Martinez's line-up identification, and (3) whether to suppress any in-court identifications that Ms. Martinez or Mr. Clipse might make.

Logic dictates, at least in part, the order in which these three subissues should be discussed. Because an impermissibly suggestive show-up would taint the line-up and in-court identifications, the attorneys need to discuss the show-up before the line-up and both the show-up and the line-up before the in-court identifications.

Logic also dictates the order of the arguments. Before it can suppress an identification, the court must find (1) that the police procedures were impermissibly suggestive and (2) if they are, that under the totality of the circumstances, the resulting identifications are unreliable. Consequently, the defendant must discuss suggestiveness first.

In deciding whether an identification is reliable, the court considers five factors: (1) the witness's opportunity to see her assailant, (2) the witness's degree of attention, (3) the accuracy of the witness's description, (4) the witness's level of certainty, and (5) the length of time between the crime and the confrontation. In this instance, logic does not dictate that the factors be discussed in a particular order. Consequently, the writer can choose how to list the factors.

PRACTICE POINTER	You should discuss the factors in the same order in which you list them.

§ 5.2.2 Decide Which Issues and Arguments Should Be Presented First

First impressions count. As a consequence, when logic does not dictate the order of your issues or arguments, put your strongest issues and your strongest arguments first. In addition, some attorneys like to end their brief with a strong argument. Although this strategy allows you to take advantage of the positions of emphasis, it also creates a risk. If the judge does not finish your brief or starts skimming, he or she might not see one of your strongest arguments.

CHAPTER 6

Argumentative Headings and the Arguments

§ 6.1 Argumentative Headings

§ 6.1.1 Use Your Argumentative Headings to Define the Structure of the Argument

Just as posts and beams define a building's structure, argumentative headings define the brief's structure. When drafted properly, they provide the judge with an outline of the argument. Read the following example. Do the headings provide you with an outline of Mr. Patterson's arguments?

EXAMPLE 1 **DEFENDANT'S ARGUMENTATIVE HEADINGS**

I. **The Court should grant Mr. Patterson's Motion to Suppress Ms. Martinez's show-up and line-up identifications and Ms. Martinez's and Mr. Clipse's in-court identifications.**

[Put general rules here.]

A. <u>Ms. Martinez's show-up identification should be suppressed because the police procedures were impermissibly suggestive and because Ms. Martinez's identification is unreliable.</u>

[Set out test.]

1. The police procedures were impermissibly suggestive because the police officer repeatedly asked Ms. Martinez whether Mr. Patterson looked like her assailant and because the officers questioned Mr. Patterson while Ms. Martinez and Mr. Clipse watched.

[Set out argument.]

2. Ms. Martinez's identification is unreliable because Ms. Martinez was able to view her assailant for only a few seconds, her attention was focused on the gun and not his face, and her description of her assailant does not match the description of Mr. Patterson.

[Set out argument.]

B. <u>Ms. Martinez's line-up identification should be suppressed because it was tainted by the show-up.</u>

[Set out argument.]

C. <u>Ms. Martinez and Mr. Clipse should not be permitted to make an in-court identification because those identifications would be tainted by the impermissibly suggestive show-up and the line-up.</u>

[Set out argument.]

In addition to defining the structure of the argument, argumentative headings also act as locators. By using the headings and subheadings, a judge can locate a particular argument.

PRACTICE POINTER   Argumentative headings also help the writer. As a practicing attorney, you will seldom have large blocks of time available for writing. Instead, you will have to squeeze in an hour here and two hours there. If you prepare your argumentative headings first, you can use those headings to write a section at a time.

§ 6.1.2 Use Your Argumentative Headings to Persuade

In addition to using argumentative headings to define the structure of your argument, use the headings to persuade.

Begin your heading by setting out a positive assertion. If you want the court to grant your motion to suppress, make that assertion: "The Court should grant the motion to suppress . . . ." In contrast, if you want the court to deny the motion to suppress, make that assertion: "The Court should deny the motion to suppress . . . ."

EXAMPLE 1   NOT A POSITIVE ASSERTION

The Court should not grant the motion to suppress . . . .
The Court should not suppress Ms. Martinez's show-up identification . . . .

EXAMPLE 2   POSITIVE ASSERTION

The Court should deny the motion to suppress . . . .
The Court should admit Ms. Martinez's show-up identification . . . .

After setting out your assertion, you will usually want to set out the facts or reasons that support your assertion. The most common format is as follows:

Assertion	because	facts or reasons that support your assertion
Ms. Martinez's line-up identification should be suppressed	because	it was tainted by the impermissibly suggestive show-up.

In those instances in which you do not set out the reasons in your heading, use subheadings or sub-subheadings to set out the reasons. Look again at the headings and subheadings in the defendant's argumentative headings. Although the writer has not included a "because" clause in the main heading, she has included them in the subheadings and sub-subheadings.

| EXAMPLE 3 | DEFENDANT'S ARGUMENTATIVE HEADINGS |

I. **The Court should grant Mr. Patterson's Motion to Suppress Ms. Martinez's show-up and line-up identifications and Ms. Martinez's and Mr. Clipse's in-court identifications.**

[Put general rules here.]

A. <u>Ms. Martinez's show-up identification should be suppressed because the police procedures were impermissibly suggestive and because Ms. Martinez's identification is unreliable.</u>

[Set out test.]

2. The police procedures were impermissibly suggestive because the police officer repeatedly asked Ms. Martinez whether Mr. Patterson looked like her assailant and because the officers questioned Mr. Patterson while Ms. Martinez and Mr. Clipse watched.

[Set out argument.]

3. Ms. Martinez's identification is unreliable because Ms. Martinez was able to view her assailant for only a few seconds, her attention was focused on the gun and not his face, and her description of her assailant does not match the description of Mr. Patterson.

[Set out argument.]

B. <u>Ms. Martinez's line-up identification should be suppressed because it was tainted by the show-up.</u>

[Set out argument.]

C. <u>Ms. Martinez and Mr. Clipse should not be permitted to make an in-court identification because such an identification would be tainted by the impermissibly suggestive show-up and the line-up.</u>

[Set out argument.]

§ 6.1.3 Make Your Headings Readable

If the judge does not read your headings, they do not serve either of their functions: They do not provide the judge with an outline of your argument, and they do not persuade. To make sure that your headings are read by the judge, keep them short and make them easy to read. As a general rule, your headings should be no more than three typed lines.

In the following example, the writer has tried to put too much information in her heading. As a result, the heading is too long, and the sentence is difficult to understand.

EXAMPLE 1 **HEADING IS TOO LONG**

A. <u>The police procedures were impermissibly suggestive because Ms. Martinez viewed only one person; the police repeatedly asked Ms. Martinez whether that person looked like her assailant; the police questioned Mr. Patterson while Ms. Martinez and Mr. Clipse watched; Mr. Patterson was simply walking down the street and not trying to escape; and Ms. Martinez was not likely to die or disappear, so there was no reason to conduct a one-person show-up.</u>

The following heading is much better. Instead of trying to put her entire argument into her heading, the writer has included only her most important points.

EXAMPLE 2 **HEADING IS SHORTER AND EASIER TO UNDERSTAND**

A. <u>The police procedures were impermissibly suggestive because the police officer repeatedly asked Ms. Martinez whether Mr. Patterson looked like her assailant and because the officers questioned Mr. Patterson while Ms. Martinez and Mr. Clipse watched.</u>

---

§ 6.1.4 Follow the Conventions: Number, Placement, and Typefaces

By convention, you should have one, and only one, main argumentative heading for each issue statement. You set out the question in your issue statement and answer the question in your main heading. Although sub-headings and sub-subheadings are optional, if you include one, you should have at least two. You may place text between the main heading and the first subheading or between a subheading and the first sub-subheading.

> **PRACTICE POINTER**
>
> Historically, only three typefaces were used. When briefs were prepared using typewriters, the main headings were set out using all capital letters, the subheadings were underlined, and the sub-subheadings were set out using regular typeface. Although many attorneys still use this system, others have adopted different systems, for example, setting out the main headings in bold rather than all capitals. Check with your local court and firm to see what is commonly done in your jurisdiction.

EXAMPLE 1 **TYPEFACES FOR MAIN HEADING,**
SUBHEADINGS, AND SUB-SUBHEADINGS

I. **First Main Heading** [Answers question set out in first issue statement.]

[If appropriate, set out paragraph and general rules here.]

A. First subheading

[If appropriate, set out test here.]

1. First sub-subheading

[Set out argument here.]

2. Second sub-subheading

[Set out argument here.]

B. Second subheading

[Set out argument here.]

II. **Second Main Heading** [If you had two issue statements, answers question set out in the second issue statement.]

A. First subheading

[Set out argument here.]

B. Second subheading

[Set out argument here.]

C. Third subheading

[Set out argument here.]

---

§ 6.2 Checklist for Critiquing the Argumentative Headings

I. *Content*

- When read together, the headings provide the judge with an outline of the argument.

II. *Persuasiveness*

- Each heading is in the form of a positive assertion.
- Each assertion is supported, either in the main heading or through the use of subheadings.
- The headings are case-specific—that is, they include references to the parties and the facts of the case.
- Favorable facts are emphasized, and unfavorable facts are de-emphasized or omitted if not legally significant.
- Favorable facts have been placed in the positions of emphasis.
- Favorable facts have been described in detail.
- Words have been selected both for their denotation and their connotation.

III. *Conventions*

- The writer has used different typefaces for main headings, sub-headings, and sub-subheadings.
- There is never just one subheading or just one sub-subheading in a section.

IV. *Writing*

- The judge can understand the heading after reading it through once. (Headings are not more than two or three lines long.)
- Punctuation has been used to divide the heading into manageable units of meaning.
- When appropriate, parallel constructions have been used.
- In both the main and subordinate clauses, the subject and verb are close together.
- The headings are grammatically correct, correctly punctuated, and proofread.

§ 6.3 The Arguments

Although most of us have had arguments, very few of us have been taught how to make arguments. We know how to express our anger and frustration; we do not know how to set out an assertion and then systematically walk our listener through our "proof." Even fewer of us have been taught how to set out our proofs persuasively.

It is, however, exactly these skills—the ability to set out an assertion, to walk your reader through your proof, and to present that proof persuasively—that you will need to develop if you are going to write an effective brief. Good advocates have the mental discipline of a mathematician. They think linearly, identifying each of the steps in the analysis, and then walk the judge through those steps in a logical order. They also have the creativity and insight of an advertising executive. They know their "market," and they know both the image they want to create and how to use language to create it. In short, they have mastered both the science and the art of advocacy.

§ 6.3.1 Identify Your Assertions and Your Support for Those Assertions

An argument has two parts: an assertion and the support for that assertion.

a. Setting Out Your Assertion

An assertion can take one of two forms. It can be procedural—setting out the procedural act you want the court to take—or it can be substantive—setting out the legal conclusion you want the court to reach.

EXAMPLE 1   **TYPES OF ASSERTIONS**

Procedural

The Court should grant the motion to suppress.

The Court should deny the motion to suppress.

Substantive

The police procedures were impermissibly suggestive.

Ms. Martinez's identification is reliable.

---

b. Supporting Your Assertion

Although your assertion is an essential part of your argument, it is not, by itself, an argument. How many judges would be persuaded by the following exchange?

Defense counsel:	Your Honor, the Court should grant the Defendant's motion to suppress.
Prosecutor:	Your Honor, we respectfully disagree. The Court should deny the motion.
Defense counsel:	No, Your Honor, the Court should grant the motion.
Prosecutor:	No. The Court should deny the motion.

An exchange in which the defendant asserts that the police procedures were impermissibly suggestive and the prosecutor asserts that they were not is equally unpersuasive. Standing alone, assertions do not persuade. They must be supported.

In law, that support can take one of several forms. You can support an assertion by citing to the constitution; by applying a statute or common law rule to the facts of your case; by comparing or contrasting the facts in your case to the facts in analogous cases; or by explaining why, as a matter of public policy, the court should rule in your client's favor.

In Example 1 below, defense counsel supports her assertion by applying the rule to the facts of Mr. Patterson's case. In Example 2, defense counsel supports her assertion by comparing the facts in Mr. Patterson's case to the facts in the analogous cases, and in Example 3, she supports her assertion by using public policy.

EXAMPLE 2 **DEFENDANT SUPPORTS HIS ASSERTION BY APPLYING THE RULES TO THE FACTS OF HIS CASE**

Assertion: The police procedures were impermissibly suggestive.

Support: Rule: One-person show-ups are inherently suggestive. *See Neil v. Biggers*, 409 U.S. 188, 199, 93 S. Ct. 375, 34 L. Ed. 2d 401 (1972).[1] When the police present the witness with a single suspect, the witness usually infers that the police believe that the person being presented committed the crime.

Application: In this case, the police presented Ms. Martinez with a single suspect: Dean Patterson. In doing so, the police suggested to Ms. Martinez that Mr. Patterson was the man who had assaulted her.

EXAMPLE 3 **DEFENDANT SUPPORTS HIS ASSERTION BY COMPARING THE FACTS IN HIS CASE WITH THE FACTS IN AN ANALOGOUS CASE**

Assertion: The police procedures were impermissibly suggestive.

Support: Analogous case: In *State v. Booth*, 36 Wn. App. 66, 67-68, 671 P.2d 1218 (1983), the police brought the witness to the scene of the arrest and showed him a single suspect, who was sitting with his back to the witness in the back seat of the police car. The court held that the police procedures were impermissibly suggestive. *Id.* at 70.

Application: As in *Booth,* in our case the police showed the witness a single suspect and asked her to identify him before she had an opportunity to see his face. The only difference between the two

---

[1] Because the briefs will be filed in a Washington court, the attorneys have used Washington's citation rules. *See* http://www.courts.wa.gov/appellate_trial_courts/supreme/?fa = atc_ supreme.style.

cases is the identity of the person in the police car. While in *Booth* it was the suspect who was in the car, in our case it was the witness.

EXAMPLE 4   **THE DEFENDANT SUPPORTS HIS ASSERTION BY USING PUBLIC POLICY**

Assertion: The police procedures were impermissibly suggestive.

Support: Policy: To protect the rights of defendants, courts should suppress unreliable identifications.

Application: Because Ms. Martinez's identifications are unreliable, Mr. Patterson will be denied his right to a fair trial if Ms. Martinez's show-up and line-up identifications are admitted.

If there is only one argument that supports your assertion, make that argument. If, however, you can make several different arguments, think about whether you want to include all those arguments. Will your brief be more persuasive if you set out only one strong argument, or will it be more persuasive if you set out three, four, or five arguments? Can you combine arguments—for example, can you combine your plain language and your analogous case arguments? Identifying the arguments is the science; deciding which arguments to include is the art.

§ 6.3.2 Select an Organizational Scheme

In making their arguments, most advocates use one of two types of reasoning: deductive or inductive. When you use deductive reasoning, you set out your assertion and then the support for that assertion. In contrast, when you use inductive reasoning, you set out your support first, and then walk the judge through your support to your conclusion.

EXAMPLE 1   **DEDUCTIVE REASONING**

Assertion: The identification is not reliable.

Support: The identification is not reliable because Ms. Martinez viewed her assailant for only two or three seconds.

The identification is not reliable because Ms. Martinez's attention was focused on the gun and not on her assailant's face.

The identification is not reliable because Ms. Martinez's description of her assailant was inaccurate.

The identification is not reliable because, at least initially, Ms. Martinez was not certain that Mr. Patterson was her assailant.

EXAMPLE 2   **INDUCTIVE REASONING**

Support: Ms. Martinez viewed her assailant for only two or three seconds.

Ms. Martinez's attention was focused on the gun and not on her assailant's face.

Ms. Martinez's description of her assailant was inaccurate.

At least initially, Ms. Martinez was not certain that Mr. Patterson was her assailant.

Conclusion: Because Ms. Martinez viewed her assailant for only two or three seconds, because her attention was focused on the gun and not on her assailant's face, because her description of her assailant was inaccurate, and because, at least initially, she was not certain that Mr. Patterson was her assailant, Ms. Martinez's show-up identification is not reliable.

If you use deductive reasoning, you will usually use a version of the following outline. Note the similarities between this outline and the outlines that you use to organize the discussion section in an objective memo. Also note that the following example shows two different ways of setting out the arguments. Under the first subheading, the assertion is set out first. Under the second subheading, the assertion is set out after the rules and the descriptions of the cases. You should use whichever format is, in your case, most likely to be effective.

EXAMPLE 3   **BLUEPRINT FOR AN ARGUMENT USING DEDUCTIVE REASONING**

   I. **Main Heading**

   [Test set out in the light most favorable to your client.]

   A. First subheading

      1. Assertion

      2. Rules set out in the light most favorable to your client

      3. Descriptions of the analogous cases

      4. Your arguments

      5. Your response to your opponent's arguments

   B. Second subheading

      1. Rules set out in the light most favorable to your client

      2. Descriptions of the analogous cases

      3. Assertion

      4. Your arguments

      5. Your response to your opponent's arguments

When you use inductive reasoning, you will usually integrate the rules, the descriptions of the cases, and your response to the other side's arguments into each of your arguments.

EXAMPLE 4   BLUEPRINT FOR AN ARGUMENT USING INDUCTIVE REASONING

I. **Main Heading**

   A. First subheading

      1. First argument

      2. Second argument

      3. Third argument

      4. Fourth argument

      5. Conclusion

   B. Second subheading

      1. First argument

      2. Second argument

      3. Third argument

      4. Conclusion

There are also several other organizational schemes that you may use. For example, if in your case the facts are your best argument, start by setting out the facts. Then show how those facts are like the facts in cases in which the court reached the conclusion you want the court to reach.

EXAMPLE 5   FACTS SET OUT FIRST

I. **Main Heading**

[Test set out in the light most favorable to your client.]

   A. First subheading

      1. Facts of your case

      2. Comparison of the facts in your case to the facts in analogous cases

      3. Courts' holdings in analogous cases

      4. Response to other side's arguments

      5. Conclusion

In the following example, defense counsel used the "facts-first" strategy in arguing that the show-up was impermissibly suggestive. Because none of the cases supported her position, defense counsel began her argument by setting out her assertion and the facts that support that assertion.

EXAMPLE 6   **EXCERPT FROM THE DEFENDANT'S BRIEF**

A.   The police procedures were unnecessarily suggestive because the police showed Ms. Martinez a single suspect, asked Ms. Martinez whether the suspect looked like her assailant, and questioned the suspect in front of Ms. Martinez and Mr. Clipse.

While driving Ms. Martinez home, Officer Yuen pulled up behind Mr. Patterson and asked Ms. Martinez whether Mr. Patterson looked like her assailant. When Ms. Martinez did not respond, Officer Yuen repeated his question, asking, "Does that look like your assailant?"

Although Ms. Martinez could not see Mr. Patterson's face, after hesitating, she agreed with Officer Yuen that Mr. Patterson looked like her assailant. At that point, Officer Yuen stopped next to Mr. Patterson, got out of the police car, and began questioning him. A few minutes later, Officer Cox and Mr. Clipse arrived, and both Officer Yuen and Officer Cox questioned Mr. Patterson while Ms. Martinez and Mr. Clipse watched.

Thus, this case can be distinguished from *State v. Kraus*, 21 Wn. App. at 392, in which the show-up identification occurred during a prompt search for the robber. In this case the show-up did not occur while the police were searching for Ms. Martinez's assailant. Instead, it occurred while the officer was driving Ms. Martinez home. In addition, unlike *Stovall*, 388 U.S. at 302, in which the police conducted the show-up because they were concerned that the suspect might die, in this case, there were no exigent circumstances. In fact, because the police had located a car that matched the description of the one driven by the assailant, they could have identified the owner of the car and any individuals who had driven it and placed them in a line-up.

In contrast, if your best argument is an argument based on an analogous case, start by describing that case.

EXAMPLE 7   **EXCERPT FROM THE STATE'S BRIEF**

A.   Merely asking the victim whether a pedestrian looks like her assailant does not make a permissible show-up impermissibly suggestive.

There are no published Washington cases in which courts have held that a show-up was impermissibly suggestive. Instead, in a Division I case, the court held that the show-up was not impermissibly suggestive when the police picked up the witness at a tavern and told him that they wanted to take him back to his apartment to see if he could identify his assailant. *State v. Rogers*, 44 Wn.

App. 510, 515-16, 722 P.2d 1249 (1986). When the witness, an elderly individual who was not wearing his glasses, arrived back at his apartment, he identified the defendant when the defendant came out of the building. *Id.* There was a uniformed police officer in front of the defendant and another uniformed police officer following behind him. *Id.*

Similarly, in *State v. Booth*, 36 Wn. App. 66, 70-71, 671 P.2d 1218 (1983), the court held that the show-up was not impermissibly suggestive when the police asked the witness to accompany them to the place where the defendant had been arrested, and the witness identified the defendant after seeing him in the back of a police car. *Id.* at 67-68; *accord State v. Guzman-Cuellar*, 47 Wn. 2d 326, 734 P.2d 966 (1987) (show-up not impermissibly suggestive when the defendant was shown to three of the four eyewitnesses while he was in handcuffs standing next to a police car).

Although you want to set out the pieces of your argument in the order that the judge expects to see them, you also want to emphasize your best arguments. Therefore, instead of using a format mechanically, use it creatively to accomplish your purpose.

PRACTICE POINTER	Initially, you may be frustrated by the fact that there are no rules for selecting issues or arguments or set formats for organizing your arguments. However, with time, you will learn to enjoy exercising your judgment and creativity.

§ 6.3.3 Present the Rules in the Light Most Favorable to Your Client

Although the structure of the argument section is similar to the structure of the discussion section, the way in which you present the rules is very different. While in an objective memo you set out the rules objectively, in a brief you set them out in the light most favorable to your client. Without misrepresenting the rules, you want to "package" them so that they support your assertion.

To set out the rules in the light most favorable to your client, use one or more of the techniques set out in the following box.

Techniques for Presenting the Rules in a Light Favorable to Your Client
A. Create a favorable context.
B. State favorable rules as broadly as possible and unfavorable rules as narrowly as possible.

> C. Emphasize favorable rules and de-emphasize unfavorable rules.
>   1. Emphasize the burden of proof if the other side has the burden; de-emphasize the burden of proof if you have the burden.
>   2. Give favorable rules more airtime and unfavorable rules less airtime.
>   3. Place favorable rules in a position of emphasis and bury unfavorable ones.
>   4. Place favorable rules in short sentences or in the main clause, and place unfavorable rules in longer sentences or in dependent clauses.
> D. Select your words carefully.

Compare the following examples, identifying the techniques that the writers used.

EXAMPLE 1 **OBJECTIVE STATEMENT OF THE RULE**

In deciding whether identification testimony is admissible, courts apply a two-part test. Under the first part of the test, the defendant must prove that the police procedures were impermissibly suggestive. If the court finds that the procedure was impermissibly suggestive, the State then has the burden of showing that, under the totality of the circumstances, the reliability of the identification outweighs the suggestive police procedure. *Manson v. Braithwaite*, 432 U.S. 98, 108, 97 S. Ct. 2243, 53 L. Ed. 2d 140 (1977).

EXAMPLE 2 **RULES STATED IN THE LIGHT MOST FAVORABLE TO THE DEFENDANT**

The United States Supreme Court has developed a two-part test to ensure a criminal defendant the procedural due process guaranteed to every individual by the Fourteenth Amendment. *Manson v. Braithwaite*, 432 U.S. 98, 108, 97 S. Ct. 2243, 53 L. Ed. 2d 108 (1977).

Under the first part of the test, the defendant need show only that the identification that he seeks to suppress was obtained through the use of unnecessarily suggestive police procedures. *Id.* Once this has been established, the onus shifts to the State to prove that, under the totality of the circumstances, the witness's identification is so reliable that it should be admitted even though it was obtained through unnecessarily suggestive means. *Id.*

| EXAMPLE 3 | **RULES STATED IN THE LIGHT MOST FAVORABLE TO THE STATE** |

Identifications should not be kept from the jury unless the procedures used in obtaining the identifications were so suggestive and unreliable that a substantial likelihood of irreparable misidentification exists. *Perry v. New Hampshire*, 565 U.S. 228, 232, 132 S. Ct. 716, 720, 181 L. Ed. 2d 694 (2012); *Simmons v. United States*, 390 U.S. 377, 384, 89 S. Ct. 1127, 22 L. Ed. 2d 402 (1969).

In deciding whether identification evidence is admissible, courts employ a two-part test. Under the first part of the test, the defendant has the burden of proving that the identification evidence that he or she seeks to suppress was obtained through impermissibly suggestive procedures. *Manson v. Braithwaite*, 432 U.S. 98, 113, 97 S. Ct. 2243, 53 L. Ed. 2d 140 (1977). Only if the defendant satisfies this substantial burden is the second part of the test applied. *Id.*

Even if the court determines that the police procedures were impermissibly suggestive, the evidence is admissible if, under the totality of the circumstances, the identifications are reliable. *Perry v. New Hampshire*, 132 S. Ct. at 720; *Simmons v. United States*, 390 U.S. at 384. Due process does not compel the exclusion of an identification if it is reliable. *Id.* Identifications should not be kept from the jury unless the procedures used in obtaining the identifications were so suggestive and unreliable that a substantial likelihood of irreparable misidentification exists. *Simmons v. United States*, 390 U.S. at 384.

Let's begin by comparing the opening sentences of all three examples. In Example 1, the writer simply states that the court applies a two-part test. There is no attempt to create a favorable context.

| EXAMPLE 4 | **OBJECTIVE STATEMENT OF THE RULE** |

In deciding whether identification testimony is admissible, courts apply a two-part test.

In contrast, in Examples 2 and 3, the writers package the rule, using policy to create a context that favors their respective clients. The key language is in boldface type.

| EXAMPLE 5 | **RULES STATED IN THE LIGHT MOST FAVORABLE TO THE DEFENDANT** |

The United States Supreme Court has developed a two-part test to ensure a criminal **defendant the procedural due process guaranteed to every individual by the Fourteenth Amendment.**

EXAMPLE 6   RULES STATED IN THE LIGHT MOST
FAVORABLE TO THE STATE

Identifications should not be kept from the jury unless the procedures used in obtaining the identifications were so suggestive and unreliable that a substantial likelihood of irreparable misidentification exists.

In addition to creating a favorable context, the parties have emphasized or de-emphasized the burden of proof depending on whether they have the burden or the other side has the burden. Compare the highlighted passages.

EXAMPLE 7   OBJECTIVE STATEMENT OF THE RULE

Under the first part of the test, **the defendant must prove** that the police procedures were impermissibly suggestive.

EXAMPLE 8   RULES STATED IN THE LIGHT MOST
FAVORABLE TO THE DEFENDANT

Under the first part of the test, **the defendant need show** only that the identification that he seeks to suppress was obtained through the use of unnecessarily suggestive police procedures.

EXAMPLE 9   RULES STATED IN THE LIGHT MOST
FAVORABLE TO THE STATE

Under the first part of the test, **the defendant has the burden of proving** that the identification evidence he seeks to suppress was obtained through impermissibly suggestive procedures.

Similarly, both sides try to lead the court to the desired conclusions. Defense counsel presumes that the defendant will meet his burden; the State presents the second part of the test as an alternative. Even if the State loses on the first part of the test, it wins on the second. Once again, the key language is in boldface type.

EXAMPLE 10   RULES STATED IN THE LIGHT MOST
FAVORABLE TO THE DEFENDANT

Once this has been established, the onus shifts to the State to prove that, under the totality of the circumstances, the witness's identification is so reliable that it should be admitted even though it was obtained through unnecessarily suggestive means.

EXAMPLE 11 **RULES STATED IN THE LIGHT MOST FAVORABLE TO THE STATE**

In deciding whether identification evidence is admissible, courts employ a two-part test. Under the first part of the test, the defendant has the burden of proving that the identification evidence that he or she seeks to suppress was obtained through impermissibly suggestive procedures. *Manson v. Braithwaite*, 432 U.S. 98, 113, 97 S. Ct. 2243, 53 L. Ed. 2d 140 (1977). **Only if the defendant satisfies this substantial burden is the second part of the test applied.** *Id.*

Even if the court determines that the police procedures were impermissibly suggestive, the evidence is admissible if, under the totality of the circumstances, the identifications are reliable. *Perry*, 132 S. Ct. at 720; *Simmons*, 390 U.S. at 384. Due process does not compel the exclusion of an identification if it is reliable. *Id.*

Finally, look at the words that each side uses.

Defendant	State
ensure	so suggestive
guaranteed	burden
onus shifts	substantial burden
so reliable	compel

Instead of using the language they saw in the cases or the first word that came to mind, both sides selected their words carefully with the goal of subtly influencing the decision-making process.

PRACTICE POINTER If you are having a hard time coming up with just the right word, look for alternative words using the thesaurus that is on your computer.

§ 6.3.4 Present the Cases in the Light Most Favorable to Your Client

When you use analogous cases to support your argument, present those cases in the light most favorable to your client. If a case supports your position, emphasize the similarities between the facts in the analogous case and the facts in your case. On the other hand, if a case does not support your position, emphasize the differences.

In the example case, both sides use *State v. Booth,* 36 Wn. App. 66, 671 P.2d 1218 (1983), a case in which the court held that the identification was reliable. The relevant portion of the court's opinion is set out in Example 1.

EXAMPLE 1   EXCERPT FROM *STATE v. BOOTH*

"The facts provide several indicia of reliability. Ms. Thomas was driving slowly, it was a clear day, and she observed Booth for approximately forty-five seconds. Her attention was greater than average because he had money in his hands and was running. In addition, her attention was particularly drawn to the car with Missouri plates because she had lived in Missouri. Finally, the identification took place thirty to forty minutes later and was unequivocal. On the basis of these facts we find that reliability outweighed the harm of suggestiveness and the identification was properly admitted."

Because the court found that the identification was reliable, the defendant wants to distinguish *Booth*. As a consequence, in discussing opportunity to view, the defendant wants to emphasize that in *Booth* the witness viewed the defendant for almost a minute, while in our case the witness viewed her assailant for only a few seconds.

EXAMPLE 2   EXCERPT FROM THE DEFENDANT'S BRIEF

An identification will not be found to be reliable unless the witness had an adequate opportunity to view the defendant. This was the situation in *Booth*. In that case, a bystander was able to view the defendant for almost a minute. *Id.* at 70. Because she was able to view the defendant for an extended period of time under good conditions, the court concluded that her identification was reliable. *Id.* In contrast, in our case Ms. Martinez viewed her assailant for only two or three seconds.

Conversely, the State wants to emphasize the similarities between the facts in its case and the facts in *Booth*. Thus, it tries to minimize the amount of time that the witness had to view the defendant.

EXAMPLE 3   EXCERPT FROM THE STATE'S BRIEF

The courts do not require that the witness have viewed the defendant for an extended period of time. *See, e.g., State v. Booth*, 36 Wn. App. 66, 671 P.2d 1218 (1983). In *Booth*, the court found the witness's identification was reliable even though the witness had viewed the defendant for less than a minute. *Id.* at 70.

---

§ 6.3.5 Present the Arguments in the Light Most Favorable to Your Client

In addition to presenting the rules and analogous cases in the light most favorable to your client, you also want to set out the arguments in the light most favorable to your client. As a general rule, set out your own arguments first, give your own arguments the most airtime, and use language that strengthens your arguments and undermines the other side's arguments.

a. Present Your Own Arguments First

You should almost always set out your own arguments first. By doing so, you can take advantage of the position of emphasis, emphasizing your argument and de-emphasizing the other side's arguments.

The following example shows what you do **not** want to do. By setting out the defendant's assertions, the State gives the defendant's arguments extra airtime. The court gets to read the defendant's argument in the defendant's brief and then again in the State's brief. In addition, do not use language that weakens your argument. Instead of saying "it is our contention," just set out your assertion: "The police procedures were not impermissibly suggestive."

EXAMPLE 1 **EXCERPT FROM THE STATE'S BRIEF: INEFFECTIVE**

The defendant argues that the police procedures were impermissibly suggestive because Officer Yuen showed Ms. Martinez a single suspect, Mr. Patterson, and because he asked Ms. Martinez whether Mr. Patterson looked like her assailant.

It is our contention that the police procedures were not impermissibly suggestive. One-person show-ups are not per se impermissibly suggestive; if the show-up occurs shortly after the commission of the crime during a search for the suspect, it is permissible. *See State v. Booth*, 36 Wn. App. 66, 70-71, 671 P.2d 1218 (1983).

The following example is substantially better. Instead of starting its arguments by setting out the defendant's assertions, the State starts by setting out a favorable statement of the rule. It then sets out its own argument, integrating its responses to the defendant's arguments into its own arguments.

EXAMPLE 2 **EXCERPT FROM THE STATE'S BRIEF: MORE EFFECTIVE**

One-person show-ups are not per se impermissibly suggestive. A show-up is permissible if it occurs shortly after the commission of a crime during a search for the suspect. *See State v. Booth*, 36 Wn. App. 66, 70-71, 671 P.2d 1218 (1983).

In the case before the Court, the show-up occurred within forty-five minutes of the assault. It also occurred before the police officers had completed their investigation: Officer Yuen saw Mr. Patterson as he was leaving the crime scene to take Ms. Martinez home.

Under these circumstances, Officer Yuen would not have been doing his job if, upon seeing a man who matched the assailant's description, he had not asked Ms. Martinez whether the man looked like her assailant. The officer's question, "Is that the man?" was not enough to turn a permissible show-up into one that was impermissibly suggestive.

b. Give the Most Airtime to Your Own Arguments

Most of the time, you will want to give more airtime to your own arguments than you do to the other side's arguments. Your goal is to respond to or counter the other side's arguments without giving them too much airtime. Compare the following examples. In the first example, the State gives too much airtime to the defendant's age. In the second, the State counters the defendant's arguments without overemphasizing them.

EXAMPLE 3   EXCERPT FROM THE STATE'S BRIEF: INEFFECTIVE

On the whole, Ms. Martinez's description was accurate. When she was interviewed, Ms. Martinez told the police that her assailant was a white male, that he was approximately 5'7" tall, that he weighed between 165 and 170 pounds, that he had blondish-brown hair, that he was wearing a dark jacket, and **that he appeared to be in his early forties. In fact, the defendant is twenty-two.**

This discrepancy in age is insignificant. It is often difficult to guess a person's age: Some people appear older than they are, and others appear younger. Thus, the court should give little weight to the fact that Ms. Martinez misjudged the defendant's age. On the basis of the other information Ms. Martinez gave to the police, the police were able to identify the defendant as the assailant.

EXAMPLE 4   EXCERPT FROM THE STATE'S BRIEF: MORE EFFECTIVE

Ms. Martinez was able to give the police a detailed description of her assailant. When she was interviewed, she told the police that her assailant was a white male with blondish-brown hair, that he was approximately 5'7" tall and weighed between 165 and 170 pounds, **that he appeared to be in his early forties**, and that he was wearing a dark green jacket.

This description is accurate in all but one respect. **Although Ms. Martinez misjudged the defendant's age**, she accurately described his hair, his height and weight, and his clothing.

c. Use Language That Strengthens Your Arguments and Undermines the Other Side's Arguments

In setting out your own arguments, do not use phrases such as "We contend that . . . ," "It is our argument that . . . ," "We believe that . . . ," or "We feel that . . . ." Just set out your assertions. The following examples from the defendant's brief demonstrate this.

EXAMPLE 5   EXCERPT FROM THE DEFENDANT'S BRIEF

Ineffective

It is our contention that the police procedures were impermissibly suggestive.

More Effective

The police procedures were impermissibly suggestive.

On the other hand, when it is necessary to set out the other side's argument, use an introductory phrase that reminds the court that the statement is just the other side's assertion or argument.

EXAMPLE 6   EXCERPT FROM THE DEFENDANT'S BRIEF

Although the State contends that Ms. Martinez's identification is reliable, Ms. Martinez had only a second or two to view her assailant.

---

d. Use the Same Persuasive Techniques You Used in Setting Out the Facts, Issues, Rules, and Analogous Cases

Finally, when appropriate, use the same persuasive techniques that you used in writing the other parts of your brief. For instance, use the positions of emphasis to your best advantage. Place your best points at the beginning or end of a section or paragraph. In addition, whenever possible, put your strong points in short sentences or, in a longer sentence, in the main clause. Finally, select your words carefully. Choose words that convey not only the right denotation but also the right connotation.

Also remember that persuasive arguments are not written; they are crafted. In first drafts, concentrate on content and organization. In subsequent drafts, work on writing persuasively.

§ 6.4 Checklist for Critiquing the Argument

I. *Content*

- Did you set out your assertions?
- Did you support your assertions?
  - If appropriate, did you apply the constitutional provision, applicable statute, or common law rule to the facts of your case?
  - If appropriate, did you compare and contrast the facts in the analogous cases to the facts in your case?
  - If appropriate, did you explain why, as a matter of public policy, the court should rule in your client's favor?
- Did you cite the key relevant authorities?
- Are your statements of the rules and descriptions of the cases accurate?

II. *Organization*

- Did you use one of the conventional organizational schemes—for example, deductive or inductive reasoning?
- Did you use an organizational scheme that allowed you to emphasize the strongest parts of your arguments?

III. *Persuasiveness*

Rules

- Did you present the rules in the light most favorable to your client?
  - Did you create a favorable context?
  - Did you state favorable rules as broadly as possible and unfavorable rules as narrowly as possible?
  - Did you emphasize favorable rules and de-emphasize unfavorable ones?
  - Did you select words both for their denotation and for their connotation?

Analogous Cases

- Did you present the cases in the light most favorable to your client?
  - Did you create a favorable context?
  - Did you state favorable holdings as broadly as possible and unfavorable holdings as narrowly as possible?

- Did you emphasize favorable facts and de-emphasize unfavorable ones?
- Did your select words both for their denotation and for their connotation?

Arguments

- Did you present your own arguments first?
- Did you give your own arguments the most airtime?
- Did you use language that strengthens your arguments and weakens your opponent's arguments?

CHAPTER 7

Finishing the Motion Brief: The Prayer for Relief and Signing the Brief

§ 7.1 The Prayer for Relief

The final section of the brief is the prayer for relief or the conclusion. In some jurisdictions, the prayer for relief is very short. The attorney simply sets out the relief that he or she wants.

EXAMPLE 1 **EXCERPT FROM THE DEFENDANT'S BRIEF**

Prayer for Relief

For the reasons set out above, Mr. Patterson respectfully requests that the Court grant his motion and suppress Ms. Martinez's show-up and line-up identifications and any in-court identifications that Ms. Martinez or Mr. Clipse might make.

In other jurisdictions, the attorney sets out the relief that he or she is requesting and summarizes the arguments.

| EXAMPLE 2 | **EXCERPT FROM THE DEFENDANT'S BRIEF** |

Conclusion

The Court should suppress Ms. Martinez's show-up identification because the police officer's questions were impermissibly suggestive and because, given Ms. Martinez's limited opportunity to view her assailant and the inaccuracies in her description, her identification is unreliable.

The Court should also suppress Ms. Martinez's line-up identification and any in-court identifications that Ms. Martinez or Mr. Clipse might make. Both the line-up and the in-court identifications have been tainted by the impermissibly suggestive show-up.

---

§ 7.2 Signing the Brief

Before the brief is submitted to the court, it must be signed by an attorney licensed to practice law in the state. The following format is used in many jurisdictions.

| EXAMPLE | **STANDARD FORMAT FOR DATING AND SIGNING A BRIEF** |

Submitted this _____ day of _____, 20 ____.

_____
Attorney for the Defendant

8

Sample Briefs

In this section, we set out two sets of briefs: the briefs from the *Patterson* case, which is used as the example case in this chapter, and the briefs from a civil case in which defense counsel has asked the court to grant defendant's Motion for Summary Judgment. Because the briefs were filed in a Washington trial court, the attorneys used the Washington court rules and the Washington citation rules.

The King County Rules, which govern the brief in Example 3, are as follows.

(B) Form of Motion and of Responsive Pleadings.

The motion shall be combined with the memorandum of authorities into a single document, and shall conform to the following format:

(i) Relief Requested. The specific relief the court is requested to grant or deny.

(ii) Statement of Facts. A succinct statement of the facts contended to be material.

(iii) Statement of Issues. A concise statement of the issue or issues of law upon which the Court is requested to rule.

(iv) Evidence Relied Upon. The evidence on which the motion or opposition is based must be specified with particularity.

Deposition testimony, discovery pleadings, and documentary evidence relied upon must be quoted verbatim or a photocopy of relevant pages must be attached to an affidavit identifying the documents. Parties should highlight those parts upon which they place substantial reliance. Copies of cases shall not be attached to original pleadings. Responsive pleadings shall conform to this format.

(v) Authority. Any legal authority relied upon must be cited. Copies of all cited non-Washington authorities upon which parties place substantial reliance shall be provided to the hearing Judge and to counsel or parties, but shall not be filed with the Clerk.

LCR 7(b)(5)(b).

§ 8.1 Briefs from the *Patterson* Case

EXAMPLE 1 **DEFENDANT'S BRIEF IN SUPPORT OF MOTION TO SUPPRESS**

1

2

3

4

5

THE SUPERIOR COURT OF
KING COUNTY, WASHINGTON ① ②

6 STATE OF WASHINGTON,   )   Case No.: 19-01-2226

7   Plaintiff,   )   DEFENDANT'S BRIEF
)   IN SUPPORT OF
8   v.   )   MOTION TO
)   SUPPRESS
9 DEAN E. PATTERSON,   )

10   Defendant.   )
   _____)

11

12

13 ③ Mr. Patterson's only crime is that he was in the
14 wrong place at the wrong time. Consequently, he asks
15 the Court to suppress Ms. Martinez's show-up and line-
16 up identifications and to prevent both Ms. Martinez and
17 Mr. Clipse from making in-court identifications. The
18 show-up was impermissibly suggestive and, because she
19 viewed her assailant for only a few seconds, Ms.
20 Martinez's identifications are unreliable. ④

21

22

Defendant's Brief   Defense Counsel's Name
in Support of   Defense Counsel's Address
Motion to Suppress–1   Defense Counsel's
                                      Phone Number

① The Superior Court Civil Rules state that the Civil Rules govern the format of briefs submitted in criminal cases. Thus, the following references to "CR" are references to the Washington Rules of Civil Procedure.

② Under the Washington rules, you must include a caption that sets out the name of the court, the names of the parties, the file number, and a title that identifies the nature of pleading or document. *See* CR 10(a).

③ In this example, defense counsel has included an introductory paragraph in which she sets out her request for relief: She wants the court to suppress Ms. Martinez's show-up and line-up identifications, and she wants to prohibit both the victim and the witness from making in-court identifications. Under the Washington rules, this type of introductory paragraph is optional.

④ Because the record was not transcribed, defense counsel cannot and has not included citations to that record. However, if you have a record, you should include references to that record. (See your local rules.)

Statement of Facts

1   ⑤At 7:30 a.m. on Monday, August 19, 2019, twenty-

2   two-year-old Dean Patterson finished his shift as a secur-

3   ity guard and walked to his apartment. After having

4   breakfast with his wife, he went to bed and slept until

5   about 1:00 p.m. At about 2:30 p.m., Mr. Patterson's

6   wife received a phone call asking her to work at the

7   local hospital where she is employed as a nurse. Mr.

8   Patterson's wife got ready, and Mr. Patterson⑥ dropped

9   her off at the hospital at about 3:10 p.m.

10   At about 3:30 p.m., Mr. Patterson called his wife to

11 find out how long she would have to work⑦; they had

12 plans to go to a movie that evening, and he wanted to

13 know whether he should change those plans. At about

14 3:50 p.m., Mr. Patterson took a load of laundry to the

15 apartment complex's laundry room. When he returned

16 to his apartment, Mr. Patterson watched part of an old

17 movie. At about 4:20 p.m., Mr. Patterson went back to

18 the laundry room to put the clothes in the dryer.

19   ⑧By this time, it was 4:30 p.m., and Mr. Patterson

20 decided to phone his wife again. He arranged to meet

21 her at 5:15 p.m. for her dinner break. Mr. Patterson

22 retrieved the laundry and then left the apartment a little

23 before 5:00 p.m. to meet his wife.

24

25

26

⑤To create a favorable context, defense counsel starts the statement of facts by describing Mr. Patterson's activities on the morning of the assault. Note how she works in the fact that Mr. Patterson is married and employed as a security guard, which would explain why Mr. Patterson owns a gun.

⑥Note how defense counsel has used Mr. Patterson or his wife as the subject of most sentences. This is one technique that can be used to tell the story from the client's point of view.

⑦Defense counsel has included the facts set out in this paragraph to paint her client in a favorable light and to explain what Mr. Patterson was doing at the time of the assault.

⑧Because defense counsel is setting out the facts in chronological order, she sets out the time at the beginning of some of the sentences.

Defendant's Brief
in Support of
Motion to Suppress–2

Defense Counsel's Name
Defense Counsel's Address
Defense Counsel's
Phone Number

1   At about 4:30 p.m. on the same day, seventeen-year-

2   old Beatrice Martinez left her apartment to walk to work.

3   As she was walking southbound on Belmont, a car ⑨ that

4   had driven by earlier pulled in front of her. The man got

5   out of his car, took one or two steps toward Ms.

6   Martinez, and then pulled a gun from his pocket. As

7   soon as she spotted the gun, Ms. Martinez screamed,

8   looked away, and then, crying, ran across the street. ⑩

9   The entire encounter was over in three or four seconds.

10   The assault was witnessed by Chester Clipse, who was

11 walking home when he saw a man in a silver SUV driving

12 slowly down the street. When the man started to pull into

13 Mr. Clipse's parking space, Mr. Clipse began walking

14 toward him to tell him that he could not park there. As

15 he did so, Mr. Clipse saw the man get out of his car and

16 walk toward a young woman who was on the sidewalk.

17 He then heard the woman scream, and as she screamed,

18 Mr. Clipse saw that the man had a gun. Mr. Clipse yelled

19 "Hey," and the man turned and ran to his car, putting the

20 gun under his coat. As the young woman ran across the

21 street, the man got back into his car, backed out, and

22 drove away. ⑪

23

24

25

26

Defendant's Brief   Defense Counsel's Name
in Support of   Defense Counsel's Address
Motion to Suppress–3   Defense Counsel's
                                           Phone Number

⑨ Because Mr. Patterson owns a vehicle that matches the description of the vehicle that the assailant drove, defense counsel describes the car using a generic term: "car." In addition, she has tried to minimize the fact that the car drove by twice.

⑩ Because she wants to argue that Ms. Martinez's identification is not reliable, defense counsel uses language that suggests that Ms. Martinez did not have an adequate opportunity to view her assailant. By putting the facts in short clauses in a single sentence, defense counsel creates the impression that events happened quickly.

⑪ Once again, defense counsel tries to give the impression that events happened quickly by setting out the facts in short clauses in a single sentence.

1   A few seconds later, a parking enforcement officer

2 drove down the street. Mr. Clipse flagged him down,

3 told him what had happened, and described the car and

4 the man. The parking enforcement officer called 911

5 and then left to try to locate the car. Because the

6 woman was still crying, Mr. Clipse took her to his land-

7 lady's apartment. He then went back outside and waited

8 for the police.

9   When the police arrived, [12] Mr. Clipse told Officers

10 Yuen and Cox what had happened. He told the officers

11 that the man was white, about 5'7" tall, and about 165

12 to 170 pounds. He also told the officers that the man

13 was wearing a green outfit and that he was in his late thir-

14 ties or early forties. [13]

15   While Mr. Clipse was talking to the police, Officer Cox

16 received a radio message indicating that the parking enfor-

17 cement officer had located a car that matched the one Mr.

18 Clipse had described. While Officer Cox took Mr. Clipse in

19 his car to see if Mr. Clipse could identify the car, Officer

20 Yuen went inside to interview Ms. Martinez.

21   Because she was still upset, Ms. Martinez was able to

22 give Officer Yuen only a general description of her assai-

23 lant. She described him as being a short, white male with

24 blondish-brown hair who was wearing glasses and a dark

25 jacket. [14] In addition, she told police that her assailant

26 was in his early forties. Mr. Patterson is twenty-two. [15]

[12] Defense counsel has used dovetailing to make clear the connection between the information in this paragraph and the information in the prior paragraph.

[13] Defense counsel has placed a favorable fact, that Clipse said the assailant was in his late thirties or early forties, in a position of emphasis.

[14] Defense counsel has "buried" the unfavorable facts, the part of Ms. Martinez's description that is accurate, in the middle of the paragraph. She then places the favorable fact, that Ms. Martinez said that her assailant was in his forties, in the position of emphasis, juxtaposed with the fact that Mr. Patterson is only twenty-two.

[15] Defense counsel has placed a favorable fact in the position of emphasis in a short sentence.

Defendant's Brief
in Support of
Motion to Suppress–4

Defense Counsel's Name
Defense Counsel's Address
Defense Counsel's
Phone Number

1   After interviewing Ms. Martinez, Officer Yuen took

2 the still-shaken Ms. Martinez to his car to take her

3 home. When they had traveled about four blocks,

4 Officer Yuen noticed a white male wearing a dark jacket.

5 As he drove up behind him, Yuen asked Ms. Martinez, "Is

6 that the man?" When Ms. Martinez did not immediately

7 answer, Yuen asked the question again: "Is that the

8 man who assaulted you?" [16]

9   Even though Ms. Martinez was unable to see the

10 man's face, [17] she agreed with the officer that the man

11 looked like her assailant. At this point, Officer Yuen

12 stopped the car, got out, and approached Mr. Patterson.

13 As he was questioning [18] Mr. Patterson, Officer Cox

14 drove up with Mr. Clipse. While Ms. Martinez and Mr.

15 Clipse watched, Officers Cox and Yuen continued ques-

16 tioning Mr. Patterson. Officer Cox then returned to Ms.

17 Martinez and Mr. Clipse and walked them back to Mr.

18 Clipse's landlady's apartment. While he did so, Yuen

19 placed Mr. Patterson under arrest.

20   Later that day, the police searched Mr. Patterson's car

21 and apartment. In the apartment, the police found the

22 gun issued to Mr. Patterson by his employer. [19] The

23 next day, the police held a line-up. Although Ms.

24 Martinez identified Mr. Patterson as the man who had

25 approached her, Mr. Clipse did not identify any of the

26 individuals in the line-up. [20]

Defendant's Brief
in Support of
Motion to Suppress–5

Defense Counsel's Name
Defense Counsel's Address
Defense Counsel's
Phone Number

[16] Defense counsel has used quotations to emphasize that the police officer used language that suggested to Ms. Martinez that Mr. Patterson was the person who had assaulted her. Note how defense counsel places the second quote in a position of emphasis.

[17] Defense counsel has placed a favorable fact, that Ms. Martinez was not able to see Mr. Patterson's face, in a position of emphasis.

[18] Instead of using a word like "talking," defense counsel has used "questioning," which suggests that the police officer was treating Mr. Patterson as if he had committed a crime.

[19] Defense counsel has tried to convert an unfavorable fact to a favorable one by emphasizing that the gun had been issued to Mr. Patterson by his employer.

[20] Defense counsel has placed the favorable fact, that Mr. Clipse did not identify Mr. Patterson as the assailant, in the main clause in the position of emphasis. The unfavorable fact, that Ms. Martinez did identify Mr. Patterson, is in the dependent clause.

1   **Issue**

2   Under the Fourteenth Amendment, should the Court

3 grant Mr. Patterson's motion to suppress㉑ Ms. Martinez's

4 show-up and line-up identifications and Ms. Martinez's and

5 Mr. Clipse's in-court identifications when (1) a police officer

6 pointed out Mr. Patterson to Ms. Martinez, repeatedly asking

7 the shaken Ms. Martinez whether Mr. Patterson looked like

8 her assailant; (2) the police questioned Mr. Patterson in

9 front of Ms. Martinez and Mr. Clipse; (3) during the second

10 or two that Ms. Martinez had to view her assailant, her atten-

11 tion was focused on his gun and not his face; and (4) both

12 Ms. Martinez's and Mr. Clipse's descriptions were inaccu-

13 rate?㉒

14   **Argument**

15   **I. The Court should grant Mr. Patterson's motion to**

16   **suppress Mr. Martinez's show-up and line-up**
        identifications and Mr. Martinez's and Mr. Clipse's

17   **in-court identifications.**㉓

18   The United States Supreme Court has developed a

19 two-part test to ensure a criminal defendant the proce-

20 dural due process guaranteed to every individual by the

21 Fourteenth Amendment. *Manson v. Braithwaite*,㉔ 432

22 U.S. 98, 113, 97 S. Ct. 2243, 53 L. Ed. 2d 140 (1977).[1]

23 _____

24   [1] Note: Because the brief is to a Washington court, defense counsel
    uses the Washington Citation Rules. *See* http://www.courts.wa.gov/
    appellate_trial_courts/supreme/?fa = atc_supreme.style.   These rules
25 require parallel cites for decisions of the United States Supreme Court.

26
                                        Defense Counsel's Name
    Defendant's Brief   Defense Counsel's Address
    in Support of   Defense Counsel's
    Motion to Suppress–6   Phone Number

㉑Defense counsel sets out the question so that it suggests the conclusion that she wants the court to reach.

㉒Defense counsel sets out the key facts in a light favorable to her client. Note that she sets out the facts that go to the first part of the test (whether the show-up was suggestive), before the facts that go to the second part of the test (whether the identifications were reliable).

㉓This heading answers the question set out in the issue statement. Although defense counsel would have liked to have included a "because" clause, doing so would have made the heading too long. As a consequence, defense counsel sets out her support for this assertion in the subheadings.

㉔Defense counsel has started the argument by setting out the general rules in a light favorable to Mr. Patterson. By doing so, she tries to create a favorable context.

1　　　Under the first part of the test, [25] the defendant need

2　show only [26] that the identification that he seeks to sup-

3　press was obtained through the use of impermissibly sug-

4　gestive police procedures. *Id.* Once the defendant has

5　established that the procedure was suggestive, [27] the

6　onus shifts to the State to prove that, under the totality

7　of the circumstances, the witness's identification is so reli-

8　able that it should be admitted even though it was

9　obtained through suggestive means. *Id.* [28]

10　　　In this case, the Court should suppress Ms.

11　Martinez's show-up identification both because the

12　police procedures were impermissibly suggestive and

13　because, under the totality of the circumstances, Ms.

14　Martinez's identification is not reliable. In addition, the

15　Court should suppress Ms. Martinez's line-up identifica-

16　tion because that line-up was tainted by the show-up.

17　Finally, the Court should rule that neither Ms. Martinez

18　nor Mr. Clipse should be allowed to make in-court iden-

19　tifications. Like Ms. Martinez's line-up identification,

20　any in-court identifications would be tainted by the

21　show-up. [29]

22　　A. <u>Ms. Martinez's show-up identification should be</u>

23　　　<u>suppressed because the police procedures were</u>
　　　<u>impermissibly suggestive and Ms. Martinez's iden-</u>

24　　　<u>tification is not reliable.</u> [30]

25

26

Defendant's Brief
in Support of
Motion to Suppress–7

Defense Counsel's Name
Defense Counsel's Address
Defense Counsel's
Phone Number

[25] Defense counsel starts the paragraph with a transition that lets the attorney know that she is setting out the first part of a two-part test.

[26] Defense counsel uses language that minimizes Mr. Patterson's burden.

[27] Defense counsel uses language that suggests that Mr. Patterson can meet his burden.

[28] Defense counsel uses language that suggests that the State's burden is a high burden.

[29] After setting out the general rules, defense counsel sets out a road-map for the rest of her arguments.

[30] In this heading, defense counsel uses the "traditional" format for an argumentative heading: She sets out her assertion followed by a "because" clause. Note that the because clause is very general: It simply repeats the two parts of the test. Defense counsel uses the sub-subheadings to provide the facts that support these assertions.

1   Courts have repeatedly condemned the practice of

2   showing a witness a single suspect. [31] *See, e.g.,* [32] *Stovall*

3   *v. Denno*, 388 U.S. 293, 302, 87 S. Ct. 1967, 18 L. Ed. 2d

4   1199 (1967), *abrogated on other grounds by United States*

5   *v. Johnson*, 457 U.S. 537, 102 S. Ct. 2579, 73 L. Ed. 2d

6   202 (1982); *State v. Rogers*, 44 Wn. App. 510, 515, 722

7   P.2d 1349 (1986); *State v. Kraus*, 21 Wn. App. 388, 391-

8   92, 584 P.2d 946 (1978). Although such show-ups are

9   not per se impermissibly suggestive, [33] identifications fol-

10   lowing such a show-up should be admitted only if the

11   show-up occurs during the prompt search for the suspect

12   and if the State proves that the witness's identification is

13   reliable. [34] *State v. Rogers*, 44 Wn. App. at 515.

14   1. <u>The police procedures were impermissibly sugges-
15   tive because the police showed Ms. Martinez one
16   suspect, asked Ms. Martinez whether that suspect
17   looked like her assailant, and questioned the suspect in front of Ms. Martinez and Mr. Clipse.</u> [35]

18   In this case, [36] Officer Yuen's actions suggested to

19   Ms. Martinez that he believed that Mr. Patterson was

20   her assailant. While driving Ms. Martinez home, Officer

21   Yuen pulled up behind Mr. Patterson and asked Ms.

22   Martinez whether Mr. Patterson looked like her assailant.

23   When Ms. Martinez did not respond, Officer Yuen

24   repeated his question, asking, "Is that the man who

25

26

Defendant's Brief
in Support of
Motion to Suppress–8

Defense Counsel's Name
Defense Counsel's Address
Defense Counsel's
Phone Number

[31] Defense counsel has set out this rule in a light favorable to Mr. Patterson.

[32] Although as a general rule you should not include "string cites"—that is, a string of citations—in this case the signal "*see, e.g.,*" and the three cites make the point that courts have repeatedly condemned the practice of showing a witness a single suspect.

[33] Defense counsel has placed an "unfavorable rule" in a dependent clause in the middle of a paragraph.

[34] Defense counsel has placed the favorable rule in the main clause at the end of the paragraph, which is a position of emphasis. In addition, by using the word "only," she has stated the rule narrowly.

[35] In drafting this heading, defense counsel sets out her assertion (that the police procedures were unnecessarily suggestive) and then includes a "because" clause in which she sets out the facts that support this assertion.

[36] While in most situations you will start your discussion of a test by setting out the applicable rules, in this case defense counsel decided to start with the facts. If your best argument is a factual argument, you can start with the facts; similarly, if your best argument is an analogous case argument, you can start with an analogous case argument. Just make sure that the judge will be able to follow your argument.

1   assaulted you?" [37] Although Ms. Martinez could not see Mr.

2   Patterson's face, after hesitating she agreed [38] with Officer

3   Yuen that Mr. Patterson looked like her assailant. At that

4   point, Officer Yuen pulled up behind Mr. Patterson, got

5   out of the police car, and began questioning him. A few

6   minutes later, Officer Cox and Mr. Clipse arrived, and

7   both Officer Yuen and Officer Cox questioned Mr.

8   Patterson while Ms. Martinez and Mr. Clipse watched.

9   Thus, this case can be distinguished from *Kraus*, 21

10 Wn. App. at 392, in which the show-up identification

11 occurred during a prompt search for the robber. [39] [40] In

12 this case, the show-up did not occur while the police

13 were searching for Ms. Martinez's assailant. Instead, it

14 occurred while the officer was driving the shaken Ms.

15 Martinez home. In addition, unlike *Stovall*, 388 U.S. at

16 302, in which the police held the show-up because they

17 were concerned that the suspect might die, in this case,

18 there were no exigent circumstances. In fact, because

19 the police had located a car that matched the description

20 of the one driven by the assailant, they could have identi-

21 fied the owner of the car and any individuals who had dri-

22 ven it and placed them in a line-up. [41]

23   2. <u>Ms. Martinez's identification is unreliable because

24   Ms. Martinez was able to view her assailant for

         only a few seconds, her attention was focused on

25   the gun and not his face, and her description of

         her assailant does not match the description of

26   Mr. Patterson.</u> [42]

Defendant's Brief
in Support of
Motion to Suppress—9

Defense Counsel's Name
Defense Counsel's Address
Defense Counsel's
Phone Number

[37] Defense counsel has emphasized this favorable fact by using a quotation and placing that quotation in a position of emphasis.

[38] Once again, defense counsel has selected words that carry not only the right denotation but also the right connotation. In particular, note defense counsel's use of the words "agreed," "watched," and "questioned."

[39] Instead of setting out the other side's argument—for example, instead of saying that the State will argue that this case is like *Kraus*—defense counsel sets out her own positive assertion, which is that Mr. Patterson's case can be distinguished from *Kraus*.

[40] Note that defense counsel does not go into detail in describing *Kraus*; she sets out only the key fact.

[41] Defense counsel ends this section with a strong argument: that the police had another way of locating the assailant.

[42] Defense counsel has used the same format for this sub-subheading as she did for the prior sub-subheading. She sets out her assertion and then the facts that support that assertion.

1   (43) The key inquiry in determining the admissibility

2   of a witness's identification is its reliability. *Manson v.*

3   *Braithwaite*, 432 U.S. 98, 114, 97 S. Ct. 2243, 53 L. Ed.

4   2d 140 (1977). In (44) determining whether an identifica-

5   tion is reliable, courts consider the witness's opportunity

6   to view the person who committed the crime, the wit-

7   ness's degree of attention, the time between the crime

8   and the confrontation, the witness's level of certainty,

9   and the accuracy of the witness's prior description. *Neil*

10   *v. Biggers*, 409 U.S. 188, 199, 93 S. Ct. 375, 34 L. Ed.

11   2d 401 (1972); *State v. Birch*, 151 Wn. App. 504, 514,

12   213 P.3d 63, 69 (2009).

13   (45) First, in this case, Ms. Martinez did not have an

14   adequate opportunity to view her assailant. Unlike(46)

15   the witness in *Rogers*, who was with his assailant for

16   almost twenty minutes, and the witness in *Booth*, who

17   observed the robber for at least forty-five seconds, Ms.

18   Martinez viewed her assailant for only a few seconds.

19   During the pretrial hearing, Ms. Martinez testified that

20   she had seen her assailant for two or three seconds before

21   she turned and ran. In addition, although Ms. Martinez

22   testified that she had noticed the car on a prior occa-

23   sion, (47) she did not testify that she had noticed the driver.

24   In a similar case, the court held that the witness had not

25   had an adequate opportunity to view the robber when

26

Defendant's Brief
in Support of
Motion to Suppress–10

Defense Counsel's Name
Defense Counsel's Address
Defense Counsel's
Phone Number

(43) Unlike the prior sub-section in which defense counsel began the section by setting out the key facts, in this section defense counsel uses the more traditional format: She sets out the specific rules and then she applies these rules to the facts of her case.

(44) In this instance, defense counsel re-ordered the list of factors so that the two most favorable factors are in the positions of emphasis.

(45) Note defense counsel's use of signposts and topic sentences. For example, defense counsel starts this paragraph with "First," and then she sets out her assertion, which is that Ms. Martinez did not have an adequate opportunity to view her assailant.

(46) Defense counsel uses the cases to support her assertion. She sets out the key facts from each of the cases and then distinguishes those cases.

(47) In this sentence, defense counsel anticipates and responds to an argument that she believes the State will make. Note that she does not set out the State's argument. She simply sets out her own argument. Also note that the unfavorable fact, that Ms. Martinez testified that she had noticed the car on a prior occasion, is in a dependent clause in the middle of the paragraph. Finally, note defense counsel's word choices. For example, defense counsel states that Ms. Martinez had "noticed" the car.

1   the witness was with the robber for five to six minutes

2   and viewed him for two or three minutes. *State v.*

3   *McDonald*, 40 Wn. App. 743, 747, 700 P.2d 327 (1985).

4   Second, Ms. Martinez's attention was not focused on

5   her assailant.⁴⁸ Unlike the witness in *Booth*, whose

6   attention was focused on the robber because he was run-

7   ning and carrying money and got into a car with license

8   plates from the witness's home state, Ms. Martinez's

9   attention was focused on the car and then on the gun

10 that her assailant was holding. As Ms. Martinez has testi-

11 fied, she looked at the gun, glanced at the man holding

12 it, and then ran.⁴⁹

13   Third, although the show-up occurred within about

14 forty-five minutes of the assault, Ms. Martinez's level of

15 certainty was low. The first time that Officer Yuen

16 asked Ms. Martinez whether Mr. Patterson looked like

17 the man who had assaulted her, she did not respond.⁵⁰

18 In addition, the second time that Officer Yuen asked her

19 the same question, she said only that Mr. Patterson

20 looked like him. She did not say, "Yes, that is him."

21   Finally, Ms. Martinez's description was inaccurate.

22 Although Ms. Martinez told the police that her assailant

23 was in his early forties, Mr. Patterson is twenty-two.⁵¹

24 While sometimes an individual will believe that an indivi-

25 dual is two, three, or even five years older than the

26

Defendant's Brief   Defense Counsel's Name
in Support of   Defense Counsel's Address
Motion to Suppress–11   Defense Counsel's
                                     Phone Number

⁴⁸ Once again, defense counsel starts the paragraph with a signpost and a topic sentence that sets out her assertion.

⁴⁹ Defense counsel has placed the favorable facts at the end of the paragraph in a position of emphasis.

⁵⁰ In discussing this factor, defense counsel does not cite to any cases: There are not any cases that specifically discuss this factor. Instead, defense counsel uses the facts. Note how defense counsel ends the paragraph. Sometimes you can use what a party did not do or did not say to support an argument.

⁵¹ While defense counsel would have liked to give this factor more airtime, there was not a good way of doing so. Thus, she makes her point and moves on.

1   individual actually is, it is extremely uncommon for some-

2   one to be off by twenty years. [52]

3   [53] In this case, Ms. Martinez identified Mr. Patterson as

4   her assailant only because Officer Yuen suggested to her

5   that Mr. Patterson was the man who had assaulted her.

6   In addition, the State cannot prove that Ms. Martinez's iden-

7   tification is reliable. Ms. Martinez did not have an adequate

8   opportunity to view her assailant, her attention was not

9   focused on her assailant, her identification was uncertain,

10 and her description was inaccurate. As a consequence,

11 Mr. Patterson's due process rights would be violated if

12 Ms. Martinez's identification is admitted.

13   B. <u>Ms. Martinez's line-up identification should be sup-
        pressed because it was tainted by the show-up.</u> [54]
14

15   When the initial identification is obtained through

16 impermissibly suggestive procedures, subsequent identi-

17 fications must also be suppressed unless the State can

18 prove that the subsequent identifications are reliable. [55]

19 *Birch,* 151 Wn. App. at 513-14 (2009); *McDonald,* 40

20 Wn. App. at 746. In *McDonald,* [56] the court reversed the

21 defendant's conviction, concluding that the procedures

22 used at the line-up were impermissibly suggestive and

23 that the State had not proved that the witness's subse-

24 quent in-court identification was reliable. *Id.* at 747.

25   Similarly, in this case the procedures were impermis-

26 sibly suggestive, and the State cannot prove that

Defendant's Brief
in Support of
Motion to Suppress–12

Defense Counsel's Name
Defense Counsel's Address
Defense Counsel's
Phone Number

[52] While you will usually provide support for your assertions, sometimes you can make a "common sense" argument.

[53] Defense counsel uses this paragraph to do three things. First, she discusses the first part of the two-part test, arguing that the show-up was suggestive. She then discusses the second part of the test. In doing so, she reminds the court that the State has the burden of proof, and then she summarizes her arguments relating to the factors. Finally, she goes back to the general rule, reminding the court of the constitutional issues.

[54] Defense counsel has set out her assertion and then a "because" clause in which she sets out her support for that assertion.

[55] In setting out this rule, defense counsel has emphasized that the State has the burden of proof.

[56] Defense counsel uses an analogous case to support her argument.

1   Ms. Martinez's subsequent identifications are reliable. See

2   section 1A(2), *supra.* [57] Ms. Martinez picked Mr. Patterson

3   out of the line-up, not because she remembered him as

4   her assailant, but because the police had suggested to

5   her that he was her assailant. [58]

6   C. <u>Ms. Martinez and Mr. Clipse should not be per-</u>

7   <u>mitted to make an in-court identification because</u>
    <u>such an identification would be tainted by the</u>

8   <u>impermissibly suggestive show-up and the line-up.</u>

9   Just as Ms. Martinez's line-up identification was tainted

10 by the impermissibly suggestive show-up, any in-court

11 identification by Ms. Martinez or Mr. Clipse would also be

12 tainted. Although the police did not ask Mr. Clipse whether

13 Mr. Patterson looked like the man who had assaulted Ms.

14 Martinez, Mr. Clipse watched as the police questioned

15 Mr. Patterson. [59] In addition, Mr. Patterson was with Ms.

16 Martinez, who may have told him that Officer Yuen

17 believed that Mr. Patterson was her assailant.

18   **Prayer for Relief**

19   For the reasons set out above, the Defendant respectfully

20 requests that the Court suppress Ms. Martinez's show-up and

21 line-up identifications and that the Court not permit Ms.

22 Martinez or Mr. Clipse to make an in-court identification.

23   Dated this 23rd day of September, 2019.

24

25   Signature
                   Attorney for the Defendant

26   Name
                   Bar No. 00000

Defendant's Brief
in Support of
Motion to Suppress—13

Defense Counsel's Name
Defense Counsel's Address
Defense Counsel's
Phone Number

---

[57] Instead of repeating an argument, you can provide the court with a cross-reference to another part of your brief.

[58] Your arguments do not need to be long. Make your point and then move on.

[59] Note that defense counsel does not set out the State's argument. She simply counters that argument by setting out her own positive assertion.

EXAMPLE 2	**STATE'S BRIEF IN OPPOSITION TO MOTION TO SUPPRESS**

1

2

3   THE SUPERIOR COURT OF
4   KING COUNTY, WASHINGTON ①

STATE OF WASHINGTON,   )   Case No.: 19-01-2226
5   )
            Plaintiff,)   STATE'S BRIEF
6   )   IN OPPOSITION TO
            v.   )   MOTION TO
7   )   SUPPRESS
)
DEAN E. PATTERSON,   )
8   )
)
9   Defendant.)
_____   )
10

11   The State asks the Court to deny the defendant's

12   motion to suppress the victim's show-up and line-up iden-

13   tifications and to allow both the victim and the witness to

14   make in-court identifications. The show-up was not sug-

15   gestive, and the victim's and the witness's identifications

16   are reliable. ②

17   **Statement of Facts**

18   On Monday, August 19, 2019, Beatrice Martinez was

19   assaulted with a deadly weapon. ③ At a show-up con-

20   ducted thirty to forty minutes after the attack, Ms.

21   Martinez identified the defendant, Dean E. Patterson, as

22

State's Brief   Name of Prosecutor
in Opposition to   Deputy Prosecuting Attorney
Defendant's   for King County
Motion to Suppress–1   Address of Prosecutor's Office

① Under the Washington rules, you must include a caption that sets out the name of the court, the names of the parties, the file number, and a title that identifies the nature of the pleading or document. *See* CR 10(a).

② In this example, the prosecutor has included an introductory paragraph in which he sets out his request for relief. Under the Washington rules, this type of introductory paragraph is optional.

③ The prosecutor starts the story where it started for the victim: with the assault.

1   her assailant. The next day, Ms. Martinez picked Mr.

2   Patterson out of a line-up, once again identifying him as

3   her assailant. ④

4   On the day of the assault, seventeen-year-old Ms.

5   Martinez left her apartment at about 4:30 p.m. to walk

6   to her after school job at Angelo's, a restaurant. As she

7   was walking north on Belmont, Martinez observed an

8   older model silver SUV with a chrome luggage rack as it

9   passed slowly by her. ⑤ Moments later, the same SUV

10 came down the street again. This time, the driver pulled

11 his car in front of Ms. Martinez, stopping his SUV so

12 that it blocked her path. As Ms. Martinez watched, ⑥

13 the driver got out of his car and walked toward her. The

14 man then took a gun from his coat pocket and pointed

15 it at Martinez. Martinez looked at the gun and then at

16 her assailant. Then, crying, she ran back across the street

17 to safety. ⑦

18   At about the same time, ⑧ Chester Clipse was walking

19 south on Belmont. As he approached his apartment, Mr.

20 Clipse saw a man in a silver SUV pull into the area where

21 he usually parked. Mr. Clipse immediately started walking

22 toward the man to tell him that he could not park there. A

23 moment later, Mr. Clipse saw the man get out of

24

25

26

State's Brief   Name of Prosecutor
in Opposition to   Deputy Prosecuting Attorney
Defendant's   for King County
Motion to Suppress–2   Address of Prosecutor's Office

④ The prosecutor uses this paragraph to introduce his theory of the case, which is that the victim has repeatedly identified the defendant as her assailant.

⑤ The prosecutor has described the facts related to the vehicle and the victim's opportunity to view that vehicle in detail, giving those facts considerable airtime. The inference that the prosecutor wants the court to draw is that, if the victim's description of the vehicle is accurate, so is her description of her assailant.

⑥ The prosecutor uses the word "watched" to suggest that the victim had a good opportunity to view her assailant. In addition, by setting out the facts in three sentences rather than one sentence, the prosecutor "slows down time."

⑦ The prosecutor has tried to create the impression that Ms. Martinez had a good opportunity to view her assailant by setting out the facts in separate sentences.

⑧ Note how the prosecutor put the orienting transitions at the beginning of the sentence.

1   his car and approach a young woman⁹ who had stopped

2   suddenly. As Mr. Clipse watched, the man pulled out a gun

3   and pointed it at the young woman.

4   Both Ms. Martinez and Mr. Clipse screamed, and the

5   man turned and ran to his car, putting the gun under his

6   coat. As the young woman ran across the street, the man

7   got back into his car, backed out, and drove away, travel-

8   ing northbound on Belmont.

9   **Issue**

10   Should the Court deny the defendant's motion to sup-

11 press⁰ when the police merely asked the victim whether

12 a pedestrian was her assailant and when the victim

13 observed her assailant on two occasions for several sec-

14 onds in broad daylight?⁰

15   **Argument**

16 **I. The Court should deny the defendant's motion to**

17 **suppress because the police procedures were not**
    impermissibly suggestive and the victim's identifica-

18 **tion is reliable.**

19   Identifications should not be kept from the jury unless

20 the procedures used in obtaining the identifications were

21 so suggestive and unreliable that a substantial likelihood

22 of irreparable misidentification exists. *See Perry v.*

23 *New Hampshire*, 565 U.S. 228, 239-40, 132 S. Ct. 716,

24 181 L. Ed. 2d 694 (2012); *Simmons v. United States*, 390

25 U.S. 377, 384, 89 S. Ct. 1127, 22 L. Ed. 2d 402 (1969).

26

State's Brief   Name of Prosecutor
in Opposition to   Deputy Prosecuting Attorney
Defendant's   for King County
Motion to Suppress–3   Address of Prosecutor's Office

⁹ The prosecutor could have used a number of different words to describe Ms. Martinez: "Ms. Martinez," "the victim," "a girl," "a woman," or "a young woman." In picking a label, the prosecutor had to weigh his desire to paint Ms. Martinez as a victim against his need to establish that her identification was reliable.

⁰ The prosecutor has framed the legal question so that it suggests the conclusion that he wants the court to reach.

⁰ The prosecutor has set out a key fact related to the first part of the two-part test and then a fact related to the second part of the test. In doing so, the prosecutor has presented those facts accurately but in a light favorable to the State.

⁰ If you have one issue statement, you should have one main heading. The issue statement sets out the question, and the heading answers that question. In this instance, the prosecutor has used the conventional format for a heading; he sets out his assertion and then a "because" clause that provides support for that assertion.

⁰ The prosecutor starts his general rule section by creating a favorable context.

⁰ Because this brief is a brief to a Washington court, the prosecutor has used the Washington citation rules.

1   In deciding whether identification evidence is admis-

2 sible, courts employ a two-part test. Under the first part of

3 the test, the defendant has the burden of proving that the

4 identification evidence that he or she seeks to suppress

5 was obtained through impermissibly suggestive proce-

6 dures. *Manson v. Braithwaite*, 432 U.S. 98, 113, 97 S. Ct.

7 2243, 53 L. Ed. 2d 140 (1977). Only if the defendant satis-

8 fies this substantial burden is the second part of the test

9 applied. *Id.* [15]

10   Even if the court determines that the police procedures

11 were impermissibly suggestive, the evidence is admissible

12 if, under the totality of the circumstances, the identifica-

13 tions are reliable. *Perry*, 565 U.S. at 239-40; *Simmons*,

14 390 U.S. at 384. Due process does not compel the exclu-

15 sion of an identification if it is reliable. *Id.* [16]

16   A. <u>Merely asking the victim whether a pedestrian was</u>

17   <u>her assailant does not make a permissible show-up</u>
     <u>impermissibly suggestive.</u> [17]

18

19   There are no published Washington cases in which

20 the court has held that a show-up was impermissibly sug-

21 gestive. [18] *See, e.g., State v. Rogers*, 44 Wn. App. 510, 722

22 P.2d 1249 (1986); *State v. Booth*, 36 Wn. App. 66, 671

23 P.2d 1218 (1983). In *Rogers*, [19] the court held that the

24 show-up was not impermissibly suggestive even though

25 the police had picked up the witness at a tavern, told

26

State's Brief   Name of Prosecutor
in Opposition to   Deputy Prosecuting Attorney
Defendant's   for King County
Motion to Suppress–4   Address of Prosecutor's Office

[15] The prosecutor uses language that empha-sizes that it is the defen-dant who has the burden of proving the first part of the test.

[16] The prosecutor ends the general rule section by responding to Mr. Patterson's due process argument. Note, though, that the prose-cutor responds to Mr. Patterson's argument without saying what Mr. Patterson argued.

[17] In drafting this head-ing, the prosecutor did not use the conventional format. He does, how-ever, make an assertion.

[18] The prosecutor starts this paragraph with a bold, but accurate statement.

[19] The prosecutor uses three cases to support his point. He discusses the first two cases in text and the third case in a parenthetical. Note that the case descriptions are short and to the point. The prosecutor sets out the court's holding and then sets out a short summary of the facts.

1   him that they wanted to take him back to his apartment

2   to see if he could identify his assailant, and then pre-

3   sented the defendant to him while the defendant was

4   standing between two uniformed police officers. 44

5   Wn. App. at 511. Similarly, [20] in *Booth*, 36 Wn. App. at

6   67-68, the court held that the show-up was not imper-

7   missibly suggestive when the police asked the witness

8   to accompany them to the place where the defendant

9   had been arrested and the witness identified the defen-

10 dant after seeing him in the back of a police car. *See*

11 *also State v. Guzman-Cuellar*, 47 Wn. 2d 326, 335-36,

12 734 P.2d 966 (1987) (show-up not impermissibly sug-

13 gestive when the defendant was shown to three of the

14 four eyewitnesses while in handcuffs standing next to

15 a police car).

16   In our case, [21] the show-up was not nearly as sugges-

17 tive as the show-ups in *Rogers*, *Booth*, or *Guzman-Cuellar*. [22]

18 Unlike the officers in *Rogers*, *Booth*, and *Guzman-Cuellar*,

19 Officer Yuen did not ask Ms. Martinez to go with him to

20 identify her assailant. Instead, the show-up occurred as he

21 was taking Ms. Martinez home. In addition, when Ms.

22 Martinez made her identification, the defendant was not

23 flanked by police officers, sitting in the back of a patrol

24 car, or in handcuffs standing next to a police car. [23]

25

26

State's Brief   Name of Prosecutor
in Opposition to   Deputy Prosecuting Attorney
Defendant's   for King County
Motion to Suppress–5   Address of Prosecutor's Office

[20] The prosecutor uses the transition to tell the court that he is moving to the next case and that case is another case that supports the assertion that he made in the principle-based topic sentence.

[21] The prosecutor uses a transition to signal that he is moving from a description of the analogous cases to a discussion of his own case.

[22] Instead of discussing the cases one by one, the prosecutor discusses them as a group.

[23] In this sentence, the prosecutor distinguishes all three cases. Note that he distinguishes them in the order in which he discussed them in the preceding paragraph.

1   If Officer Yuen had not asked Ms. Martinez whether

2 the pedestrian looked like her assailant, he would not

3 have been doing his job. [24] To protect others, Officer

4 Yuen needed to determine whether the man who

5 matched Ms. Martinez's description was, in fact, Ms.

6 Martinez's assailant. The officer's question, "Is that the

7 man?" was not enough to turn a permissible show-up

8 into one that was impermissibly suggestive.

9   B. Ms. Martinez's identification was reliable: She had
10   observed her assailant on two occasions; her atten-
           tion was focused on her assailant; and, except for
11   her statement about her assailant's age, her descrip-
           tion was accurate. [25]
12

13   Even if the police procedures were suggestive, [26] the

14 identification is admissible unless [27] the procedures are

15 "so impermissibly suggestive as to give rise to very sub-

16 stantial likelihood of irreparable misidentifications."

17 Simmons; accord Perry, 565 U.S. at 232. In deciding

18 whether the identification is reliable, courts consider

19 the witness's opportunity to view the criminal at the

20 time of the crime, the witness's degree of attention,

21 the accuracy of the witness's description, the level of cer-

22 tainty demonstrated by the witness at the confrontation,

23 and the length of time between the crime and the con-

24 frontation. Neil v. Biggers, 409 U.S. 188, 199-200, 93 S.

25 Ct. 375, 34 L. Ed. 2d 401 (1972).

26

[24] In addition to making arguments based on analogous cases, the prosecutor also makes a policy argument.

[25] The prosecutor also uses an alternative format for this heading. Instead of using the word "because," he uses a colon. The statement that precedes the colon is the assertion, and the facts set out after the colon are the support for the assertion.

[26] The prosecutor uses language that tells the court that this argument is an alternative argument.

[27] The prosecutor sets out the rule broadly: "the identification is admissible unless. . . ."

State's Brief   Name of Prosecutor
in Opposition to   Deputy Prosecuting Attorney
Defendant's   for King County
Motion to Suppress–6   Address of Prosecutor's Office

1   Courts do not require that the witness view the defen-

2   dant for an extended period of time. [28] *State v. Booth*, 36

3   Wn. App. 66, 671 P.2d 1218 (1983). For example, in

4   *Booth*, the court concluded that the witness's identification

5   was reliable when the witness had viewed the defendant

6   for less than a minute. [29] *Id.* at 71. Because the witness's

7   attention had been drawn to the fleeing man and because

8   she viewed him in broad daylight, the court found that the

9   identification was reliable. *Id.* Similarly, in our case, Ms.

10   Martinez's attention had been drawn to her assailant. [30]

11   Shortly before the assault, Ms. Martinez watched [31] as

12   her assailant drove slowly by her.

13   Consequently, when he drove by her again, her atten-

14   tion was focused on him. She watched as he drove his car

15   in front of her, blocking her path. In addition, she watched

16   as he got out of his car and walked toward her. Thus,

17   although she looked at him for only two or three seconds

18   once he pulled out the gun, [32] before that time, she had a

19   good opportunity to view him and her attention had been

20   focused on him. In addition, courts do not require that the

21   witness's description be completely accurate. [33] *State v.*

22   *Kraus*, 21 Wn. App. 388, 584 P.2d 946 (1978). In *Kraus*,

23   the court held that the witness's identification was reliable

24   despite the fact that the witness had stated that the robber

25   was wearing a dark jacket and the defendant was wearing

26

State's Brief   Name of Prosecutor
in Opposition to   Deputy Prosecuting Attorney
Defendant's   for King County
Motion to Suppress–7   Address of Prosecutor's Office

[28] After listing the factors, the prosecutor goes through the factors one at a time.

[29] In describing *Booth*, the prosecutor sets out only the key facts and the court's holding.

[30] In comparing the facts in *Booth* to the facts in the case before the court, the prosecutor repeats key language from the case: "the witness's attention had been drawn."

[31] The prosecutor has selected words—for example, "watched" and "focused"—that suggest Ms. Martinez had a good opportunity to view her assailant.

[32] The prosecutor has placed the unfavorable fact in a dependent clause.

[33] The prosecutor organizes the discussion of the second factor in the same way that he organized his discussion of the first factor. First, he sets out a topic sentence that sets out the rule in a light favorable to the State. Second, he uses cases to illustrate how courts have applied that rule. In setting out his case descriptions, he includes only the key facts, and he sets out those facts in a light favorable to his client. Finally, he applies the rule to the facts of his case.

1   a light-colored jacket. *Id.* at 393. Similarly, in *State v.*

2   *Maupin*, 63 Wn. App. 887, 822 P.2d 355 (1992), the

3   court held that the witness's identification was reliable

4   even though the witness was not able to tell the police

5   the rapist's race. *Id.* at 892.

6   In this case, Ms. Martinez was able to give the police a

7   detailed description of her assailant. When she was inter-

8   viewed, she told the police that her assailant was a white

9   male with blondish-brown hair, that he was approxi-

10 mately 5'7" tall and weighed between 165 and 170

11 pounds, that he appeared to be in his early forties, and

12 that he was wearing a dark jacket. This description is

13 accurate in all but one respect. Although Ms. Martinez

14 misjudged the defendant's age, she accurately described

15 his car, his hair, his height and weight, and his clothing.

16   In addition, Ms. Martinez's identification occurred

17 shortly after the assault, and Ms. Martinez was certain in

18 her identification. Although she did not answer Officer

19 Yuen's question the first time that he asked her, as soon as

20 ·she got a better look at the defendant, she identified him

21 as her assailant. [34] As she stated during the suppression hear-

22 ing, "Once I got a good look at him I was sure it was him." [35]

23   Taken together, these facts establish that, even if the

24 show-up was suggestive, Ms. Martinez's identification was

25 reliable. [36] Ms. Martinez had a good opportunity to view

26

State's Brief   Name of Prosecutor
in Opposition to   Deputy Prosecuting Attorney
Defendant's   for King County
Motion to Suppress–8   Address of Prosecutor's Office

[34] In this sentence, the prosecutor responds to defense counsel's argument that the officer's statement influenced Ms. Martinez's identification.

[35] The prosecutor ends this section with a favorable quote.

[36] The prosecutor ends this part of the argument by summarizing the points that he made.

1 her assailant; her attention was focused on her assailant;

2 she accurately identified her assailant's build and clothing;

3 and once she got a good look at the defendant, she was cer-

4 tain that he was her assailant. Accordingly, the Court should

5 not suppress Ms. Martinez's show-up identification.

6   C. <u>Because the show-up was not impermissibly sug-

7   gestive, the Court should not suppress Ms.
     Martinez's line-up identification or prevent Ms.

8   Martinez or Mr. Clipse from making in-court
     identifications.</u> [37]

9

10   The Court should not suppress Ms. Martinez's line-up

11 identification, nor should it prevent Ms. Martinez or Mr.

12 Clipse from making an in-court identification. [38] Because

13 the show-up was not impermissibly suggestive, see subsec-

14 tion IA, it did not taint either the line-up or any potential in-

15 court identifications.

16   Although Mr. Clipse may have seen the police talking

17 with the defendant, such an act by itself is not enough

18 to make a show-up impermissibly suggestive. [39] *See*

19 *Guzman-Cuellar*, 47 Wn. 2d at 333; *Rogers*, 44 Wn. App.

20 at 512; *Booth*, 36 Wn. App. at 72. In addition, like

21 Ms. Martinez, Mr. Clipse had a good opportunity to view

22 Ms. Martinez's assailant. His attention was drawn to the

23 assailant because the man was pulling into his parking

24

25

26

[37] The prosecutor has also used an alternative format for this heading. He has placed the "because" clause at the beginning rather than the end.

[38] The prosecutor starts this section by setting out his assertion.

[39] The prosecutor has intentionally kept this argument short. If he wins his first argument, the prosecutor will also win this argument; however, if he loses the first argument, he will, probably, also lose this argument.

State's Brief   Name of Prosecutor
in Opposition to   Deputy Prosecuting Attorney
Defendant's   for King County
Motion to Suppress–9   Address of Prosecutor's Office

1   spot, and, except for his description of the assailant's age,

2   Mr. Clipse's description was accurate.

3   **Prayer for Relief**

4   For the reasons set out above, the State respectfully

5   requests that the Court deny the defendant's motion to

6   suppress and admit Ms. Martinez's show-up and line-up

7   identifications and permit Ms. Martinez and Mr. Clipse

8   to make in-court identifications.

9   Dated this 30th day of September, 2019.

10   _____

11   Assistant Prosecuting Attorney
                          Washington Bar No. 00000
12

13

14

15

16

17

18

19

20

21

22

23

24

25

26

State's Brief   Name of Prosecutor
in Opposition to   Deputy Prosecuting Attorney
Defendant's   for King County
Motion to Suppress–10   Address of Prosecutor's Office

§ 8.2 Briefs from a Civil Case Seeking Motion for Summary Judgment

---

EXAMPLE 3   **DEFENDANT'S BRIEF IN SUPPORT OF A MOTION FOR PARTIAL SUMMARY JUDGMENT**

1

2

3

4   IN THE SUPERIOR COURT OF THE STATE OF
       WASHINGTON FOR KING COUNTY ❶

5

6   BARBARA DONELY et al.,   )   Case No.:
)   19-1-02399-2 SEA
7   Plaintiffs,   )
)   BRIEF IN SUPPORT
8   v.   )   OF DEFENDANT'S
)   MOTION FOR
9   SUNNY ORCHARD   )   PARTIAL SUMMARY
10 RESTAURANT GROUP, INC.   )   JUDGMENT
    a Delaware Corporation,   )
11   )
)
12   Defendant.   )
    _____   )

13

14   **Relief Requested**

15   Sunny Orchard requests that the Court grant its

16   motion for partial summary judgment and dismiss the

17   plaintiffs' strict liability claims because (1) there are no

18   genuine issues of material fact, (2) the relevant product

19   is the orange juice, (3) as a matter of law Sunny

20   Orchard did not manufacture the juice, and (4) as a

❶ The King County Local Rules govern the form of the brief.

Brief in Support   Attorney for Defendant,
of Motion for   Sunny Orchard Restaurant, Inc.
Partial Summary Judgment–1   Address and
                                                  Phone Number

1   matter of law Sunny Orchard did not market the orange

2   juice under its trade name or brand name. Sunny

3   Orchard is not asking the Court to dismiss the plaintiffs'

4   negligence claims. ② ③

5   **Statement of Facts**

6   The defendant, Sunny Orchard Restaurant Group

7   (Sunny Orchard), operates 132 family-friendly restau-

8   rants in 15 states. ④ Def's Answer to 1st Amended

9   Compl. ⑤ ¶1.3. One of the items that Sunny Orchard ⑥

10 serves at its restaurant is orange juice that it purchases

11 from the California Juice Company (California Juice).

12 Def's Responses to Pls' 1st Interr. No. 1.

13   ⑦ California Juice delivers the juice in one-gallon con-

14 tainers to Sunny Orchard's distribution center in Tukwila,

15 Washington, which then fill orders from individual restau-

16 rants. Def's Resp. to Pls' 1st Interr. No. 3. When a restau-

17 rant receives the juice, it places the juice containers in a

18 walk-in cooler. *Id.* As needed, the juice is taken from the

19 walk-in cooler and poured into a juice dispenser from

20 which servers get the juice that they serve to customers.

21 *Id.*

22

23

24

25

26

Brief in Support
of Motion for
Partial Summary Judgment–2

                Attorney for Defendant,
          Sunny Orchard Restaurant, Inc.
                    Address and
                   Phone Number

---

② In addition to setting out the relief that he wants, the defendant's attorney summarizes his arguments. Each of the listed items are discussed in a separate section of the argument.

③ In this sentence the defendant's attorney reminds the court that the plaintiffs have set out two causes of action: one for negligence and one for strict liability. The defense attorney's hope is that the court will be more likely to grant this motion if it knows that the plaintiffs will still get "their day in court" on the negligence claims. (Note: The defense attorney thinks he may be able to win on the negligence claim.)

④ The defendant's attorney tries to paint his client in a favorable light by including the fact that the restaurants are "family friendly."

⑤ The Washington Style Sheet does not prescribe the abbreviations that should be used in referring to documents filed with the court.

⑥ In this case, the defendant's attorney has decided to refer to his client as "Sunny Orchard" and to use the label "plaintiffs" for the plaintiffs.

⑦ In this paragraph, the defendant's attorney sets out, in a matter-of-fact way, the distribution process. Ultimately, the attorney wants to establish that the defendant does not alter or change the juice. It is simply a link in the chain of distribution.

1   [8]Sunny Orchard does not refer to the orange juice

2   offered in its restaurants as "Sunny Orchard juices," Def's

3   Responses to Pls' 1st Interr. No. 10, and if asked whether

4   the juice being served was squeezed at the restaurant, the

5   servers are assumed to answer truthfully by saying, "No."

6   Def's Responses to Pls' 1st Interr. No. 15. Although the

7   menu and servers describe the orange juice as "fresh"

8   and "orchard-squeezed," [9] any use of the name "Sunny

9   Orchard" in conjunction with a description of the juice

10   refers only to the fact that the juice is served within, at, or

11   by a Sunny Orchard restaurant. Def's Responses to Pls'

12   1st Interr. No. 11. The orange juice that is sold in the gift

13   shop, which is the same orange juice offered to Sunny

14   Orchard customers, is labeled with the California Juice

15   and not the Sunny Orchard brand name. *Id.* [10]

16   [11]Sunny Orchard first offered the "Picnic Banquet

17   Breakfast," which included orange juice in a souvenir

18   glass, in 2005. Def's Responses to Pls' 1st Interr. No.

19   13. While at first the glass was decorated with the

20   Sunny Orchard logo, the logo was removed four years

21   ago. Def's Responses to Pls' 1st Interr. No. 17. Since

22   then, the glasses have featured a seasonal design that

23   changes four times a year. *Id.*

24   On May 12, 2019, the plaintiffs [12] had breakfast at

25   Sunny Orchard's Seattle restaurant. All six plaintiffs

26

Brief in Support   Attorney for Defendant,
of Motion for   Sunny Orchard Restaurant, Inc.
Partial Summary Judgment–3   Address and
                                            Phone Number

[8] In this paragraph the defendant's attorney sets out the facts that he knows he will need in responding to the plaintiffs' arguments. Note that paragraph is not in a position of emphasis.

[9] The attorney has put an unfavorable fact in a dependent clause in the middle of the sentence that is in the middle of the paragraph.

[10] The attorney ends this paragraph with a favorable fact.

[11] In this paragraph the defense attorney sets out the fact that he will need to respond to the plaintiffs' argument that Sunny Orchard marketed the juice under its brand or trade name. Note that the attorney puts the favorable facts at the end of the paragraph in a position of emphasis and the unfavorable fact in a dependent clause.

[12] While defendant's attorney could have used the phrase "members of the family," he chooses to go with the more "clinical" term, "plaintiffs."

1   ordered the Picnic Banquet Breakfast, which comes with

2   the orange juice that Sunny Orchard purchases from

3   California Juice. Complaint, ¶2.4. The juice was brought

4   to the table in a pitcher that had a kerchief tied on the

5   handle and poured into the decorative glasses, which

6   had been garnished with a slice of orange and a sprig of

7   mint. Def's Responses to Pls' 1st Interr. No. 16. Three

8   days later, the Washington State Department of

9   Community Health (WSDH) issued a warning to consu-

10 mers not to drink unpasteurized orange juice products

11 distributed under the California Juice brand name

12 because the orange juice had the potential to be contami-

13 nated with *Salmonella*. Complaint, ¶3.1. The plaintiffs

14 allege, Complaint, ¶5.4, and Sunny Orchard admits,

15 that two of the plaintiffs, Barbara Donely and Daniel

16 Steddic, contracted *Salmonella* from the juice that they

17 drank at the Sunny Orchard restaurant. Requests for

18 Admission, Nos. 13, 14, 16. This has been the only con-

19 firmed claim of a foodborne, illness-related injury at a

20 Sunny Orchard restaurant in at least five years. Def's

21 Responses to Pls' 1st Interr. No. 20. ⑬

22   **Statement of Issues**

23   Under the Washington Product Liability Act, RCW

24 7.72, is Sunny Orchard entitled to judgment as a matter

25 of law on the plaintiffs' strict liability claim when (1) the

26

Brief in Support   Attorney for Defendant,
of Motion for   Sunny Orchard Restaurant, Inc.
Partial Summary Judgment–4   Address and
                                                 Phone Number

⑬In this paragraph, the defendant's attorney tries to minimize the process that the servers used in serving the juice. Compare the way in which the plaintiffs' attorney presents these facts in Example 4 with the way in which the defendant's attorney presents them here.

Although the attorney could have added a paragraph break, he did not do so. Because the facts set out in this paragraph do not favor California Restaurants, he decided to de-emphasize them by putting them in a long paragraph.

By setting out the facts in chronological order, the defendant's attorney highlights the fact that the restaurant did not know about the contamination until after it served the juice.

The defendant's attorney does not give any airtime to the fact that two of the plaintiffs became ill after drinking juice at a Sunny Orchard restaurant. Compare the way in which the plaintiffs' attorney presents these facts in Example 4 with the way in which the defendant's attorney presents them here.

Defense counsel ends this paragraph, and the statement of facts, with a favorable fact.

Note that the defendant's statement of facts is much shorter than the plaintiffs'. The defendant's attorney wants to suggest that the facts in the case are not in dispute and that the only issues are legal issues.

1   plaintiffs became ill after drinking orange juice at a Sunny

2   Orchard restaurant; (2) Sunny Orchard purchased the

3   contaminated orange juice from California Juice; (3) all

4   Sunny Orchard did was pour the juice from the original

5   containers into a dispenser and then into a pitcher and

6   garnished glasses; and (4) the menu does not represent

7   that Sunny Orchard made the juice and the Sunny

8   Orchard logo is not on the glasses? [14]

9   **Evidence Relied Upon**

10   This motion is based on the First Amended Complaint

11 for Product Liability and Punitive Damages; Defendant's

12 Answer to First Amended Complaint for Product Liability

13 and Punitive Damages; Plaintiffs' First Requests for

14 Admission, and Defendant's Objections and Responses

15 to the Same; and Plaintiffs' First Interrogatories and

16 Requests for Production, and Defendant's Objections and

17 Responses to the Same.

18   **Authority**

19 **I. The Court should grant sunny orchard's motion**
20   **for partial summary judgment because there are**
       no issues of fact and, as a matter of law, Sunny
21   **Orchard did not manufacture the orange juice or**
       market the juice under its brand name. [15]
22

23   Summary judgment is appropriate when "the plead-

24 ings, depositions, answers to interrogatories, and admis-

25 sions on file, together with the affidavits, if any, show

26 that there is no genuine issue as to any material fact

Attorney for Defendant,
Sunny Orchard Restaurant, Inc.
Address and
Phone Number

[14] The defendant's attorney has framed the question so that it suggests the conclusion that he wants the court to reach.

In drafting this issue statement, the defendant's attorney had to decide whether to include the key facts, which makes for a long issue statement, or to set out legal conclusions. The attorney decided to go with the first option and set out the key facts.

[15] Once again, the attorney for defendant had to make a decision. Should he just set out his assertion—THE COURT SHOULD GRANT SUNNY ORCHARD'S MOTION FOR PARTIAL SUMMARY JUDGMENT—or should he include a "because" clause? Including the "because" makes the issue statement much longer.

1 and that the moving party is entitled to judgment as a

2 matter of law." CR 56(c). [16] In making a decision, courts

3 must consider all facts submitted and all reasonable infer-

4 ences from them in the light most favorable to the non-

5 moving party. *Sanders v. State*, 169 Wn. 2d 827, 844,

6 240 P.3d 120 (2010).

7 However, the nonmoving party may not rely on spec-

8 ulation, on argumentative assertions that unresolved fac-

9 tual issues remain, or on having its affidavits considered

10 at face value. *Seven Gables Corp. v. MGM/UA Entm't Co.*,

11 106 Wn. 2d 1, 13, 721 P.2d 1 (1986). After the defendant

12 submits adequate affidavits, the burden shifts to the non-

13 moving party to provide specific facts that sufficiently

14 rebut the moving party's contentions and disclose the

15 existence of a material issue of fact. *Id.* The Court should

16 grant Sunny Orchard's motion for summary judgment if

17 there are no genuine issues of material fact. *See Sanders*,

18 169 Wn. 2d at 844.

19 In this case, there are no genuine issues of material

20 fact. Both sides agree that the plaintiffs contracted

21 *Salmonella* after drinking the orange juice that Sunny

22 Orchard purchased from California Juice. Requests for

23 Admission, Nos. 13, 14, 16. [17] Because there are no gen-

24 uine issues of material fact, the questions before the Court

25 are questions of law. [18] *See Almquist v. Finley Sch. Dist.*,

26 114 Wn. App. 395, 404, 57 P.3d 1191 (2002). In this

Brief in Support
of Motion for
Partial Summary Judgment–6

Attorney for Defendant,
Sunny Orchard Restaurant, Inc.
Address and
Phone Number

[16] The defendant's attorney starts the Authority section by setting out the general rules, which in this case are the rules governing summary judgment. However, because judges know the rules governing summary judgment, this section can be very short. The attorney simply sets out the key rules in a light favorable to his client.

[17] The defendant's attorney starts this paragraph with an assertion: that there are no genuine issues of material fact. He then provides support for this assertion by citing to the Requests for Admission.

[18] At this point, the attorney does not know whether the plaintiffs will argue that there is a question of fact. If they do, he will respond to those arguments in a reply brief or in oral argument.

1   case, as a matter of law, the relevant product is the orange

2   juice, and Sunny Orchard did not manufacture that

3   orange juice or market that orange juice under its trade

4   or brand name.

5   A. <u>The relevant product is the orange juice because it
       was the orange juice that gave rise to the product</u>

6   <u>liability claim.</u> [19]

7

8   Under RCW 7.72.010(3), the relevant product is "that

9   product or its component part or parts, which gave rise to

10 the product liability claim." [20] In this case, the plaintiffs

11 allege that their injuries were caused by the orange juice

12 that they drank at one of Sunny Orchard's restaurants.

13 Complaint, ¶2.4. They do not allege that they were

14 harmed by the glass in which the orange juice was served,

15 by the garnishes that were placed on the glass, or by any

16 of the other items that were served as part of the Picnic

17 Banquet Breakfast. [21] *Id.* Therefore, under the definition

18 set out in the act, the relevant product is the orange

19 juice because it contained the *Salmonella* "which gave

20 rise to the product liability claim." RCW 7.72.010(3).

21   B. <u>Sunny Orchard is not a "manufacturer" because all
       that it did was serve orange juice that it purchased</u>

22   <u>from California Juice.</u>

23

24   Although Sunny Orchard is a product seller, it is not a

25 manufacturer. An entity is a manufacturer only if it

26

Brief in Support   Attorney for Defendant,
of Motion for   Sunny Orchard Restaurant, Inc.
Partial Summary Judgment–7   Address and
                                           Phone Number

[19] The attorney uses the conventional format for this argumentative heading. He sets out his assertion and then a "because" clause in which he provides support for that assertion.

[20] In this brief, the attorney does not include a general rule section in which he provides the judge with an overview of the Washington Products Liability Act. Instead, he jumps right into the analysis. While this strategy would work well with judges who are familiar with the Act, it might not work for judges who are not. Thus, unless the attorney knows that the judge is familiar with the Act, he should add a general rule section.

[21] The defendant's attorney uses detail to emphasize what the plaintiffs have not alleged.

1 "designs, produces, makes, fabricates, constructs, or rema-

2 nufactures the relevant product. . . . " RCW 7.72.010(2).

3   In the only Washington Products Liability Act case

4 that discusses whether a defendant who serves food

5 falls within the definition of a manufacturer, the defen-

6 dant altered the food item that caused the injury.

7 *Almquist v. Finley Sch. Dist.*, 114 Wn. App. 395, 57 P.3d

8 1191 (2002). In *Almquist*, the defendant, the Finley

9 School District (District), did not just serve the tainted

10 ground beef. *Id.* at 404. Instead, it thawed the beef,

11 cooked the beef, drained it, rinsed it, added seasonings,

12 and then added other ingredients to create tacos. *Id.*

13   In light of these facts, the court concluded that the

14 District's cooking process fell neatly into each of the defi-

15 nitions for "design," "produce," "make," "fabricate," and

16 "construct." The District designed the school lunch and,

17 using the tainted meat, it produced, made, fabricated,

18 and constructed the taco lunch. *Id.* at 405. As the court

19 noted in its opinion, "[t]he reason for excluding non-

20 manufacturing retailers from strict liability is to distin-

21 guish 'between those who have actual control over the

22 product and those who act as mere conduits in the

23 chain of distribution.'" *Id.*

24   Unlike the District, which altered the frozen ground

25 beef, Sunny Orchard simply served juice that it purchased

26 from California Juice. It did not do anything to prepare the

The defendant's attorney starts this sub-section by setting out the specific rule in a light favorable to the defendant. Note the attorney's use of the phrase "only if."

The defendant's attorney starts his discussion of the analogous case with a principle-based topic sentence.

Because he wants to distinguish *Almquist*, the defendant's attorney goes into detail in describing the process that the District used in preparing and mixing the tainted beef with other ingredients.

The defendant's attorney ends this paragraph with a quotation that supports his client's argument.

The defendant's attorney uses this paragraph to distinguish *Almquist*.

Brief in Support
of Motion for
Partial Summary Judgment–8

Attorney for Defendant,
Sunny Orchard Restaurant, Inc.
Address and
Phone Number

1   juice—for example, it did not thaw frozen concentrate,

2   and it did not add anything to the orange juice. All it did

3   was add an orange slice and a sprig of mint to the glass.

4   The orange juice remained in exactly the same form

5   from the time Sunny Orchard purchased it from

6   California Juice until Sunny Orchard served it to its custo-

7   mers. Therefore, Sunny Orchard acted as a mere conduit

8   in the chain of distribution. [27]

9   C. <u>The orange juice was marketed under California
10   Juice's brand name and not Sunny Orchard's
       brand name.</u>
11

12   Finally, Sunny Orchard did not market the orange

13 juice under its trade name or brand and, therefore, it is

14 not a manufacturer under RCW 7.72.040(2)(e). [28]   The

15 key case is *Johnson v. Recreational Equip., Inc.*, 159 Wn.

16 App. 939, 247 P.3d 18 (2011), a case in which the plaintiff

17 brought a products liability action against the seller of an

18 allegedly defective carbon fiber fork that fractured and

19 detached from her bicycle. *Id.* at 943. Because both the

20 bicycle and the carbon fiber fork were marketed under

21 REI's brand name, "Novara," the court held REI strictly

22 liable for the injuries caused by the defective product. *Id.*

23   Unlike REI, which marketed both the bicycle and the

24 carbon fiber fork under its brand name, Sunny Orchard

25 did not market the juice under its brand name. [29]   It did

26 not advertise the juice as Sunny Orchard juice, and, on

[27] The attorney concludes this paragraph by repeating language that he quoted in the last sentence of the preceding paragraph. This type of repetition can be effective.

Although there are other arguments that the defendant's attorney might make, most judges say that they want short, concise briefs. Thus, the attorney makes his key points and then stops. If the plaintiffs make other arguments, he can respond to those arguments in a reply brief or during the oral arguments.

[28] The attorney begins this section of his brief by setting out his assertion and then introducing the key case.

[29] The attorney uses this paragraph to distinguish *REI*. In doing so, he sets out the facts that support his position.

Brief in Support   Attorney for Defendant,
of Motion for   Sunny Orchard Restaurant, Inc.
Partial Summary Judgment–9   Address and
                                                  Phone Number

1   its menu it simply states that the juice is "sunny-fresh,

2   orchard-squeezed juice." Pls.' First Am. Compl. ¶3.12;

3   Def.'s Resp. to Pls.' Interrog. No. 11. In addition, the

4   Sunny Orchard logo is not on the pitcher or the glasses

5   in which the juice is served. Finally, the orange juice

6   that is sold in the gift shop, which is the same orange

7   juice offered to Sunny Orchard customers, is labeled

8   with the California Juice brand name and not the Sunny

9   Orchard brand name. [30] *Id.* Even if the court were to

10 find that the Picnic Banquet Breakfast is labeled under

11 the Sunny Orchard name, the product that gave rise to

12 the product liability claim is the orange juice containing

13 *Salmonella* and, therefore, it is irrelevant whether the

14 Picnic Banquet Breakfast meets the trade name or

15 brand name exception.

16   **Prayer for Relief**

17   For the reasons set out above, Sunny Orchard

18 respectfully requests that the Court grant its motion for

19 partial summary judgment on the plaintiffs' strict liability

20 claims.

21   Respectfully submitted this 2nd
22   day of October, 2019.

23

24   /s/

25   Attorney's Name
        Attorney for the defendant, Sunny
26   Orchard Restaurant Group, Inc.
        Bar No.

[30] In this sentence the attorney counters an argument that he expects that the plaintiffs will make.

Brief in Support
of Motion for
Partial Summary Judgment–10

Attorney for Defendant,
Sunny Orchard Restaurant, Inc.
Address and
Phone Number

EXAMPLE 4   PLAINTIFFS' BRIEF IN OPPOSITION TO MOTION FOR PARTIAL SUMMARY JUDGMENT

1

2

3

4

5

IN THE SUPERIOR COURT OF THE STATE OF WASHINGTON IN AND FOR THE COUNTY OF KING

BARBARA DONELY et al.,	)	Case No.:
	)	19-1-02399-2 SEA
Plaintiffs,	)	
	)	BRIEF IN OPPOSITION TO
v.	)	DEFENDANT'S MOTION
	)	FOR PARTIAL SUMMARY
SUNNY ORCHARD	)	JUDGMENT
RESTAURANT GROUP, INC.	)	
a Delaware Corporation,	)	
	)	
Defendant.	)	
_____	)	

6

7

8

9

10

11

12

13

14

Relief Requested ➊

15   The Plaintiffs ➋ request that the Court deny

16 Defendant's Motion for Partial Summary Judgment on

17 the Plaintiffs' strict liability claims under the

18 Washington Product Liability Act (Act) because there are

19 genuine issues of fact. In addition, even if there are no

20 genuine issues of fact, Defendant is strictly liable both

21 because it manufactured the relevant product and

22 because it marketed the relevant product under its

23 brand or trade name.

Brief in Opposition to   Attorney for Plaintiffs
Defendant's Motion for   Address and
Partial Summary Judgment–1   Phone Number

➊ The Washington Rules require a section in which the party submitting the brief sets out the relief that it is requesting. *See* LCR 7(b)(5)(b).

➋ Although the attorney for the plaintiffs would like to have referred to his clients by name, because the plaintiffs have different last names, she decided to use the more generic label.

Statement of Facts

1. Exposure to *Salmonella* Typhimurium and Resulting Injuries ③

④Plaintiffs Barbara and James Donely reside in Omaha, Nebraska. Pls.' First Am. Compl. ¶1.1. Plaintiffs Michael and Beverly Steddic reside in Seattle, Washington, and are the parents of Daniel and Charlotte Steddic, the Donelys' grandchildren. Pls.' First Am. Compl. ¶1.2. Defendant, Sunny Orchard Restaurant Group, Inc., is a Delaware public corporation headquartered in California. It operates 132 restaurants in fifteen states. Pls.' First Am. Compl. ¶1.3.

On Mother's Day, May 12, 2019, ⑤ the Plaintiffs visited one of Sunny Orchard's Seattle restaurants where all six members of the family ordered the "Picnic Banquet Breakfast," which Defendant states in its advertising and menu is like "having a family picnic in a sun-filled orchard!" Def's Responses to Pls' 1st Interr. No. 12. The featured item on the menu is a pitcher of "sunny-fresh, orchard-squeezed juice." Pls.' First Am. Compl. ¶3.12; Def.'s Resp. to Pls.' Interrog. No. 11.

2. Barbara Donely's Injuries and Medical Care

⑥Two days after eating at Defendant's restaurant, Ms. Donely became so ill that she had to be hospitalized for seven days. Pls.' First Am. Compl. ¶3.14(a). During this time, Ms. Donely underwent a series of tests: a

③Because her statement of facts is long, the plaintiffs' attorney has divided it into subsections and then labeled those subsections.

④The plaintiffs' attorney begins her statement of facts with a paragraph in which she identifies the parties.

⑤While the fact that the plaintiffs ate at the restaurant on Mother's Day is not legally significant, the plaintiffs' attorney has included it because it helps her tell her clients' story.

⑥While Defendant's attorney did not devote any space to the plaintiffs' injuries, the plaintiffs' attorney sets out those facts in detail. While these facts are not legally significant, they help the plaintiffs' attorney tell her clients' story.

Brief in Opposition to   Attorney for Plaintiffs
Defendant's Motion for   Address and
Partial Summary Judgment–2   Phone Number

1   stool culture confirmed the presence of *Salmonella*

2   *Typhimurium*. Pls.' First Am. Compl. ¶3.14(c); Def.'s

3   Resp. to Pls.' First Req. for Admis. No. 13.

4   3. Daniel Steddic's Injuries and Medical Care

5   While at school on the Monday after he ate at

6   Defendant's restaurant, nine-year-old Daniel Steddic ⑦

7   developed abdominal cramps and diarrhea. Pls.' First

8   Am. Compl. ¶3.15. Because his symptoms worsened

9   overnight, the next morning his parents took him to the

10 emergency room, where he was admitted with a tem-

11 perature of 103 degrees. *Id.* Daniel ⑧ was in the hospital

12 for three days and was diagnosed with gastroenteritis

13 caused by *Salmonella Typhimurium*, a condition called

14 Salmonellosis. Pls.' First Am. Compl. ¶3.22; Def.'s Resp.

15 to Pls.' First Req. for Admis. No. 14.

16   4. *Salmonella Typhimurium* Outbreak Investigation

17   During the week of May 12, 2019, the Washington

18 State Department of Community Health (WSDH) investi-

19 gated nine *Salmonella* infections that resulted from con-

20 sumption of "fresh, orchard-squeezed" orange juice at

21 one of Defendant's Seattle restaurants. Attach. No. 1 to

22 Pls.' Interrogs. 2; Def.'s Resp. to Pls.' First Req. for

23 Admis. No. 1. One of the unopened gallon bottles of

24 orange juice taken from Defendant's restaurant tested

25 positive for *Salmonella Typhimurium*. Def.'s Resp. to

26 Pls.' First Req. for Admis. No. 15. Pulsed-field gel

⑦ The plaintiffs' attorney emphasizes that one of the plaintiffs is a young child.

⑧ While as a general rule you do not want to refer to a party by just his or her first name, that rule does not apply to children.

Brief in Opposition to   Attorney for Plaintiffs
Defendant's Motion for   Address and
Partial Summary Judgment–3   Phone Number

1   electrophoresis (PFGE) testing concluded that the

2   *Salmonella* bacteria isolated from this unopened bottle

3   was "a genetically indistinguishable match" to the

4   *Salmonella* bacteria isolated from Ms. Donely's and

5   Daniel's stool cultures. Def.'s Resp. to Pls.' First Req. for

6   Admis. No. 16.

7
    5. Handling of "Sunny-Fresh, Orchard-Squeezed"
8   Orange Juice

9   ⑨Defendant's Operations Manual sets out detailed

10 instructions for the assembly and service of the "fresh,

11 orchard-squeezed juice" that is served as part of the

12 Picnic Banquet Breakfast. Attach. No. 2 to Pls.'

13 Interrogs. First, servers fill a pitcher with juice from the

14 refrigerated dispenser and tie a gingham kerchief around

15 the handle of the pitcher. Attach. No. 2 to Pls.' Interrogs.

16 Second, servers place the pitcher on a tray and arrange

17 "Sunny Orchard decorative glasses" around the pitcher

18 in a semi-circle. Attach. No. 2 to Pls.' Interrogs. Third, ser-

19 vers garnish the glasses by placing a slice of orange on the

20 edge of the glass and tucking the stem of a mint sprig

21 under the fruit slice; at the table, a cherry is added to chil-

22 dren's glasses. Attach. No. 2 to Pls.' Interrogs. In empha-

23 sizing the importance of these garnishes, the Operations

24 Manual states that "it would just not be Sunny Orchard

25 'orchard-squeezed juice' without the proper 'picnic'

26 garnishes. Our guests expect and pay for these extra-

⑨Unlike Defendant's attorney, the plaintiffs' attorney goes into detail in describing the process that Defendant uses in preparing and serving the juice. The use of "First," "Second," "Third," helps the plaintiffs' attorney emphasize that the process involves a number of steps.

Brief in Opposition to   Attorney for Plaintiffs
Defendant's Motion for   Address and
Partial Summary Judgment–4   Phone Number

1   steps [sic]." Attach. No. 2 to Pls.' Interrogs. Fourth, when

2   they get to the table, servers place a napkin with

3   Defendant's logo on it in front of each guest and then

4   place the glass on the napkin. Attach. No. 2 to Pls.'

5   Interrogs. Finally, servers pour juice from the pitcher

6   into each glass. As they do so, they say "I hope that you

7   enjoy our fresh, orchard-squeezed juice." Attach. No. 2

8   to Pls.' Interrogs. ⑩ ⑪

9   Since introducing the Picnic Banquet Breakfast in

10 2005, Defendant has served the juice in "decorative

11 glasses." While these glasses now feature seasonal

12 designs, originally the glasses had Defendant's logo

13 printed on them. ⑫ Def.'s Resp. to Pls.' Interrog. No.

14 12. The Defendant advertises the glasses as "seasonal

15 souvenir glasses," and states that many customers collect

16 the glasses by visiting the Defendant's restaurants several

17 times a year. Def.'s Resp. to Pls.' Interrog. No. 12.

18   **Issue Statement**

19   Should the Court deny Defendant's motion for partial

20 summary judgment when the plaintiffs purchased the

21 Picnic Banquet Breakfast from Defendant, and the fea-

22 tured product of that breakfast, orange juice served

23 from a pitcher with a kerchief tied around the handle

24 into decorative glasses garnished with an orange

25 slice and a sprig of mint, was contaminated with

26 *Salmonella*? ⑬

Brief in Opposition to   Attorney for Plaintiffs
Defendant's Motion for   Address and
Partial Summary Judgment–5   Phone Number

⑩ Although the plaintiffs' attorney could have added a paragraph break, she decided not to. She thought that the long paragraph would highlight the fact that the process was a long one.

⑪ Plaintiffs' attorney ends the paragraph with a favorable fact, which she emphasizes by including a quotation.

⑫ The plaintiffs' attorney has put the favorable fact in the main clause.

⑬ The plaintiffs' attorney frames the question so that it suggests the conclusion that she wants the court to reach.

Although these details make the issue statement longer, they are key facts.

Because she wants to remind the court that some of her clients became seriously ill, she puts the reference to *Salmonella* at the end of the sentence.

1   **Evidence Relied Upon**

2   This Motion is based on Plaintiffs' First Requests for

3   Admission and Defendant's Responses Thereto, Plain-

4   tiffs' First Interrogatories and Requests for Production

5   and Defendant's Responses Thereto and their attach-

6   ments, and the pleadings on file with this Court.

7   **Argument**

8   **I. The Court should deny the defendant's motion**

9   **for partial summary judgment because there**
     are genuine issues of material fact and the

10   **defendant is not entitled to judgment as a mat-**
     ter of law.

11

12   A court should deny a motion for summary judg-

13   ment unless it concludes "that there is no genuine issue

14   as to any material fact and that the moving party is

15   entitled to a judgment as a matter of law." CR 56(c). In

16   deciding the motion, the court considers the evidence

17   and all reasonable inferences drawn therefrom in the

18   light most favorable to the nonmoving party. *Seybold v.*

19   *Neu*, 105 Wn. App. 666, 675, 19 P.3d 1068 (2001). It is

20   the moving party—in this case, the defendant—that

21   bears the initial burden of showing that there is no genu-

22   ine issue of fact. *See id.*

23   A. <u>There is a genuine issue of material fact.</u>

24   In this case, there is a genuine issue of material fact.

25   Although Defendant argues that the relevant product is

26   the orange juice, the plaintiffs assert that the relevant

Brief in Opposition to   Attorney for Plaintiffs
Defendant's Motion for   Address and
Partial Summary Judgment–6   Phone Number

Because the plaintiffs' attorney has one issue statement, she has one main heading. The issue statement sets out the question, and the heading answers that question.

While the "because" clause makes the heading longer, the plaintiffs' attorney decided to include it because it allows her to emphasize that there are issues of fact, and once she mentions issue of fact, she also needs to mention her alternative argument.

Because judges know the rules governing summary judgment, the plaintiffs' attorney does not go into detail in setting out those rules. She simply sets out the key rules, emphasizing those rules that favor her client.
Compare the way in which plaintiffs' attorney sets out the rules for summary judgment with the way that the defendant's attorney set out the rules in Example 3.

In this instance, the attorney just sets out her assertion. There is no concise way of setting out the facts.

To show that there is an issue of fact, the plaintiffs' attorney sets out each side's assertion. Note that Defendant's assertion is in the dependent clause and the plaintiffs' assertion is in the main clause.

1   product is the Picnic Banquet Breakfast. In addition, they

2   assert that the component part giving rise to their injuries

3   is the juice that was served from a pitcher with a kerchief

4   on the handle into decorative glasses garnished with a

5   slice of orange and a sprig of mint. [19]

6   *Almquist v. Finley Sch. Dist.*, 114 Wn. App. 395, 57 P.3d

7   1191 (2002), can be distinguished from this case. [20] While

8   in that case the plaintiffs argued that there was an issue of

9   fact, the court noted that the plaintiffs had not raised that

10   issue at the trial court level and that, in arguing the motion

11   for summary judgment, the plaintiffs had referred to the

12   product as the tainted meat and not as the taco lunch. [21]

13   *Id.* at 404. In contrast, in this case the plaintiffs have raised

14   the issue. The jury should be allowed to decide whether the

15   relevant product is the juice or whether it is the product that

16   Defendant sold and the plaintiffs purchased: the Picnic

17   Banquet Breakfast. [22]

18   B. Defendant is a Manufacturer. [23]

19   The Washington Product Liability Act (WPLA) imposes

20   strict liability on manufacturers of defective products.

21   RCW 7.72.030(2). [24] The WPLA defines both "manufac-

22   turer" and "product." The term manufacturer includes a

23   "product seller who designs, produces, makes, fabricates,

24   constructs, or remanufactures the relevant product or

25   component part of a product before its sale," RCW

26   7.72.010(2), and a product is "any object . . . produced

[19] The plaintiffs' attorney goes into detail in setting out the facts that support her assertion that the relevant product is the breakfast and that the component part is the juice as it was packaged and served.

[20] Because Defendant cites *Almquist* as authority, plaintiffs' attorney distinguishes it. Note the attorney's use of a strong topic sentence.

[21] The plaintiffs' attorney responds to Defendant's argument without repeating that argument.

[22] Unfortunately, there are no cases that say that the issue is an issue of fact. Thus, the plaintiffs' attorney must rely on assertions.

[23] Once again, plaintiffs' attorney has chosen to set out an assertion without a "because" clause.

[24] Unlike the defendant's attorney, plaintiff's' attorney starts her argument by setting out the applicable sections of the law.

Brief in Opposition to   Attorney for Plaintiffs
Defendant's Motion for   Address and
Partial Summary Judgment–7   Phone Number

1 for introduction into trade or commerce." RCW 7.72.010

2 (3). In addition, the WPLA defines the term "relevant pro-

3 duct." *Id.* The relevant product is "that product or its com-

4 ponent part or parts, which gave rise to the product liability

5 claim." *Id.* In discussing these definitions, the *Almquist*

6 court emphasized that the statute applies to all sellers

7 who do "more than merely pass along, unchanged, a pre-

8 viously packaged product." 114 Wn. App. *Id.* at 401.

9   Because WPLA does not define the words "designs,"

10 "produces," "makes," "fabricates," "constructs," or "rema-

11 nufactures," courts have used the dictionary definitions.

12 *Almquist*, 114 Wn. App. at 404-05. For example, in

13 *Almquist*, the court stated that the School District had a

14 "design" for cooking the meat: its recipe. In addition, the

15 court held that the District's cooking process fell within

16 the definitions for "produce," "make," "fabricate," and

17 "construct." *Id.* at 405.

18   Like the School District, Defendant had a design for

19 preparing and serving the juice that was included in the

20 Picnic Banquet Breakfast. Defendant's Operations

21 Manual sets out in detail the way in which the servers

22 should prepare and serve the juice. The juice is dispensed

23 into a pitcher with a kerchief tied around the handle, the

24 glasses are garnished with a slice of orange and a sprig of

25 mint, and the servers are instructed not only on how to

26 serve the juice but also on what to say as they are serving

The plaintiffs' attorney ends this paragraph with a quote that supports her position.

Note the attorneys' use of transition.

The attorney starts this paragraph with an assertion: that this case is like *Almquist*. She then uses the facts from her case to support her assertion; at the end of the paragraph she compares the facts in *Almquist* to the facts in her client's case. In doing so, the attorney counters the arguments that defense counsel made in his brief, and she tries to create a new rule, that a manufacturer is someone who creates a new product.

Brief in Opposition to   Attorney for Plaintiffs
Defendant's Motion for   Address and
Partial Summary Judgment–8   Phone Number

1   it. Thus, just as the School District produced and made a

2   new product 28   when it combined the meat with other

3   ingredients, Defendant produced and made a new pro-

4   duct when it combined juice, fruit slices, mint sprigs, cher-

5   ries, and various service items and breakfast foods to

6   produce and make its Picnic Banquet Breakfast.

7   Because the Defendant designed, produced, and made

8   the relevant product, it is a manufacturer.

9   29 The *Almquist* court also concluded that the School

10   District "was not merely a retailer" because it "did not

11   simply resell frozen ground beef, seasonings, and tortillas

12   as a grocery store would." 114 Wn. App. at 405. Instead

13   of simply reselling a product, the District took a product

14   and altered it. *Id.* at 405-06. 30   Similarly, in this case,

15   Defendant did not act as a retailer, reselling juice, fruit

16   slices, mint, cherries, and the various service items and

17   breakfast foods as separate goods. Instead, it assembled

18   and served these items in an elaborate way, as evidenced

19   by the multi-step procedure outlined in the Operations

20   Manual. The Operations Manual's own words—that res-

21   taurant "guests expect and pay for these extra-steps

22   [sic]"—show that Defendant transformed these items

23   into a unique and valuable product, a product that it

24   manufactured.

25

26

28 Note how the attorney repeats the phrase "produced and made a new product."

29 In this paragraph, the attorney for the plaintiffs sets out an additional/alternative argument. She uses *Almquist* to argue that Defendant did more than resell a product.

30 To emphasize her point, the plaintiffs' attorney goes into detail in describing the facts.

Brief in Opposition to
Defendant's Motion for
Partial Summary Judgment–9

Attorney for Plaintiffs
Address and
Phone Number

1   C. <u>In the alternative, the Defendant marketed the Picnic Banquet Breakfast under its brand or trade name.</u>

2

3   Even if Defendant is not deemed a manufacturer, it is

4   still strictly liable. [31] Under the Act, a non-manufacturing

5   product seller is strictly liable for a defective product

6   when it markets that product under its brand or trade

7   name. RCW 7.72.040(2)(e).

8   In this case, Defendant falls within the definition of a

9   "product seller" because it sells various food products to

10   the public. *See* RCW 7.72.010(1). In addition, it marketed

11   the Picnic Banquet Breakfast in its advertising and on its

12   menu, stating that the Picnic Banquet Breakfast is

13   "[l]ike having a family picnic in a sun-filled orchard!"

14   While Defendant has not done what REI did and created

15   a special brand name, *Johnson v. Recreational Equip., Inc.*,

16   159 Wn. App. 939, 247 P.3d 18 (2011), it has done the

17   equivalent. [32] It has used a word from its corporate

18   name, "orchard," and used it in its advertising for the

19   orange juice: The juice is "sunny-fresh" and "orchard-

20   squeezed." In addition, Defendant serves the juice in dec-

21   orative glasses that customers associate with Defendant's

22   restaurants. Thus, even if deemed a non-manufacturing

23   product seller, under the Act, Defendant is strictly liable.

24

25

26

[31] The plaintiffs' attorney starts this subsection by setting out her assertion. In doing so, she makes it clear that she is arguing in the alternative. She then sets out the specific rule.

[32] In this sentence and the following sentence, plaintiffs' attorney counters Defendant's argument. Note that the attorney does not repeat Defendant's argument. She simply sets out her own argument.

Brief in Opposition to   Attorney for Plaintiffs
Defendant's Motion for   Address and
Partial Summary Judgment–10   Phone Number

1

Prayer for Relief

2   For the reasons set forth above, the Plaintiffs respect-

3   fully request that the Court deny Defendant's motion for

4   partial summary judgment on the Plaintiffs' strict liability

5   claims.

6   Respectfully submitted this 11th day of
                        October, 2019.

7

8   /s/ ——
                        Attorney's name

9   Attorney for the plaintiffs

10

11

12

13

14

15

16

17

18

19

20

21

22

23

24

25

26

Brief in Opposition to   Attorney for Plaintiffs
Defendant's Motion for   Address and
Partial Summary Judgment–11   Phone Number

Appellate Briefs

It is the stuff of movies and childhood fantasies. You are standing before the United States Supreme Court making an impassioned argument. You are arguing that *Roe v. Wade* should not be overruled; that the new immigration rules are constitutional; or that the government should, or should not, require every citizen to purchase health care.

Although such high-stakes oral advocacy is exciting and dramatic, in most cases the brief is as important, if not more important. While Hollywood and authors like John Grisham might be more inclined to write a scene depicting oral advocacy, in the real legal world it is frequently the written brief that makes the difference.

In Part III, we continue our discussion of written advocacy, which was begun in Part II, and take it to the next level: the appellate brief. Much of what we discussed about writing a motion brief applies to appellate briefs. Thus, this Part focuses on those aspects of writing a brief that are unique to writing an appellate brief: finding and applying the rules on appeal, types of appeals, scope of review, standard of review, and harmless error.

9

Practicing Before an Appellate Court

In most jurisdictions, there are court rules that govern appellate practice. For example, appellate practice before the United States Supreme Court is governed by the Rules of the Supreme Court of the United States (Sup. Ct. R.), and appellate practice before the United States Courts of Appeal is governed by the Federal Rules of Appellate Procedure (Fed. R. App. P.). Similarly, states have rules that govern appellate practice within that state.

In addition to locating and reading the general rules, also look for local rules. For example, if you are writing a brief in a case that will be heard by the Ninth Circuit Court of Appeals, look at both the Federal Rules of Appellate Procedure and the Ninth Circuit's rules. If you do not comply with both the general and local rules, the court might refuse to hear your appeal or petition for review or reject your brief.

PRACTICE POINTER The easiest place to find a particular set of rules is the jurisdiction's or court's website. For example, you can find the Rules of the Supreme Court of the United States at https://www.supremecourt.gov/filingandrules/rules_guidance.aspx and the Ninth Circuit rules at https://www.ca9.uscourts.gov/rules/.

§ 9.1 Types of Appellate Review

In most jurisdictions, court rules provide for two types of appellate review: an appeal as of right (Fed. R. App. P. 4) and discretionary review (Fed. R. App. P. 5). For example, in both the federal and state systems, a defendant convicted of a crime has the right to appeal to an intermediate court of appeals or, if the state does not have an intermediate court of appeals, to the state's highest court. However, in the federal system and most states, review by the jurisdiction's highest court is discretionary. Thus, a defendant seeking review of a decision of an intermediate court of appeals would have to file a petition for review or a writ of certiorari requesting such review. If the highest court grants review, the parties would then prepare briefs in which they argue the case on its merits. In determining whether to grant discretionary review, courts will generally look to whether the case involves a conflict between circuits or divisions, raises an important constitutional question, or raises an issue of great public import. For example, Supreme Court Rule 10 sets out the rules governing the Court's discretionary review on a writ of certiorari.

EXAMPLE   **SUPREME COURT RULE 10**[1]

Review on a writ of certiorari is not a matter of right, but of judicial discretion. A petition for a writ of certiorari will be granted only for compelling reasons. The following, although neither controlling nor fully measuring the Court's discretion, indicate the character of the reasons the Court considers:

(a) a United States court of appeals has entered a decision in conflict with another United States court of appeals on the same important matter; has decided an important federal question in a way that conflicts with a decision by a state court of last resort; or has so far departed from the accepted and usual course of judicial proceedings, or sanctioned such a departure by a lower court, as to call for an exercise of this Court's supervisory power;

(b) a state court of last resort has decided an important federal question in a way that conflicts with the decision of another state court of last resort or of a United States court of appeals;

(c) a state court or a United States court of appeals has decided an important question of federal law that has not been, but should be, settled by this Court, or has decided an important federal question in a way that conflicts with relevant decisions of this Court.

A petition for a writ of certiorari is rarely granted when the asserted error consists of erroneous factual findings or the misapplication of a properly stated rule of law.

---

[1] https://www.law.cornell.edu/rules/supct/rule_10

> **PRACTICE POINTER**　Different jurisdictions might use different labels to refer to the parties. For example, in cases involving an appeal as of right, the parties might be referred to as the *appellant* and *appellee* or as the *appellant* and *respondent*. In contrast, in a case involving discretionary review, the parties might be referred to as the *petitioner* and *respondent*. Thus, before writing your brief, check the applicable rules to determine which labels apply.

§ 9.2 Time Limits for Filing the Notice of Appeal or Petition for Discretionary Review

In pursuing an appeal of right or seeking discretionary review, a party must adhere to the timelines as set out in the applicable rules. For example, Fed. R. App. P. 4 sets out the time for filing an appeal as of right in a federal court of appeal. Note that the time limits differ depending on the nature of the case and the party seeking an appeal. In a civil case, the party filing the appeal must file its notice of appeal within thirty days of the date the judgment or order appealed was entered. Fed. R. App. P. 4(a)(1)(A). However, if the United States, its officer, or its agency is a party, the party filing the appeal must file its notice of appeal within sixty days of the date the judgment or the order was entered. Fed. R. App. P. 4(a)(1)(B).

In contrast, in a criminal case, the defendant must file his or her notice of appeal "within 10 days after the later of: (i) the entry of either the judgment or the order being appealed; or (ii) the filing of the government's notice of appeal." Fed. R. App. P. 4(b)(1)(A). When the government is entitled to appeal, "its notice of appeal must be filed in the district court within 30 days after the later of: (i) the entry of the judgment or order being appealed; or (ii) the filing of the notice of appeal by any defendant." Fed. R. App. P. 4(b)(1)(B).

If a party is seeking review by the United States Supreme Court, it must file its petition for review on certiorari within ninety days after the entry of judgment. Sup. Ct. R. 13.1.

§ 9.3 The Notice of Appeal or Notice for Discretionary Review

In addition, in most jurisdictions there is a court rule that sets out the procedure for filing a notice of appeal or a notice for discretionary review. For example, Fed. R. App. P. 3 sets out the rules for filing and serving the Notice of Appeal when a party has an appeal as of right. A sample template for a notice of appeal is set out in Form 1 of the appendix to the Federal Rules of Appellate Procedure. Supreme Court Rule 12 sets out the method of seeking review on certiorari.

§ 9.4 Scope of Review

In determining the scope of review, courts consider two factors. First, as a general rule, an appellate court will review only those issues or decisions listed in the notice of appeal or in the petition for discretionary review or writ of certiorari. Second, as a general rule, an appellate court will review only those errors that were raised, or preserved, at trial. This second rule gives the trial court the opportunity to rule on alleged errors in the first instance and helps ensure that attorneys will not stay silent, hoping for a favorable result at trial while using an appeal as a "fallback" position. There are, however, exceptions to this rule. In some jurisdictions, the requirement that issues be preserved for appeal by raising them at trial and exceptions to the requirement are developed through case law. *See, e.g.,* Bennet Evan Cooper, *Federal Appellate Practice: Ninth Circuit, 2018-2019 ed.* (2018). In other jurisdictions, the rules and their exceptions are set out in a statute or a court rule. For example, in North Carolina, this rule and its exceptions are set out in a statute.

> (a) Except as provided in subsection (d), error may not be asserted upon appellate review unless the error has been brought to the attention of the trial court by appropriate and timely objection or motion . . . .
>
> (b) Failure to make an appropriate and timely motion or objection constitutes a waiver of the right to assert the alleged error on appeal, but the appellate court may review such errors affecting substantial rights in the interest of justice if it determines it is appropriate to do so.

N.C. Gen. Stat. Ann. §15A-1446(a)-(b) (2018).

Some of the errors that can be raised on appeal, even absent an objection or motion, are a lack of jurisdiction, a failure of the pleading to state the essential elements of a violation, and insufficient evidence. N.C. Gen. Stat. Ann. §15A-1446(d)(1), (4) and (5). In contrast, in Washington State, this rule and its exceptions are set out in the Rules of Appellate Procedure (RAP) 2.5.

§ 9.5 The Record on Appeal

After filing the notice of appeal or notice for discretionary review, the appellant or petitioner must then "designate the record on appeal," that is, select the portions of the trial record that the appellate court needs to decide the issues on appeal. Generally, the record consists of the original papers and exhibits filed in the trial court and transcripts of the proceedings that are relevant to the issues on review. In addition, under Fed. R. App. P. 10(a)(3), the appellant needs to include a certified copy of the docket entries prepared by the United States District Court clerk. While the appellant bears the burden of ensuring that the record is adequate for review of the issues raised, the responding party may supplement the record.

PRACTICE POINTER Remember that there may be local rules that govern the record on appeal. For example, under a Ninth Circuit rule, if the appellant does not plan on ordering the entire transcript, either the parties have to agree on the portions that will be ordered, or the appellant must let the appellee know which portions it plans to order along with a statement of issues it plans to raise. Ninth Cir. R. 10-3.1(a).

§ 9.6 Types of Briefs

The next step in the process is the preparation of the brief. As a general rule, the party seeking review (the appellant or petitioner) files an opening brief and serves a copy of that brief on the appellate court and the opposing party. After reading the appellant's (or petitioner's) brief, the opposing party (the appellee or respondent) prepares its brief, in which it addresses and responds to the issues and arguments raised in the appellant's (or petitioner's) brief. After the appellee (or respondent) has completed its brief, it serves it on both the court and the appellant (or petitioner). The appellant (or petitioner) then has the opportunity to file a reply brief, which answers arguments made in the appellee's (or respondent's) brief. In some jurisdictions, the court rules also permit the appellee (or respondent) to file a reply brief; the defendant in a criminal case to file a *pro se* brief; and interested parties to file an amicus brief, which is a brief submitted by a group or an individual who has a strong interest in the subject matter of the case, but who is not a party.

10

Audience, Purpose, and Conventions

Just as it is important to understand the audience and purpose of an objective memorandum, opinion letter, and motion brief, it is also important to understand the audience and purpose of an appellate brief. If you understand your audience and your purpose in writing to that audience, you will be able to make sound decisions about what to include and exclude and about how to best present your arguments.

§ 10.1 Audience

The primary audience for an appellate brief is the panel of judges that will be deciding the appeal. This means that if you are seeking review in an intermediate court of appeals, you will usually be writing to a panel of three judges, and if you are seeking review in the United States Supreme Court, to nine justices. When you are writing for your intermediate court of appeals, you may or may not know who your judges will be. In the United States Courts of Appeals and in many state intermediate courts, there are more than three judges on the court, and you are not told which judges will be on your panel until all of the briefs are filed and your case has been set on the court's docket. In contrast, when you are writing to the United States Supreme Court or your state supreme court, you will know who will be hearing your case.

Even if you do not know which judges will be hearing your case, research your court before writing. You can do this research by reading recent decisions issued by the court or by talking with other attorneys who are familiar with the court. In addition, you can usually locate information about individual judges on the court's homepage or on other websites. Often these pages will provide a photograph of each judge and information about his or her education and legal experience.

The judges are not, however, your only audience. In most appellate courts, each appeal is assigned to a particular judge, who then assigns the case to one of his or her law clerks. After reading the briefs and independently researching the issues, the clerk prepares a memo to the judge (usually called a "bench memo" or a "prehearing memo") that summarizes the law and each side's arguments and, in some courts, recommends how the appeal should be decided. Because law clerks can shape how the judges view the appeal, they are some of your most significant readers. In addition, you are writing for your client and for opposing counsel. You want to write your brief in such a way that your client feels that his or her story is being told and that opposing counsel knows that he or she is up against a well-prepared, thoughtful, and vigorous advocate.

As you write, you also need to keep in mind that most appellate judges have substantial workloads. Many intermediate appellate judges hear between 100 and 150 cases a year, and write opinions in approximately one-third of those cases. If each party submits a thirty-page brief, each judge would have to read between 6,000 and 9,000 pages in the course of a year. Thus, although you might think that a longer brief is a better brief, most appellate judges would disagree. For most appellate judges, the best briefs are those that make their points clearly and concisely.

Also keep in mind that appellate judges must work within certain constraints, the most significant of which is the standard of review. Although in some cases the court's review is *de novo*, in most cases the review is more limited. Instead of deciding the case on its merits, the appellate court reviews only the trial court's decision to see if the trial judge abused his or her discretion or if there is substantial evidence to support the jury's verdict. (For more on standard of review, see section 11.2.2(c).)

Finally, in some cases the appellate court is itself bound by mandatory authority. State intermediate courts of appeal are bound by the decisions of the state's highest court, and both the state courts and the United States Courts of Appeals are bound by decisions of the United States Supreme Court interpreting and applying the United States Constitution.

§ 10.2 Purpose

In writing an appellate brief, you want to accomplish two things: You want to educate the judges about the facts of your case and the applicable law, and you want to persuade a majority of the judges to rule in your client's favor. Thus, in addition to explaining the underlying facts, the relevant procedural history, and the law, you must also persuade the appellate court either that the decision of the trial court was correct and should be affirmed or that the trial court's decision was wrong and should be reversed or reversed and remanded.

§ 10.3 Conventions

Just as the process of bringing an appeal is governed by rules, so is the format of an appellate brief. These rules are usually quite specific, governing everything from the types of briefs that can be filed to the sections that must be included, the order of the required sections, and how to reference the parties and the record. The following excerpt from Fed. R. App. P. 28 is representative.

EXAMPLE 1   **RULE 28. BRIEFS**

(a) APPELLANT'S BRIEF. The appellant's brief must contain, under appropriate headings and in the order indicated:

   (1) a disclosure statement if required by Rule 26.1;

   (2) a table of contents, with page references;

   (3) a table of authorities—cases (alphabetically arranged), statutes, and other authorities—with references to the pages of the brief where they are cited;

   (4) a jurisdictional statement, including:

      (A) the basis for the district court's or agency's subject matter jurisdiction, with citations to applicable statutory provisions and stating relevant facts establishing jurisdiction;

      (B) the basis for the court of appeals' jurisdiction, with citations to applicable statutory provisions and stating relevant facts establishing jurisdiction;

      (C) the filing dates establishing the timeliness of the appeal or petition for review; and

      (D) an assertion that the appeal is from a final order or judgment that disposes of all parties' claims, or information establishing the court of appeals' jurisdiction on some other basis;

   (5) a statement of the issues presented for review;

   (6) a concise statement of the case setting out the facts relevant to the issues submitted for review, describing the relevant procedural history, and identifying the rulings presented for review, with appropriate references to the record (see Rule 28(e));

   (7) a summary of the argument, which must contain a succinct, clear, and accurate statement of the arguments made in the body of the brief, and which must not merely repeat the argument headings;

   (8) the argument, which must contain:

      (A) appellant's contentions and the reasons for them, with citations to the authorities and parts of the record on which the appellant relies; and

(B) for each issue, a concise statement of the applicable standard of review (which may appear in the discussion of the issue or under a separate heading placed before the discussion of the issues);

(9) a short conclusion stating the precise relief sought; and

(10) the certificate of compliance, if required by Rule 32(g)(1).

(b) APPELLEE'S BRIEF. The appellee's brief must conform to the requirements of Rule 28(a)(1)-(8) and (10), except that none of the following need appear unless the appellee is dissatisfied with the appellant's statement:

(1) the jurisdictional statement;

(2) the statement of the issues;

(3) the statement of the case; and

(4) the statement of the standard of review.

(c) REPLY BRIEF. The appellant may file a brief in reply to the appellee's brief. Unless the court permits, no further briefs may be filed. A reply brief must contain a table of contents, with page references, and a table of authorities—cases (alphabetically arranged), statutes, and other authorities—with references to the pages of the reply brief where they are cited.

(d) REFERENCES TO PARTIES. In briefs and at oral argument, counsel should minimize use of the terms "appellant" and "appellee." To make briefs clear, counsel should use the parties' actual names or the designations used in the lower court or agency proceeding, or such descriptive terms as "the employee," "the injured person," "the taxpayer," "the ship," "the stevedore."

(e) REFERENCES TO THE RECORD. References to the parts of the record contained in the appendix filed with the appellant's brief must be to the pages of the appendix. If the appendix is prepared after the briefs are filed, a party referring to the record must follow one of the methods detailed in Rule 30(c). If the original record is used under Rule 30(f) and is not consecutively paginated, or if the brief refers to an unreproduced part of the record, any reference must be to the page of the original document. For example:

- Answer p. 7;
- Motion for Judgment p. 2;
- Transcript p. 231.

Only clear abbreviations may be used. A party referring to evidence whose admissibility is in controversy must cite the pages of the appendix or of the transcript at which the evidence was identified, offered, and received or rejected.

(f) REPRODUCTION OF STATUTES, Rules, Regulations, etc. If the court's determination of the issues presented requires the study of statutes, rules, regulations, etc., the relevant parts must be set out in the brief or in an addendum at the end, or may be supplied to the court in pamphlet form.

(g) [RESERVED]

(h) [RESERVED]

(i) BRIEFS IN A CASE INVOLVING MULTIPLE APPELLANTS OR APPELLEES. In a case involving more than one appellant or appellee, including consolidated cases, any number of appellants or appellees may join in a brief, and any party may adopt by reference a part of another's brief. Parties may also join in reply briefs.

(j) CITATION OF SUPPLEMENTAL AUTHORITIES. If pertinent and significant authorities come to a party's attention after the party's brief has been filed—or after oral argument but before decision—a party may promptly advise the circuit clerk by letter, with a copy to all other parties, setting forth the citations. The letter must state the reasons for the supplemental citations, referring either to the page of the brief or to a point argued orally. The body of the letter must not exceed 350 words. Any response must be made promptly and must be similarly limited.

PRACTICE POINTER

Remember to check local rules. For example, in the Ninth Circuit, an appendix containing the record is not included with the brief. Instead, excerpts of the record are filed. *See* Ninth Cir. R. 10-2(b). References to the excerpts of the record are referred to by "ER" followed by a page number.

Also, a brief filed in the Ninth Circuit must contain a statement regarding the defendant's bail status, Ninth Cir. R. 28-2.4, and a statement of any known related cases pending before the court. Ninth Cir. R. 28-2.6. Moreover, the appellee cannot omit the jurisdictional statement section; an appellee must include either a statement of jurisdiction or a statement agreeing with the appellant's statement of jurisdiction. Ninth Cir. R. 28-2.2(c).

Although these rules are representative, some jurisdictions have other requirements. For example, in Washington State, the appellant must include assignments of error. RAP 10.3(g).

In addition to rules governing the content of briefs, there are rules governing the format of the briefs, including length, typeface, and paper size. For example, with the advent of word processing programs, courts have enacted very specific rules as to length to avoid having attorneys try to skirt the length limits by changing typefaces, font sizes, and margins.

EXAMPLE 2   FED. R. APP. P. 32 FORM OF BRIEFS, APPENDICES, AND OTHER PAPERS

(a) **Form of a Brief.**

. . .

(2) Cover. Except for filings by unrepresented parties, the cover of the appellant's brief must be blue; the appellee's, red; an intervenor's or amicus curiae's, green; any reply brief, gray; and any supplemental brief, tan. The front cover of a brief must contain:

(A) the number of the case centered at the top;

(B) the name of the court;

(C) the title of the case (see Rule 12(a));

(D) the nature of the proceeding (e.g., Appeal, Petition for Review) and the name of the court, agency, or board below;

(E) the title of the brief, identifying the party or parties for whom the brief is filed; and

(F) the name, office address, and telephone number of counsel representing the party for whom the brief is filed.

(3) Binding. The brief must be bound in any manner that is secure, does not obscure the text, and permits the brief to lie reasonably flat when open.

(4) Paper Size, Line Spacing, and Margins. The brief must be on 8 1/2 by 11 inch paper. The text must be double-spaced, but quotations more than two lines long may be indented and single-spaced. Headings and footnotes may be single-spaced. Margins must be at least one inch on all four sides. Page numbers may be placed in the margins, but no text may appear there.

(5) Typeface. Either a proportionally spaced or a monospaced face may be used.

(A) A proportionally spaced face must include serifs, but sans-serif type may be used in headings and captions. A proportionally spaced face must be 14-point or larger.

(B) A monospaced face may not contain more than 10 1/2 characters per inch.

(6) Type Styles. A brief must be set in a plain, roman style, although italics or boldface may be used for emphasis. Case names must be italicized or underlined.

(7) Length.

(A) Page Limitation. A principal brief may not exceed 30 pages, or a reply brief 15 pages, unless it complies with Rule 32 (a)(7)(B) and (C).

(B) Type-Volume Limitation.

(i) A principal brief is acceptable if:

- it contains no more than 14,000 words; or
- it uses a monospaced face and contains no more than 1,300 lines of text.

(ii) A reply brief is acceptable if it contains no more than half of the type volume specified in Rule 32(a)(7)(B)(i).

(iii) Headings, footnotes, and quotations count toward the word and line limitations. The corporate disclosure statement, table of contents, table of citations, statement with respect to oral argument, any addendum containing statutes, rules or regulations, and any certificates of counsel do not count toward the limitation.

(C) Certificate of Compliance.

(i) A brief submitted under Rules 28.1(e)(2) or 32(a)(7) (B) must include a certificate by the attorney, or an unrepresented party, that the brief complies with the type-volume limitation. The person preparing the certificate may rely on the word or line count of the word-processing system used to prepare the brief. The certificate must state either:

- the number of words in the brief; or
- the number of lines of monospaced type in the brief.

. . .

In addition to the rules, there might be other, unwritten conventions governing the format of the brief. For example, in some jurisdictions, attorneys may use a particular format for the table of authorities or for the questions presented, or there might be conventions regarding the capitalization of words like "court." Therefore, in addition to reading and following the rules, always check with the court clerk and other attorneys to find out what is expected.

11

First Steps: Getting the Case and Preparing to Write the Brief

§ 11.1 Getting the Case

For the rest of this Part, presume that it is your second year in law school and that you are working as an intern at the Office of the Federal Public Defender in Seattle, Washington. One of the cases the office is handling is *United States v. Josephy*. The facts of the case are as follows.

At about 9:30 a.m. on June 25, 2019, an individual placed a 911 call from a pay phone at the Bellis Fair Mall in Bellingham, Washington, which is about a five-minute drive from the Travel House Inn. The individual, who said that his name was Zachary Dillon, told the 911 operator that Peter Josephy was involved in drug trafficking between Canada and the United States and that Josephy was currently at the Travel House Inn, where he was going to sell a large amount of marijuana to a man named Oliver. Dillon also told the operator that police should go to the Travel House Inn right away because Josephy would only be there for another hour or two.

When the 911 operator asked Dillon to describe Josephy, Dillon stated that Josephy was a Native American, that Josephy had black hair, that Josephy was in his mid to late twenties, and that Josephy was driving a blue Chevy Blazer. Dillon also told the operator that he did not know Oliver's last name but that Oliver was in his thirties, that he was six feet tall, and that he had brown hair and a beard. Dillon was not able to give the operator the license number of the Blazer, and he said that he did not know what the men were wearing. In addition, Dillon would not tell the operator where he lived or give the operator his home or cell phone number.

After the 911 operator conveyed the information from the phone call to a Bureau of Alcohol, Tobacco, and Firearms (ATF) agent, the agent, Agent Bhasin, checked several databases, trying to locate a Zachary Dillon. Agent Bhasin was not, however, able to find anyone by that name in the greater Bellingham area.

At about 10:00 a.m., Agent Bhasin drove to the Travel House Inn to investigate. When he arrived at 10:15 a.m., Agent Bhasin located a blue Chevy Blazer parked in the parking lot. After running the license plate number and determining that the Blazer was registered to Peter Jason Josephy and that Josephy was registered at the motel, Agent Bhasin requested a K-9 unit (an agent and a dog trained to alert to the presence of drugs) as backup.

At about 10:45 a.m., Mr. Josephy and a man later identified as Oliver Preston walked out of one of the rooms and went into the office, where Mr. Josephy paid the bill. The two men left the office, talked for two or three minutes just outside the office, and then parted ways. Mr. Josephy walked to his car and got in. As Mr. Josephy started his car, Agent Bhasin pulled behind his car, and another agent, Agent O'Brien, pulled in front.

Agent Bhasin then got out of his car, approached the driver's side of Mr. Josephy's car, and asked Mr. Josephy to get out of the car. Although Mr. Josephy complied with this request, he refused Agent Bhasin's request for permission to search the vehicle. Agent Bhasin then instructed the agent with the dog to walk the dog around the outside of the vehicle. After the dog alerted to the vehicle, Agent Bhasin searched the vehicle and located four kilos of marijuana in the wheel well. Agent Bhasin then arrested Mr. Josephy.

Before trial, Mr. Josephy moved to suppress the marijuana on the grounds that (1) a seizure occurred when Agent Bhasin pulled behind Mr. Josephy's car and Agent O'Brien pulled in front and (2) the tip was not sufficient to provide the agents with a reasonable suspicion that Mr. Josephy had possession of a controlled substance with intent to sell. Although the trial court agreed with Mr. Josephy that a seizure occurred when the agents blocked Mr. Josephy's car with their own vehicles, the trial court denied the motion to suppress on the grounds that the tip was sufficient to provide the agents with a reasonable suspicion that Mr. Josephy was in Unlawful Possession of a Controlled Substance with the Intent to Deliver in violation of 21 U.S.C. §841(a)(1) (2018).

The case proceeded to trial, and during jury selection, the judge asked whether any jurors had concerns regarding their ability to serve as jurors for the duration of the trial. Juror No. 12, Mr. Williams, stated that his tribal council was scheduled to meet on Thursday and Friday, that he would like to attend the meeting, but that he could skip the meeting if he needed to do so. Juror No. 2, Mr. Feldman, stated that he was flying to Africa on Saturday and that his boss was unhappy that he was missing work.

However, Mr. Feldman stated that his boss would just have "to live with it." Juror No. 18, Mr. Woods, stated that his eighty-seven-year-old mother had had a massive heart attack and was in the hospital and that he did not know whether he needed to go out of town the following week. No other jurors mentioned a problem regarding the trial schedule.

The prosecutor then asked whether anyone had had negative experiences with law enforcement officers. Juror No. 5, Ms. Whitefish, stated that she had been pulled aside for questions each time she crossed the border. Ms. Whitefish attributed the extra questioning to her age and her belief that college students are stopped more frequently than others. Juror No. 11, Mr. Martin, said that he had been stopped on a number of occasions for routine problems with his car—for example, a taillight that was not working. During further questioning, Mr. Martin stated that the police stopped people with long hair more often than they did people with short hair and that he was bothered by the fact that the police tended to target people with long hair.

After the questioning ended, and both the prosecutor and the defense counsel accepted the panel for cause, the parties used their peremptory challenges. The prosecutor excused Juror No. 2, Mr. Feldman; Juror No. 5, Ms. Whitefish; and Juror No. 12, Mr. Williams.

Although the prosecutor then accepted the panel, defense counsel made a *Batson*[1] objection, arguing at sidebar that the government's exclusion of Ms. Whitefish and Mr. Williams, the only two Native Americans on the panel, violated Mr. Josephy's right to equal protection.

The district court concluded that Mr. Josephy had made a prima facie case of discrimination regarding race and asked whether the prosecutor had race-neutral reasons for excluding Ms. Whitefish and Mr. Williams.

The prosecutor offered the following reasons: (1) he excused Ms. Whitefish because he believed that she would have difficulty being impartial given her personal experiences at the border, and (2) he excused Mr. Williams because he believed that Mr. Williams would have difficulty focusing on the facts of the case because he needed to attend the tribal council meeting on Thursday and Friday. The trial court held that these reasons were neutral reasons.

Defense counsel then argued that, given the fact that the prosecutor had used his peremptory challenges to excuse the only Native Americans in the jury pool, the prosecutor's proffered reasons were pretexts for purposeful discrimination. The district court concluded that the prosecutor had not engaged in purposeful discrimination and denied Mr. Josephy's *Batson* objection. At the close of trial, the jury found Mr. Josephy guilty.

---

[1] *Batson v. Kentucky,* 476 U.S. 79, 86-87 (1986). A *Batson* violation occurs when (1) the defendant establishes a prima facie case of purposeful discrimination in the government's use of peremptory challenges by showing that the challenged juror is a member of a cognizable class and that the circumstances raise an inference of discrimination; (2) the government fails to meet its burden to provide a race-neutral explanation for its strike; or (3) the government offers a race-neutral reason, but the defense meets its burden of showing that a review of all relevant circumstances shows purposeful discrimination. *Id.*; *see also Johnson v. California,* 545 U.S. 162, 169 (2005).

Soon after the entry of judgment and sentence, Ms. Elder, Mr. Josephy's attorney, met with Mr. Josephy to explain his options. She described the appeals process, telling him how long he had to file an appeal, how long it would take for his case to be heard by the court of appeals, and the provisions for staying his sentence while his case was on appeal. In addition, she explained that if he did not appeal or if his appeal was denied, his current convictions might affect his sentence for any future crimes.

After considering his options, Mr. Josephy decided that he wanted to appeal. As a result, Ms. Elder filed a notice of appeal within the required time limits and ordered the relevant portions of the record.

§ 11.2 Preparing to Write the Brief

§ 11.2.1 Reviewing the Record for Error

Like many attorneys, Mr. Josephy's attorney, Ms. Elder, uses a four-step process to review the record for errors. First, she reviews her trial notes, writing down the errors that she had identified during the trial. Second, Ms. Elder goes through the record, document by document, page by page, and exhibit by exhibit, noting the following:

- Each motion that she made that was denied.
- Each motion that the prosecutor made that was granted.
- Each objection that she made that was overruled.
- Each objection that the prosecutor made that was granted.
- Each request for a jury instruction that she made that was denied.
- Each request for a jury instruction that the prosecutor made that was granted.

For example, during this step, Ms. Elder notes the following *Batson* objection, which the court overruled.

EXAMPLE | **EXCERPT FROM THE TRANSCRIPT OF A SIDEBAR DURING VOIR DIRE**

THE COURT: Does the defendant have an objection?

DEFENSE: Unfortunately, we do, Your Honor. As you know, Mr. Josephy is Native American, and the prosecutor improperly excluded both Juror No. 5, Ms. Whitefish, and Juror No. 12, Mr. Williams, the only two Native Americans on the panel.

THE COURT: Under *Batson*, the defendant is required, of course, to make a prima facie showing of purposeful discrimination based on race. Because the defendant has established a prima facie case, the prosecutor has the burden of showing that he had a neutral explanation for striking the juror. Can I hear from the prosecutor?

PROSECUTOR: Yes, Your Honor. I excused Ms. Whitefish because I think that her experiences at the border would make it difficult for her to judge this case fairly and impartially. I excused Mr. Williams because I think that his other obligation may make it difficult for him to focus on the trial. These are neutral reasons for excluding these people from this panel.

THE COURT: I agree. Defense Counsel, would you like to respond?

DEFENSE: The reasons stated are not neutral; they are only a mask for unconstitutional race discrimination. Mr. Williams said that it would not be a problem for him to be on the jury, and Ms. Whitefish indicated that she was not bothered by the fact that all college students seemed to be subjected to tighter screening. Given the pattern of strikes, the reasons that the prosecutor has given are pretexts.

THE COURT: Your objection is noted, Counsel, but the Court finds no purposeful discrimination here.

Third, Ms. Elder looks for the other, less obvious types of errors.

- Were Mr. Josephy's constitutional rights violated? (Was he read his *Miranda* rights? Was he represented by counsel at all significant stages in the process?)
- Was Mr. Josephy tried within the appropriate time period? Was he given the right to confront the witnesses against him? Is his sentence cruel and unusual?
- Is the statute under which Mr. Josephy was charged constitutional?
- Was there misconduct on the part of the judge, opposing counsel, or the jury?

Finally, Ms. Elder examines her own actions. Did she fail to raise a viable defense or fail to make an objection that she should have made? If she did, Mr. Josephy might be able to argue that he was denied effective assistance of counsel.

Having identified the potential errors, Ms. Elder moves to the next step in the process: researching the potential errors to determine which she should raise in her brief.

§ 11.2.2 Selecting the Issues on Appeal

As an appellate judge, whom would you find more credible: the attorney who alleges twenty-three errors or the one who alleges three?

Most appellate judges take the attorney who lists two, three, or four errors more seriously than the attorney who lists a dozen or more. Instead of describing the attorney who lists numerous errors as "thorough" or "conscientious," judges use terms such as "inexperienced," "unfocused," and "frivolous." When so many errors are listed, the appellate court is likely to think that the problem is with the attorney bringing the appeal and not with the trial court.

But how do you decide which errors to discuss in your brief? Once again, Ms. Elder uses a four-step process. She determines (1) whether there was in fact an error, (2) whether that error was preserved, (3) what the standard of review is, and (4) whether the error was harmless.

a. Was There an Error?

The first question is whether there was, in fact, an error. Does the Constitution, a statute, or the case law allow you to make a credible argument that the trial court erred? To answer this question, you usually need to do some research. For example, in *United States v. Josephy*, Ms. Elder needs to do some preliminary research to determine whether she can make a good faith argument that the tip was not sufficient to establish a reasonable suspicion that Mr. Josephy was in possession of drugs with intent to sell them and whether she can make a good faith argument that the district court improperly overruled her *Batson* objection. Because her research indicates there are arguments to be made on both issues, she continues with her analysis.

In contrast, the other research that Ms. Elder did was not as fruitful. For example, after doing some preliminary research, Ms. Elder determines that she cannot make a good faith argument that the district court erred in denying her objection to one of the statements that Agent Bhasin made during direct examination. As a result, Ms. Elder abandons that issue. Without a good faith basis for raising the issue, she risks, at a minimum, annoying the court and, at worst, a potential Rule 11 action for making a frivolous claim.

> **PRACTICE POINTER** Under Fed. R. Civ. P. 11(b), an attorney signing a brief "certifies that to the best of the attorney's knowledge, information or belief, formed after an inquiry reasonable under the circumstances" that "the claims, defenses, and other legal contentions therein are warranted by existing law or by a nonfrivolous argument for the extension, modification, or reversal of existing law or the establishment of new law[.]" A violation of Rule 11 can lead to sanctions, including monetary sanctions, sufficient to deter the repetition of such conduct. Fed. R. Civ. P. 11(c).

b. Was the Error Preserved?

It is not enough that there was an error. Unless the error involved an issue of constitutional magnitude, that error must have been preserved. Defense counsel must have objected or in some other manner brought the alleged error to the attention of the trial court and given the trial court the opportunity to correct the error. As noted in section 9.4, in some jurisdictions the rules regarding preservation of error for appeal are developed through case law; in others they are addressed explicitly in a statute or court rule.

In *United States v. Josephy*, both issues were preserved for appeal: Ms. Elder preserved the issue relating to the search incident to arrest by making a motion to suppress and the issue relating to jury selection by making a *Batson* objection.

c. What Is the Standard of Review?

The next step relates to the standard of review. In deciding whether there was an error, what standard will the appellate court apply? Will it review the issue *de novo*, making its own independent determination, or will it defer to the trial court, affirming the trial court unless, for example, the trial court's finding was clearly erroneous or the trial court judge abused his or her discretion.

As a general rule, an appellate court will review questions of law *de novo*. As a consequence, when the issue is whether the jury was properly instructed, the appellate court will make its own independent determination. The standard is different when the question is one of fact. In most circumstances, an appellate court will not disturb factual findings unless such findings are "clearly erroneous" or "contrary to law," and the court will not overturn a jury's verdict if it is supported by substantial evidence. Similarly, an appellate court will give great deference to the trial court's evidentiary rulings and will not reverse the trial court unless the trial court judge abused, or manifestly abused, his or her discretion.

Here is how Kevin Casey, Jade Camara, and Nancy Wright have defined the terms.[2]

De novo review:	When an appellate court conducts a *de novo* review, the appellate court does not defer to the trial court. It decides the issue as if it was the first court to decide the issue. In most instances, courts review questions of law *de novo*.
Abuse of discretion:	When an appellate court uses the abuse of discretion standard, it looks to see whether the trial court judge committed clear error when he or she ruled on an objection or motion. For example, the appellate courts use the abuse of discretion standard when reviewing evidentiary rulings, including whether to admit or exclude expert testimony.
Substantial evidence:	When an appellate court reviews a jury verdict, it looks to see whether the verdict is supported by substantial evidence. In addition, an appellate court

---

[2] Kevin Casey, Jade Camara & Nancy Wright, *Standards of Appellate Review in the Federal Circuit: Substance and Semantics*, 11 Fed. Circuit B.J. 279 (2002).

must uphold an agency's decision if that decision is supported by substantial evidence. There is substantial evidence when, viewing the evidence in favor of the prevailing party, a reasonable person could have reached the same conclusion.

Clearly erroneous: An appellate court uses the clearly erroneous standard when reviewing a trial court's findings of fact. The appellate court defers to the trial court, particularly on findings of fact that relate to the credibility of a witness and will reverse only when it has a definite and firm conviction that a mistake has occurred.

Because very few issues are pure questions of law or pure questions of fact, you might be able to argue the standard of review. While the appellant (or petitioner) will usually want to argue that the appellate court should review the question *de novo,* the appellee (or respondent) will usually want to argue that the appellate court should affirm unless the trial court's ruling was clearly erroneous or the trial court abused its discretion.

PRACTICE POINTER The standard of review can also be affected by the case's procedural posture. For example, the standard of review a federal circuit court uses in deciding a direct appeal will differ from the standard of review the court uses in deciding a case in which a party is seeking habeas relief from a state court ruling.

The rules set out above are general; for specific issues, you must research the standard of review. Sometimes this research will be easy. In one of its opinions, the court will set out the standard that is to be applied. At other times, the research is much more difficult. Although the court decides the issue, it does not explicitly state what standard it is applying. In such cases, read between the lines. Although the court does not explicitly state that it is reviewing the issue *de novo*, is that what the court has done? Also, look for helpful secondary sources. For example, if your appeal is in the Ninth Circuit, look at *Standards of Review/Ninth Circuit Court of Appeals*, United States Court of Appeals (9th Circuit) available at https://www.ca9.uscourts.gov/content/view.php?pk_id = 0000000368.

PRACTICE POINTER One way to research the standard of review is to use one or more standards as a search term. For example, search for "de novo" or "abuse!" or "discretion."

d. Was the Error Harmless?

The final question that must be asked is whether an alleged error was harmless—that is, whether the error, even if established, would not warrant a reversal. As courts have often said, an appellant is entitled to a fair trial, not a perfect one.

> The reversal of a conviction entails substantial social costs: it forces jurors, witnesses, courts, the prosecution, and the appellants to expend further time, energy, and other resources to repeat a trial that has already once taken place. . . . These societal costs of reversal and retrial are an acceptable and often necessary consequence when an error . . . has deprived the appellant of a fair determination of the issue of guilt or innocence. But the balance of interest tips decidedly the other way when the error has had no effect on the outcome of the trial.

William Rehnquist, *Harmless Error, Prosecutorial Misconduct, and Due Process: There's More to Due Process Than the Bottom Line*, 88 Colum. L. Rev. 1298, 1301 (1988).

As a consequence, as an advocate, you will usually not want to assign error to a decision that, although incorrect, was harmless. For instance, although the court might have acted improperly when it admitted a particular piece of evidence or testimony, that error might not be prejudicial if that same evidence or testimony was properly elicited from another witness.

In some instances, the court does not do a harmless error analysis; persuading the appellate court that a trial error occurred is all that is needed to obtain a reversal. For example, in *United States v. Josephy*, if Ms. Elder can persuade the Court of Appeals that the district court erred in denying her motion to suppress, reversal would be required because the conviction for possession of a controlled substance with intent to deliver cannot stand if the marijuana was inadmissible. Similarly, if she is able to persuade the Court of Appeals that the district court erred in overruling her *Batson* objection, the remedy would be a new trial (*see Gray v. Mississippi*, 481 U.S. 648, 668 (1987) (holding that there is no harmless error analysis when there has been a *Batson* violation)).

Generally, however, you will need to consider whether the error was harmless. In so doing, keep in mind that courts apply different tests for different types of errors. For example, as a general rule, courts apply one test for nonconstitutional errors and a different, more stringent, test for constitutional errors. In addition, different jurisdictions can apply different tests: When reviewing a nonconstitutional error, some courts look to whether the error had a substantial and injurious effect on the verdict, while others look to whether, within reasonable probabilities, the outcome of the trial would have been materially affected had the error not occurred.

In contrast, when reviewing a constitutional error, most courts apply either the contribution test or the overwhelming untainted evidence test. Under the contribution test, the appellate court looks at the tainted evidence to determine whether that evidence could have contributed to the fact finder's determination of guilt. If it could have, reversal is required. Courts that apply the overwhelming untainted evidence test take a different approach. Instead of looking at the tainted evidence, they look at the untainted evidence. If the untainted evidence is sufficient to support a finding of guilt, reversal is not required. Note, however, that in a criminal case, the government has the burden of showing the error was harmless.

> **PRACTICE POINTER** An argument that the erroneous admission or exclusion of evidence requires reversal necessarily rests on how the evidence related to the specific elements of the cause of action or charge. However, arguments can also be developed by looking at how the evidence was addressed in closing arguments: How much weight was it given? Was it emphasized, repeated, or touched on only briefly? Was it characterized as being a small piece in a larger puzzle or as being critical to the case?

Having gone through these four steps, Ms. Elder is ready to select the issues on appeal. She does, in fact, decide to challenge the district court's denial of her motion to suppress and the district court's decision to overrule her *Batson* objection.[3] The first issue, whether the investigatory stop was supported by a reasonable, articulable suspicion, is a question of law; thus, review is *de novo*. However, for the second issue, whether the court correctly overruled the defense's *Batson* objection, the appellate court will give deference to the district court's finding that defense counsel did not establish unlawful discrimination in the prosecutor's use of peremptory challenges even though those findings relate to a constitutional issue.

§ 11.2.3 Preparing an Abstract of the Record

Before beginning to write, Ms. Elder does one last thing: She creates an abstract of the record by going through the trial transcript and taking notes on each piece of relevant testimony. For each piece of relevant testimony, she notes the name of the individual who gave the testimony, she writes down the page numbers on which the testimony appears, and she summarizes the testimony.

---

[3] As noted earlier, Ms. Elder will not need to include a harmless error analysis for either of these issues.

EXAMPLE	**EXCERPT FROM MS. ELDER'S ABSTRACT OF THE RECORD**

Direct Examination of Gregory Bhasin.

P. 4:   Gregory Bhasin, ATF agent; several years of experience investigating cross-border drug cases; 1.5 years in Blaine office.

P. 30-31:   At about 9:30 received a call from 911 operator in Bellingham. Man who said his name was Zachary Dillon had called and said that a man called Peter Josephy was involved in selling drugs that had been brought into the U.S. from Canada.

P. 32-33:   Dillon says that Josephy will be at Travel House Inn for another hour or so. Gives physical description of Josephy's car, Josephy, and the man Josephy is selling the drugs to.

P. 32-35:   Dillon would not give 911 operator his address or a phone number. Records check does not indicate that anyone by the name of Zachary Dillon lives in the greater Bellingham area.

P. 42:   Agent Bhasin goes to the Travel House Inn and finds a blue Blazer in the parking lot. Checks license plate—car registered to Peter Josephy.

Although preparing such an abstract is time-consuming, the process forces Ms. Elder to go through the record carefully, identifying each piece of relevant testimony. It also makes brief writing and preparation for oral argument easier. Instead of having to search through the entire record looking for the testimony she needs, Ms. Elder can refer to her abstract to find the page number.

§ 11.2.4 Preparing the Record on Appeal

After having determined which issues she will raise on appeal, Ms. Elder goes back through the trial record, identifying those parts that she wants included as the record on appeal. She selects pleadings and documents filed with the district court: the charging document, the Motion to Suppress, the Findings of Fact and Conclusions of Law and Order Denying the Motion to Suppress, the jury's Verdict Form, the Judgment and Sentence, and the Notice of Appeal. In addition, she includes the transcript of the evidentiary hearing on the motion to suppress and the transcript of voir dire.

Because she was not assigning error to anything that happened during the trial, Ms. Elder does not have the trial record transcribed. In addition, because there were no relevant exhibits, she does not include any of them in the record on appeal.

§ 11.2.5 Researching the Issues on Appeal

How an individual researches an issue depends in large part on that individual's familiarity with the area of law. For example, in this case, Ms. Elder is an experienced criminal defense lawyer with extensive trial experience who knows the law relating to a *Batson* analysis. As a consequence, when she starts her research, she already knows the names of the key cases—for example, *Batson v. Kentucky*, 476 U.S. 799 (1986); *Flowers v. Mississippi*, 139 S. Ct. 2228, 2242 (2019); and *Johnson v. California*, 545 U.S. 162, 169 (2005). Ms. Elder rereads these and other cases and then cite checks the cases that are most on point to locate more recent cases. In contrast, attorneys who are less familiar with criminal law would have to take a different approach: They would need to begin their research by doing some background reading on a free website, in a hornbook, or in a federal practice book that discusses the analysis the Ninth Circuit uses to determine if a *Batson* violation has occurred. Using the citations that they obtain while doing this background reading, these attorneys would need to locate, read, and cite check the key cases. In addition, they might want to look for a law review or bar journal article that discusses *Batson*.

12

Planning the Brief

Having researched the issues, Ms. Elder is ready to begin drafting the brief. She does not, however, start writing until she has spent several hours analyzing the facts and the law, developing a theory of the case, and selecting an organizational scheme.

§ 12.1 Analyzing the Facts and the Law

To write an effective brief, Ms. Elder must have mastered both the facts of the case and the law. For example, before she begins drafting the arguments relating to the motion to suppress, she needs to know what each witness said, and did not say, at the suppression hearing and every finding of fact and conclusion of law that the court entered. Similarly, before she begins drafting the arguments related to the *Batson* issue, she needs to know what questions the potential jurors were asked during voir dire, and she needs to read carefully all of the relevant cases and think not only about how she might be able to use them to support her argument but also about how the government might use them in its arguments.

Ms. Elder also needs to think about what relief she wants and the various ways in which she might persuade the court to grant that relief. Here, ends–means reasoning, outlined below, often works well. In doing an ends–means analysis for the *Batson* issue, Ms. Elder starts with the conclusion that she wants the court to reach and then works backward through the steps in the analysis.

Relief wanted: Conviction reversed.

How to have conviction reversed: Have the appellate court reverse the district court.

How to have the appellate court reverse the district court: Show that the district court improperly overruled Mr. Josephy's *Batson* objection.

How to show that the district court erred: Establish a prima facie case of discrimination and show that the reasons the prosecutor gave were a pretext for discrimination.

How to show the district court erred in not finding the reasons were a pretext for discrimination:

Show that the reasons are not supported by the record.
and/or
Use a comparative analysis to show that the prosecutor did not use peremptory challenges to excuse similarly situated non-Native Americans by comparing the answers given by Native Americans with answers given by non-Native Americans.
and/or

Show the court failed to do the required analysis when it made a cursory ruling without setting out its reasons clearly on the record.

In contrast, the prosecutor's ends–means analysis for the *Batson* issue would look like this:

Relief wanted: Jury verdict affirmed.

How to get the jury verdict affirmed: Show that the district court did not err when it overruled defense counsel's *Batson* objection.

How to show district court did not err: Show that the government met its burden of offering a race-neutral reason for excusing Mr. Williams and Ms. Whitefish and that the defendant did not carry his burden of showing discrimination.

How to show that the prosecution met its burden of offering a race-neutral reason for excusing Ms. Whitefish and Mr. Williams: Show that the reasons are not based on stereotypes about Native Americans, but are based on specific responses from Ms. Whitefish based on her experiences at the border and from Mr. Williams based on his outside obligations the following week.

How to show defense did not carry its burden of showing that the pro-secutor's reasons were a pretext for discrimination: Dismissing the only two jurors of the defendant's race does not, by itself, establish pretext.

How to show using peremptory challenges to excuse the two Native American jurors was not racially based in this case: Show that the defendant's comparative analysis does not satisfy his burden of showing the government's reasons were a pretext for discrimination.

Show that the court did the required analysis on the record by spe-cifically addressing each of the three steps.

Each side would do a similar ends–means analysis for the other issue, whether the trial court erred in denying Mr. Josephy's motion to suppress the drugs found in his vehicle.

§ 12.2 Developing a Theory of the Case

We noted the importance of the theory of the case in Chapter 3 and described some of the ways attorneys approach constructing a theory of the case. If you have not read that chapter, please read it now.

In this instance, Ms. Elder has three options.

(1) She can try to construct a theory of the case that is broad enough to cover both the *Batson* challenge and the motion to suppress. To use this option, Ms. Elder would need to step back and see if there is a theory of the case that connects the two issues and whether that theory would appeal to the judges in both their heads and hearts.

(2) She can try to construct two theories of the cases: one for the *Batson* issue and one for the motion to suppress. Under this option, Ms. Elder would want each theory of the case to appeal to the judges' heads and hearts.

(3) She would have separate legal theories for the two issues but a
    common theme that appeals to the judges' hearts.

If she picks the first option, Ms. Elder's theory of the case would suggest
that Mr. Josephy, as a Native American, was denied his constitutional right
to a fair trial when the district court improperly denied his motion to suppress and denied his *Batson* challenge.

Under the second option, Ms. Elder would start with the first issue and
argue that law enforcement officers impinged on the Fourth Amendment
rights of an ordinary citizen when they conducted a search without a particularized objective suspicion of criminal activity. For the second issue, her
theory of the case would be that the district court permitted the government
to use its peremptory challenges in a discriminatory way, once again denying a member of a minority group his right to equal protection under the
Fourteenth Amendment.

Under the third option, Ms. Elder would argue that, once again, the government denied a Native American his constitutional right to a fair trial
when (1) law enforcement officers impinged on Mr. Josephy's Fourth
Amendment rights by searching his car without a particularized objective
suspicion of criminal activity; and (2) the district court permitted the government to use its peremptory challenges in a discriminatory way. As you have
undoubtedly noted, these approaches are similar. Where they differ is that
the first one focuses on big picture, the forest, while the second two are nar-
rower, each one focusing on a different tree.

§ 12.2.1 Exercise: Developing a Theory of a Case

The following paragraphs are from *Cowdery v. City of Seattle*, a case in which
a police officer, Cowdery, sued the City of Seattle alleging that the City had
been grossly negligent when it failed to provide him with adequate protec-
tive clothing and when it failed to notify him in a timely manner that he had
been exposed to the HIV virus and hepatitis C.

The case arose out of an incident in which a man with a mental illness got
out of his seat on a bus and shot the driver as the bus was moving onto a very
high bridge. The driver lost control, and the bus went over the bridge, landing
on the ground about 100 feet below the bridge. Cowdery was one of the first
responders and is credited with saving several lives. While helping a man
with a badly mangled leg, Cowdery became covered in the man's blood.
Unfortunately, at the hospital, medical personnel discovered that the man
had both the HIV virus and hepatitis C. While the hospital notified the police
department, the police department did not relay the information to Cowdery.

In the months following the bus accident, Cowdery filed a number of
claims under the City's version of workers' compensation. While two of
the claims were granted, the others were denied. Subsequently, Cowdery
filed this lawsuit. The following are the opening paragraphs from
Cowdery's and the City's briefs.

Read each of the following examples. What is Cowdery's theory of the case? What is the City's theory of the case?

EXAMPLE 1   **COWDERY'S STATEMENT OF FACTS**

Before joining the Seattle Police Department, Officer Cowdery served as an Army medic for six years; in this role, he participated in the Gulf War. Cowdery Decl. ¶4-5. After leaving the Army, Officer Cowdery began serving Seattle as a police officer for nearly five years. During his five years of service, Officer Cowdery received many commendations and awards. Cowdery Decl. ¶3.

On November 27, 2018, a chain of events began that would alter Officer Daniel Cowdery's career as a police officer. On that day, a bus crashed off of the Aurora Bridge, creating the first link in a tragic series of events. Within minutes of the department's radio call, Officer Cowdery and his partner arrived at the scene. Expecting to encounter a twisted wreck of steel and glass, Officer Cowdery put on two pairs of the latex gloves the police department had provided.

However, the flimsy gloves proved to be inadequate for the chaos and tore quickly. Officer Cowdery continued to re-glove until all of the available gloves had been used. Cowdery Decl. ¶7. Still wearing the torn gloves, the glass and debris cut Officer Cowdery's hands; his knees became cut.

One of the victims that Officer Cowdery tended to was a man with a badly mangled leg. Although the man was bleeding profusely and Officer Cowdery was wearing his last pair of badly torn gloves, Officer Cowdery used his training as a medic to assist him. Compl. ¶3.3-3.4. In helping him, Officer Cowdery cut his hands and his knees, and his uniform became so saturated with the man's blood that he was required to dispose of it as bio-hazardous waste. Cowdery Decl. ¶10.

EXAMPLE 2   **DEFENDANT'S STATEMENT OF FACTS**

Plaintiff Daniel Cowdery was hired as a police officer with the Seattle Police Department in 2015. Between December 3, 2018, and September 23, 2019, plaintiff filed five workers' compensation claims.

Plaintiff filed his first claim on December 3, 2018. In this claim, the plaintiff listed his injury as "blood exposure." Ex. 3, Self-Insurer Accident Report W 311422. Although the plaintiff was exposed to blood while assisting at the scene of a bus accident, he never contracted HIV or hepatitis. Compl. ¶3.5; Ex. 5, ER Notes and Report. Accordingly, his claim was denied. Ex. 4, Order and Notice Denying Claim W 311422.

On January 8, 2019, the plaintiff filed a second claim for injuries sustained during a demonstration held in downtown Seattle. In this claim, the plaintiff listed his injury as "pneumonitis." Ex. 9, Self-Insurer Accident Report W 341766. Plaintiff's second claim was approved. *See* Ex. 13, Order and Notice Allowing Claim W 341766.

On March 25, 2019, the plaintiff filed a third claim, once again, for pneumonitis. *See* Ex. 12, Self-Insurer Accident Report W 311703. This claim was combined with the second claim. *See* Ex. 14, Order and Notice stating that Claim W 311703 Duplicates Claim W 341766.

On September 23, 2019, the plaintiff filed a fourth claim. In this claim, the plaintiff claimed a back injury after he fell off his bike while on a routine patrol. *See* Ex. 10, Self-Insurer Report W 342968. This claim was denied because the plaintiff failed to provide a licensed physician's report or medical proof of the injury. *See* Ex. 11, Order and Notice denying Claim W 343968.

That same day, the plaintiff filed a fifth claim, this time for depression. *See* Ex. 6, Self-Insurer Report W 342948. The Department of Labor and Industries determined that this fifth claim was a duplicate of his first claim and denied the claim. *See* Ex. 7, Order and Notice Stating that Claim W 342948 Duplicates Claim No. W 311422.

---

§ 12.3 Selecting an Organizational Scheme

Because you must have the same number of issue statements and argumentative headings (see Chapters 5 and 6), the last thing that Ms. Elder does before she begins writing is to select an organizational scheme. She needs to decide how many issue statements and, thus, how many main headings she wants to have, and she needs to decide how to order those issue statements and main headings.

§ 12.3.1 Deciding on the Number of Issues and Headings

In almost every brief, there is more than one way to organize the arguments. As a consequence, before you begin writing, you need to decide whether you want to set out only one issue statement and one main argumentative heading, or whether you want to set out several issue statements and a corresponding number of main argumentative headings. In addition, if you have more than one issue statement, you need to decide how to order those issues. Finally, you need to decide whether you want to use subheadings and, if you do, how many.

In *United States v. Josephy*, Ms. Elder decides to argue both that the district court erred when it denied her motion to suppress, and that the district court erred in overruling her *Batson* objection. Unless she decides to adopt the first option as her theory of the case and treat these two issues as parts of a larger issue, she will need two issue statements and two main argumentative headings. One of the issue statements and main argumentative headings would relate to Mr. Josephy's motion to suppress, and the other issue statement and main argumentative heading would relate to the district court's denial of the *Batson* challenge.

> **PRACTICE POINTER** As a general rule, do not write a separate issue statement for each line of argument or each part of a test. For instance, do not have an issue statement and main argumentative heading for the first part of the *Batson* test, a second issue statement and main argumentative heading for the second part of the test, and a third issue statement and main argumentative heading for the third part of the test. The only exception to this general rule is if you are arguing only one issue, for example, just the *Batson* issue.

The next question is whether you want to use subheadings and sub-subheadings. Most judges encourage attorneys to use subheadings. When they read the table of contents, the main headings and subheadings provide them with an outline of the arguments, and when they are reading the arguments themselves, the headings and subheadings remind them where they are in the argument. One final point: While in some instances you may have only one main heading, if you use subheadings, convention dictates that you need at least two. Likewise, if you use sub-subheadings, you will need at least two.

§ 12.3.2 Ordering the Issues and Arguments

In many cases, logic dictates the order in which you set out the issues and the arguments related to those issues. Threshold questions—for example, issues relating to subject matter jurisdiction, service of process, and the statute of limitations—must be discussed before questions relating to the merits of the case. Similarly, the parts of a test should usually be discussed in order and, when one argument builds on another, the foundational argument should be set out first.

When logic does not dictate the order of the issues and arguments, you will usually want to start with your strongest argument. By doing so, you ensure that the judges will read your strongest argument and that your strongest argument is in a position of emphasis. You can then go through the rest of your issues and arguments in the order of their strength, or you can begin and end with strong issues and arguments, sandwiching your weaker arguments in the middle.

> **PRACTICE POINTER** While the appellee needs to respond to the issues raised by the appellant, the appellee does not need to, and usually will not want to, use the appellant's organizational scheme. Instead, the appellee will usually want to select an organizational scheme that allows it to set out its strongest argument first.

In *United States v. Josephy,* both logic and strategy dictate the ordering of the issues and arguments related to those issues. If the appellate court determines that the evidence should have been suppressed, it will not reach the *Batson* issue. In addition, while a "win" on the *Batson* issue would result in a remand for a new trial, more likely than not a win on the suppression issue would end up with the charges being dismissed.

Having thoroughly analyzed the facts and the law, developed a theory of the case, and selected an organizational scheme, Ms. Elder is now ready to write. While many attorneys do not write the sections of the brief in the order in which they appear in the brief, we do. No matter how you decide to draft the brief, keep in mind that writing an appellate brief is a recursive process, with the completion of one section often requiring revision of another section. For example, once she drafts the arguments, Ms. Elder might find she needs to include additional facts in her statement of the facts or that she needs to revise her issue statements.

13

Beginning the Appellate Brief: The Cover, Tables, Jurisdictional Statement, and the Statement of Issues

§ 13.1 The Cover, Tables, and Jurisdictional Statement

§ 13.1.1 Preparing the Cover

The first page of a brief is the title page, or cover. As in most other jurisdictions, federal courts have rules that govern the cover. For instance, the rules prescribe the types of information that must be on the cover, the order of that information, and the color. *See* Fed. R. App. P. 32(a)(2). The briefs in Chapter 18 comply with the rule for briefs submitted to the Ninth Circuit Court of Appeals.

§ 13.1.2 Preparing the Table of Contents

The second page of the brief should be the table of contents. Once again, the rules specify the information that should be included and the format that should be used. *See* Fed. R. App. P. 28(a)(2) and the sample briefs in Chapter 18.

> **PRACTICE POINTER**
>
> If you are writing a brief to the United States Supreme Court, the issues, or questions presented, would be set out, by themselves, on the page directly after the cover. *See* Sup. Ct. R. 24(1)(a).

§ 13.1.3 Preparing the Table of Authorities

Immediately following the table of contents is the table of authorities. In this section, list each of the cases, constitutional provisions, statutes, rules, and secondary authorities cited in the brief. As a general rule, cases are listed first, in alphabetical order, followed by constitutional provisions, statutes, court rules, and secondary authorities. *See* Fed. R. App. P. 28(a)(3).

In listing the authorities, use the citation form prescribed by your court rules (your jurisdiction might or might not have adopted the *ALWD Citation Manual* or *The Bluebook*) and include references to each page in the brief where the authority appears. Both Lexis and Westlaw have programs that you can use to check your citations and prepare the table of authorities.

> **PRACTICE POINTER**
>
> If you use a program to create your table of authorities, make sure that the table that the program generates is complete, accurate, and in compliance with the applicable rules. For example, some programs might not catch citations embedded in parentheticals, where one case cites to another case. In addition, make sure that the citations are in proper order (cases before secondary authorities) and in proper form (case names in italics or underlined), and make sure that the table of authorities is easy to read: Use white space between each citation, and make sure that the citation does not run up against the page references. Finally, do not finalize your table of authorities until you have finished editing, revising, and proofreading the body of your brief. Even a small change can change the pagination.

§ 13.1.4 Drafting the Jurisdictional Statement

Under Fed. R. App. P. 28(4), briefs filed in federal courts must have a jurisdictional statement that includes the following:

(A) the basis for the district court's or agency's subject matter jurisdiction, with citations to applicable statutory provisions and stating relevant facts establishing jurisdiction;

(B) the basis for the court of appeals' jurisdiction, with citations to applicable statutory provisions and stating relevant facts establishing jurisdiction;

(C) the filing dates establishing the timeliness of the appeal or petition for review; and

(D) an assertion that the appeal is from a final order or judgment that disposes of all parties' claims, or information establishing the court of appeals' jurisdiction on some other basis[.]

PRACTICE POINTER Under the federal rules, an appellee's brief need not include a jurisdictional statement unless the appellee disagrees with the appellant's jurisdictional statement. *See* Fed. R. App. P. 28(b)(1). However, in the Ninth Circuit, the appellee cannot omit the jurisdictional statement section; an appellee must include either a statement of jurisdiction or a statement agreeing with the appellant's statement of jurisdiction. Ninth Cir. R. 28-2.2(c).

---

§ 13.2 Statement of Issues Presented for Review

§ 13.2.1 Drafting the Statement of Issues Presented for Review

The Federal Rules of Appellate Procedure require that the appellant include a statement of the issues presented for review. *See* Fed. R. App. P. 28(a)(5). The Federal Rules of Appellate Procedure do not require the appellee to include a statement of the issues. *See* Fed. R. App. P. 28(b)(2). However, in most instances, the appellee will want to set out the issues in such a way that they support its theory of the case.

Look, for example, at the following issue statements from *Hishon v. King & Spaulding*, 467 U.S. 69 (1984), a case in which the United States Supreme Court was asked to decide whether law firms were subject to federal civil rights laws prohibiting discrimination in employment on the basis of sex, race, religion, or national origin.

EXAMPLE 1   **PETITIONER'S STATEMENT OF THE ISSUE**

Whether King and Spaulding and other large institutional law firms that are organized as partnerships are, for that reason alone, exempt from Title VII of the Civil Rights Act of 1964, and are free (a) to discriminate in the promotion of associate lawyers to partnership on the basis of sex, race or religion; and (b) to discharge those associates whom they do not admit to partnership based on reasons of sex, race or religion under an established "up-or-out" policy.

EXAMPLE 2   RESPONDENT'S STATEMENT OF THE ISSUES

1. Whether law partners organized for advocacy are entitled to constitutionally protected freedom of association.
2. Whether Congress intended through Title VII of the Civil Rights Act
   of 1964 to give the Equal Employment Opportunity Commission, a
   politically appointed advocacy agency engaged in litigation, jurisdiction over invitations to join law firm partnerships.

The petitioner's issue statement sets out its theory of the case: According
to the petitioner, the issue is whether law firms are free to discriminate on the
basis of sex, race, religion, or national origin. Similarly, the respondent's issue
statements set out its theory. To the respondent, this is not a case about discrimination. Instead, it is a case about whether the partners in a law firm are
entitled to their constitutionally protected right of freedom of association and
about whether members of a politically appointed advocacy agency have the
right to determine who is invited to join a law firm.

§ 13.2.2 Select a Format

Most court rules do not prescribe the format that should be used for the
issue statement. As a consequence, in writing your issue statement or statements, you can use the "under-does-when" format, the "whether" format,
or a multi-sentence format. See section 5.1.2.

EXAMPLE 1   "UNDER-DOES-WHEN" FORMAT

Did the district court err in denying Mr. Josephy's *Batson* challenge objection when the prosecutor used his peremptory challenges to excuse both
Mr. Williams and Ms. Whitefish, the only two Native Americans in the jury
pool, and, in overruling the objection, the trial judge's only statement was,
"Your objection is noted, Counsel, but the Court finds no purposeful discrimination here"?

EXAMPLE 2   "WHETHER" FORMAT

Whether the district court erred in denying Mr. Josephy's *Batson* objection
when the prosecutor used his peremptory challenges to excuse both
Mr. Williams and Ms. Whitefish, the only two Native Americans in the jury
pool, and, in overruling the objection, the court's only statement was, "Your objection is noted, Counsel, but the Court finds no purposeful discrimination here"?

| EXAMPLE 3 | MULTI-SENTENCE FORMAT |

The prosecutor excused a Native American juror who assured the court he could miss a scheduled meeting, but he did not excuse a white juror who might have had to leave town because his elderly mother was in the hospital. In addition, the prosecutor excused a Native American juror who said she was not bothered by searches at the border that she attributed to her age, but he did not excuse a white juror with long hair who admitted to being bothered by police officers who targeted individuals who had long hair. The judge's only ruling was, "Your objection is noted, Counsel, but the Court finds no purposeful discrimination here." Given the fact that Mr. Josephy is a Native American, did the district court err when it overruled Mr. Josephy's *Batson* objection?

Although you can use any format, once you select a format, use it for each of your issues. Do not write one issue using the "under-does-when" format and another using the "whether" format. Also, remember that you are not bound by opposing counsel's choices. You do not need to use the format that he or she used, and you do not need to have the same number of issues. Select the format and number of issues that work best for your client.

> **PRACTICE POINTER**   Some issue statements work equally well under any of the three formats, while others do not. Consequently, although you might have a preferred format, if you have an issue that just does not work with that particular format, don't force it. Use the format that will work for all of the issues raised.

§ 13.2.3 Make the Issue Statement Subtly Persuasive

A good issue statement is subtly persuasive: Not only does your issue statement set up your theory of the case, but it also subtly suggests the conclusion you want the court to reach and provides support for that conclusion.

In writing the issue statements for an appellate brief, you can use three techniques to make your statements subtly persuasive: (1) you can state the question so that it suggests the conclusion you want the court to reach; (2) you can emphasize the facts that support your theory of the case; and (3) you can emphasize or de-emphasize the burden of proof or standard of review.

a. State the Question So That It Suggests the Conclusion You Want the Court to Reach

Begin by framing the legal question so that it suggests the conclusion you want the court to reach. For example, in writing the issue statement for

United States v. Josephy, Ms. Elder frames the question so that it suggests that the district court erred in overruling her *Batson* objection, while the government frames the question so that it suggests that the district court did not err.

EXAMPLE 1   APPELLANT'S STATEMENT OF THE LEGAL QUESTION

Did the district court err in denying Mr. Josephy's *Batson* challenge . . . ?

EXAMPLE 2   APPELLEE'S STATEMENT OF THE LEGAL QUESTION

Did the district court properly overrule the defendant's *Batson* objection . . . ?

Note that while the appellant uses "denying" and "Batson challenge," the appellee uses "overrule" and "Batson objection." Because some courts use one phrase and other courts use the other phrase, each side could select the phrase that is most favorable to its position. In this instance, the appellee uses "overrule" and "objection" because appellate courts usually defer to a trial court's decision to sustain or overrule an objection. In contrast, the appellant uses "denying" and "Batson challenge" because that phrase suggests that the case involves more than just a routine evidentiary issue.

Similarly, attorneys think carefully about the language they will use in connection with the suppression issue. The appellee uses a general statement of the rule that courts apply: whether the officers had a reasonable suspicion that the defendant was involved in criminal activity. However, although Ms. Elder includes this language, she frames her argument using the more favorable language from Ninth Circuit cases, which define a reasonable suspicion as a "particularized and objective basis for suspecting the particular person stopped of criminal activity." For more on word choice, see section 14.3.3(e).

PRACTICE POINTER	One way to see what phrase the courts use in a particular situation is to run a search for the possible alternative terms in a fee-based service like Westlaw or Lexis or a free service that has copies of opinions.

There are, of course, other ways of framing the legal question.

EXAMPLE 3 **OTHER WAYS THAT THE APPELLANT COULD SET OUT THE LEGAL QUESTION**

Under the Equal Protection Clause, was Mr. Josephy denied his right to a jury trial when . . . ?

Were the reasons that the prosecutor gave for excusing the only two Native Americans in the jury pool a pretext for discrimination when . . . ?

Did the prosecutor violate Mr. Josephy's constitutional rights when . . . ?

EXAMPLE 4 **OTHER WAYS THAT THE APPELLEE COULD SET OUT THE LEGAL QUESTION**

Did the government properly exercise its right to use peremptory challenges when . . . ?

Did the defendant fail to prove purposeful discrimination when . . . ?

Given that the district court was in the best position to judge the prosecutor's action, did the district court properly overrule the *Batson* objection when . . . ?

---

b. Emphasize the Facts That Support Your Theory of the Case

In addition to stating the question so that it suggests a favorable conclusion, also emphasize the facts that support your theory of the case. For instance, in the following example, Ms. Elder has emphasized the facts that suggest the prosecutor's proffered reasons were a pretext for discrimination by including the jurors' names and stating that these two jurors were the only two Native Americans in the jury pool. In addition, Ms. Elder has emphasized the facts that suggest that the district court did not do the required "sensitive analysis" by stating that the district court's ruling consisted of a single statement and quoting that statement.

EXAMPLE 1 **APPELLANT'S USE OF FACTS**

Did the district court err in denying Mr. Josephy's *Batson* challenge when the prosecutor used his peremptory challenges to excuse both Mr. Williams and Ms. Whitefish, the only two Native Americans in the jury pool, and, in denying the challenge, the judge's only statement was, "Your objection is noted, Counsel, but the Court finds no purposeful discrimination here"?

In contrast, in drafting its issue statement, the government emphasizes the facts that support its theory of the case. In particular, in the first part of its issue statement, the government sets up its argument that it excused Ms. Whitefish because of her age and her experiences, and not because she is a Native American, by including in its issue statement references to

Ms. Whitefish's age and the problems that she encountered at the border. Similarly, the government sets up its argument that it did not engage in purposeful discrimination when it excused Mr. Williams by highlighting the fact that the government excused both a Native American and a white juror for similar reasons. Finally, note that while Ms. Elder refers to the jurors by name, which allows her to include a name that appears to be a Native American name (Ms. Whitefish) in her issue statement, the government does not refer to the jurors by name.

EXAMPLE 2   **APPELLEE'S USE OF FACTS**

Whether Mr. Josephy failed to prove that the government engaged in purposeful discrimination when (1) the government excused a twenty-one-year-old Native American juror who volunteered that she had experienced problems each time she had crossed from the United States into Canada and (2) the government excused both a Native American juror who told the judge that he had a tribal council meeting at the end of the week and a white juror who was worried about missing work.

---

c. *Emphasize or De-emphasize the Burden of Proof and Standard of Review*

Another way to make your issue statement subtly persuasive is to use the burden of proof and standard of review to your advantage. As a general rule, if the other side has the burden of proof, emphasize that fact. In contrast, if you have the burden of proof, de-emphasize that fact. Similarly, if the standard of review favors your client, include a reference to it in your issue statement; if it does not, do talk about the standard of review in the argument, but not in the issue statement.

EXAMPLE 1   **BECAUSE THE APPELLANT HAS THE BURDEN OF PROOF, MS. ELDER DOES NOT MENTION THE BURDEN OF PROOF IN HER ISSUE STATEMENT**

Did the district court err in denying Mr. Josephy's *Batson* challenge when . . . ?

EXAMPLE 2   **BECAUSE THE APPELLANT HAS THE BURDEN OF PROOF, THE GOVERNMENT EMPHASIZES THAT FACT IN ITS ISSUE STATEMENT**

Whether the defendant failed to prove that the government had engaged in purposeful discrimination when, ...

> **PRACTICE POINTER** — In some jurisdictions, courts or individual judges have stated that the parties should not be referred to as appellant/petitioner or appellee/respondent. Instead, courts or judges have stated that the parties should be referred to by name, by a label that identifies their relationship to other parties (for example, employer and employee or doctor and patient), or by the label that describes their status at the trial court (for example, plaintiff and defendant). Thus, before deciding what to call the parties, check your local rules.

§ 13.2.4 Make Sure the Issue Statement Is Readable

An issue statement that is not readable is not persuasive. Thus, during the revising process, check your issue statement to make sure a judge can understand it after reading it just once. First, look at length. If your issue statement is more than four or five lines long, try to shorten it. The longer the statement, the more difficult it becomes to read. Second, make sure that you have presented the information in manageable "chunks." One way to make a long issue statement easier to read is to use the three slots in a sentence:

_____,   _____   _____.

Introductory phrase   main clause   modifier(s)

Another way is to use enumeration: In listing the key facts, use numbers or letters to introduce each item in the list of facts.

Finally, make sure your statement of the issue does not contain any grammatical errors. In particular, make sure that your subject and verb agree and that, in listing the facts, you have used parallel constructions for all of the items in the list.

See section 8.7 in *Just Writing, Fifth Edition*. See section 4.4 in this book for a checklist for critiquing issue statements.

14

Statement of the Case

Over and over again, judges emphasize the importance of the facts. At both the trial and appellate court levels, judges want to know what the facts are and how the law should be applied to them.

Because the facts are so important, good advocates spend considerable time crafting their statement of the case. They think carefully about which facts they want to include, how those facts should be organized, and how the facts can be presented in the light most favorable to their client.

For more on the importance of the statement of facts, see Chapter 4.

§ 14.1 Check the Rules

Just as there are rules governing the cover, tables, and statement of issues, there is also a rule governing the statement of the case. Under the federal rules, an appellant's brief must contain the following:

Fed. R. App. P. 28(a)

* * *

(6) a statement of the case briefly indicating the nature of the case, the course of proceedings, and the disposition below;

(7) a statement of facts relevant to the issues submitted for review with appropriate references to the record (see Rule 28(e))[.]

Although the rules do not require that an appellee include a statement of the case and statement of facts (*see* Fed. R. App. P. 28(b)(3)-(4)), most attorneys include them so that they can set out the procedure and facts in a light favorable to their clients.

§ 14.2 Draft the Statement of the Case

Under the federal rules, the statement of the case precedes the statement of facts. *See* Fed. R. App. P. 28(a)(6). In most instances, you will want to include the following facts in your statement of the case: (1) a statement describing the nature of the action, (2) a description of any relevant motions and their dispositions, and (3) a statement telling the court whether the case was heard by a judge or by a jury. For example, in *United States v. Josephy*, the statement of the case would look something like this:

EXAMPLE   APPELLANT'S STATEMENT OF THE CASE

STATEMENT OF THE CASE

On June 25, 2019, Peter Jason Josephy was charged with one count of Unlawful Possession of a Controlled Substance with the Intent to Deliver under 21 U.S.C. §841(a)(1) (2018) (CR 7). After an evidentiary hearing, the district court denied Mr. Josephy's motion to suppress evidence obtained during a warrantless search (CR 26; ER 30).

The case proceeded to jury trial, the Honorable Alesha J. Moore presiding (CR 28). During voir dire, Mr. Josephy challenged the government's use of two of its peremptory challenges to excuse the only two Native Americans on the jury panel (ER 123-24). The district court concluded that while Mr. Josephy had established a prima facie case of discrimination, the reasons given by the government were race neutral and that Mr. Josephy had not established purposeful discrimination (ER 124). Thus, the court denied Mr. Josephy's *Batson* challenge.

PRACTICE POINTER   Notice that each statement is supported by a reference to the record. CR stands for Clerk's Record—that is, a document filed with the trial court, and ER stands for Excerpt of Record—that is, those portions of the trial transcript filed in connection with the appeal. Check your court rules to see what labels are used in your jurisdiction.

§ 14.3 Draft the Statement of Facts

Even in an appellate brief, the facts are vitally important. Depending on the issues before the court, the judges will be looking to the evidence to see whether the trial court judge's findings of fact were clearly erroneous, whether the evidence supports the jury's verdict, and whether the record establishes that the judge did or did not abuse his or her discretion. In addition, just as you used your statement of facts in a motion brief to prime the judge to see the case in a light favorable to your client and to introduce your theory of the case (see Chapter 3), you do the same in an appellate brief. And, as with a motion brief, drafting the statement of facts for an appellate brief is a multi-step process.

§ 14.3.1 Select the Facts

Like the statement of facts in an objective memo and a motion brief, the statement of facts in an appellate brief contains three types of facts: legally significant facts, emotionally significant facts, and background facts.

a. Legally Significant Facts

Because the court rules require that the statement of the facts include the facts relevant to the issues being raised, in writing the statement of facts include all of the legally significant facts, both favorable and unfavorable. For example, in *United States v. Josephy,* the parties must include all of the facts that will be relevant in determining whether ATF agents had a reasonable suspicion that Mr. Josephy was engaged in criminal activity and all of the facts that will be relevant in determining whether the district court erred in overruling Ms. Elder's *Batson* challenge. For example, in setting out the facts relating to the *Batson* challenge, Ms. Elder must include the fact that the prosecutor used one of his peremptory challenges to excuse a white juror who had scheduling problems, and the prosecutor must include the fact that he excused all of the Native Americans in the jury pool.

b. Emotionally Significant Facts

Although you must include all of the legally significant facts, you do not need to include all of the emotionally significant facts. Although as a defensive move you might sometimes include an emotionally significant fact that is unfavorable, recharacterizing it or minimizing its significance, most of the time you will not. It is more common to include only those emotionally significant facts that favor your client.

The harder question is how to handle emotionally significant facts that are unfavorable to the other side. Should you sling mud, or should you take a higher road and omit any reference to those facts? The answer is that it depends: It depends on the fact, on the case, and on the attorney. If the case is strong and the fact's connection to the case is tenuous, most attorneys would not include the fact. If, however, the case is weak and the fact's connection is closer, many attorneys will include it—some using it as a sword, others using it much more subtly.

c. Background Facts

Background facts play a different role in persuasive writing than they do in objective writing. In an objective statement of facts, the writer includes only those facts that are needed for the story to make sense. However, in drafting a persuasive statement of facts, you want to do more. You want to use background facts to create a favorable context. See section 14.3.3(b).

§ 14.3.2 Select an Organizational Scheme

After selecting the facts, the next step is to pick an organizational scheme. Should the facts be presented chronologically or topically, or would a scheme that combines topical and chronological organization work better?

Unlike an objective statement of facts in which the only selection criterion was logic, in writing a persuasive statement of facts there are three criteria: (1) you want to select a scheme that is logical, (2) you want to select a scheme that is consistent with the order in which you set out the arguments, and (3) you want to select a scheme that allows you to present the facts in a light favorable to your client.

In *United States v. Josephy*, logic dictates that Ms. Elder start with the facts relating to the seizure and not with the facts relating to the *Batson* challenge: The seizure occurred before the jury selection. In addition, starting with the facts relating to the search is consistent with the way in which Ms. Elder has decided to order the arguments. Because the court would probably dismiss the charges if it finds that the search was illegal, Ms. Elder has decided to discuss the search before she discusses the *Batson* challenge. Finally, starting with the facts that relate to the seizure allows Ms. Elder to present the facts in a light favorable to Mr. Josephy. Even though the facts relating to the *Batson* objection are more compelling than the facts relating to the search, Ms. Elder decides that, on balance, it works best to start with the facts relating to the search. However, instead of starting with the tip, she decides to start with the seizure, which favors her client.

In contrast, for the prosecutor, the best choice is to set the facts out in chronological order. Setting out the facts in chronological order is logical and consistent with the order in which the prosecutor plans to discuss the issues. In addition, setting out the facts in chronological order allows the prosecutor to start with the facts that are most favorable to the government: the fact that Zachary Dillon called and told the police that Mr. Josephy was involved in selling drugs that had been brought into the United States from Canada.

§ 14.3.3 Present the Facts in the Light Most Favorable to the Client

Although the statement of facts must be accurate, it need not be objective. Therefore, as an advocate, you want to present the facts in the light most favorable to your client. In doing so, you can use the following strategies, which we first discussed in section 4.3.

**Strategies for Writing
a Persuasive Statement of Facts**

a. Prime the judges to rule in your client's favor.
b. Create a favorable context.
c. Tell the story from the client's point of view.
d. Emphasize the facts that support your theory of the case and de-emphasize those that do not.
   1. Airtime
   2. Detail
   3. Positions of emphasis
   4. Sentence and paragraph length
   5. Main and subordinate clauses
   6. Active and passive voice
e. Choose words carefully.
f. Be subtly persuasive.

PRACTICE POINTER While the statement of the facts should be persuasive, do not misstate, mischaracterize, or overstate the facts. Because one of your greatest assets as an advocate is your professional reputation, do not do anything that might damage it or undermine your credibility.

a. Prime the Judges to Rule in Your Client's Favor

As we talked about in section 4.3.1, you can use the statement of facts to "prime" the judge to see your client, the facts, and the arguments in a light favorable to your client. First impressions do matter. And, much of the time, first impressions are lasting impressions, coloring everything that follows.

b. Create a Favorable Context

The opening paragraph or paragraphs of your statement of facts are like the opening scenes in a movie. They create both a context and a "mood" for the story that you are about to tell and for the arguments that you want to make. It is, therefore, important to think carefully about where you want to start the story and about the language that you want to use.

For instance, in the example problem set out in Part II, Mr. Patterson's attorney wanted to start the story by creating a picture of Mr. Patterson and his activities on the day that the assault occurred. In doing so, the attorney hoped to present her client as a young and attentive husband who could not and would not have assaulted the victim, Ms. Martinez. Put differently, she wanted to prime the judge to see her client as someone who could not have committed the crime.

EXAMPLE 1   OPENING PARAGRAPHS OF THE DEFENDANT'S STATEMENT OF FACTS IN *PATTERSON*

At 7:30 on Monday morning, August 19, 2019, twenty-two-year-old Dean Patterson finished his shift as a security guard and walked to his apartment. After having breakfast with his wife, Patterson went to bed and slept until about 1:00 p.m. At about 2:30 p.m., Patterson's wife received a phone call asking her to work at the local hospital, where she is employed as a nurse. She got ready, and Patterson dropped her off at the hospital at about 3:10 p.m.

At about 3:30 p.m., Patterson called his wife to find how long she would have to work. They had plans to go to a movie that evening, and he wanted to know whether he should change those plans. At about 3:50 p.m., Patterson took a load of laundry to the apartment complex's laundry room. When he returned to his apartment, Patterson watched part of an old movie. At about 4:20 p.m., Patterson went back to the laundry room to put the clothes in the dryer. By this time, it was 4:30 p.m., and Patterson decided to phone his wife again. He arranged to meet her at 5:15 p.m. for her dinner break. Patterson picked up the laundry and then left the apartment to walk to the hospital to meet his wife.

In contrast, in *Patterson*, the State started its statement of facts where the story started for the victim. In the first paragraph of its statement of facts, the State described the assault and then the show-up and line-up.

EXAMPLE 2   OPENING PARAGRAPH OF THE STATE'S STATEMENT OF FACTS IN *PATTERSON*

On Monday, August 19, 2019, Beatrice Martinez was assaulted with a deadly weapon. At a show-up held thirty to forty minutes after the attack, Martinez positively identified the defendant, Dean E. Patterson, as her assailant. The next day, Martinez picked Patterson out of a line-up, once again positively identifying him as her assailant.

For more on the statement of facts in *Patterson*, see Chapter 4.

Although the differences are more subtle, context is equally important in *United States v. Josephy*. For example, in drafting the opening paragraph, Ms. Elder wants to present Mr. Josephy in a favorable light by creating the impression that Mr. Josephy was engaged in a lawful activity when ATF agents pulled behind and in front of his car. The following examples show two different ways in which Ms. Elder can create this favorable context.

EXAMPLE 3   **ONE WAY OF STARTING THE STATEMENT OF FACTS IN THE APPELLANT'S BRIEF**

On the evening of June 24, 2019, Peter Jason Josephy checked into the Travel House Inn in Bellingham, Washington (ER 44). When he checked in, Mr. Josephy filled out a registration form on which he listed the make and model of his car and his license number (ER 44).

The next morning, Mr. Josephy checked out a few minutes before the 11:00 a.m. checkout time (ER 22). After a brief conversation with his acquaintance, a man later identified as Oliver Preston, both men walked out of the hotel. Parting ways in front of the hotel, Mr. Preston walked toward his car and Josephy walked to his car and got in (ER 43).

As Mr. Josephy started his car, ATF vehicles pulled in front of and behind Mr. Josephy's car (ER 44). As a result, Mr. Josephy was not able to pull forward or back up (ER 44).

EXAMPLE 4   **ANOTHER WAY OF STARTING THE STATEMENT OF FACTS IN THE APPELLANT'S BRIEF**

At 10:45 a.m. on June 25, 2019, Peter Josephy left his room at the Travel House Inn in Bellingham, checked out, and, after talking to a friend for three or four minutes, walked to his car and got in (ER 22, 43). As Mr. Josephy started his car, one Alcohol, Tobacco, and Firearms (ATF) agent pulled behind Mr. Josephy's car, and another ATF agent pulled in front (ER 44). As a result, Mr. Josephy could not move his car (ER 44).

In contrast, the government wants to start its statement of the facts by portraying Mr. Josephy as a drug dealer. The following examples show two ways of creating this favorable context for the prosecution.

EXAMPLE 5   **ONE WAY OF STARTING THE STATEMENT OF FACTS IN THE APPELLEE'S BRIEF**

At about 9:30 a.m. on June 25, 2019, Zachary Dillon called 911 and reported that Peter Josephy was involved in selling drugs that had been brought into the United States from Canada (ER 30). Two hours later, Alcohol, Tobacco, and Firearms (ATF) agents searched Mr. Josephy's car and found four kilos of marijuana in the wheel well (ER 49).

EXAMPLE 6   **ANOTHER WAY OF STARTING THE STATEMENT OF FACTS IN THE APPELLEE'S BRIEF**

At 9:30 a.m. on June 25, 2019, the Bellingham Police Department received a tip that Peter Josephy was involved in selling marijuana that had been brought into the United States from Canada (ER 30). During the 911 call, which was recorded, the caller identified himself as Zachary Dillon (ER 31). Although Mr. Dillon did not know where Josephy lived, he said that Josephy was currently at the Travel House Inn, a local motel (ER 32).

> **PRACTICE POINTER**   In the preceding *Patterson* examples, the authors did not include references to the record because, at the time that they drafted their briefs, there was no record. The parties wrote the briefs before the trial court held an evidentiary hearing. In contrast, in the *Josephy* examples, the authors did include references to the record because there was a record and the appellate rules required citations to that record.

c. Tell the Story from Your Client's Point of View

One of the most powerful persuasive devices is point of view. Consequently, as a general rule, you will want to present the facts from your client's point of view. One way of doing this is to tell the story as your client would tell it, using your client's name as the subject in most sentences. Look again at the following examples. In Example 1, Mr. Josephy's name is used as the subject in five of the seven sentences. In contrast, in Example 4, Ms. Elder used Mr. Josephy as the subject in the first sentence but the ATF agents as the subjects in the second sentence. Although Ms. Elder wanted to emphasize that Mr. Josephy was engaged in lawful activities, she wanted to emphasize that Mr. Josephy was the victim of what she will argue were the agents' unlawful acts. Thus, in the second sentence, she puts the agents in the subject slots of the sentence and Mr. Josephy in the object slot.

In the following examples, the subjects are in boldface type.

EXAMPLE 1   **ONE WAY OF STARTING THE STATEMENT OF FACTS IN THE APPELLANT'S BRIEF**

On the evening of June 24, 2019, **Peter Jason Josephy** checked into the Travel House Inn in Bellingham, Washington (ER 44). When he checked in, **Mr. Josephy** filled out a registration form on which he listed the make and model of his car and his license number (ER 44).

The next morning, **Mr. Josephy** checked out a few minutes before the 11:00 a.m. checkout time (ER 22). After a brief conversation with his acquaintance, Oliver Preston, **both men** walked out of the hotel. Parting ways in front of the hotel, **Mr. Preston** walked toward his car, and **Mr. Josephy** walked to his car and got in (ER 43).

As **Mr. Josephy** started his car, **ATF vehicles** pulled in front of and behind **Mr. Josephy's** car (ER 44). As a result, **Mr. Josephy** could not move his car (ER 44).

EXAMPLE 2   **ANOTHER WAY OF STARTING THE STATEMENT OF FACTS IN THE APPELLANT'S BRIEF**

At 10:45 a.m. on June 25, 2019, Peter Josephy left his room at the Travel House Inn in Bellingham, checked out, and, after talking to a friend for three or four minutes, walked to his car and got in (ER 43). As Mr. Josephy started his car, **one Alcohol, Tobacco, and Firearms (ATF) agent** pulled behind Mr. Josephy's car, and **another ATF agent** pulled in front, preventing Mr. Josephy from leaving the parking lot (ER 44).

While in a criminal case defense counsel usually tells the story from the client's point of view, the government has more options: If there is a victim, the government can tell the story from the victim's point of view or, if there is not a victim, it can tell the story from the point of view of government agents. In addition, when the defendant did something egregious, the prosecutor can use the defendant as the actor. In Example 3 below, the prosecutor uses the informant as the subject in the first sentence and the ATF agents as the subjects in the second sentence. In Example 4, the prosecutor uses the Bellingham Police Department as the subject of the first sentence and "caller" and "he" as the subjects of the second and third sentences.

EXAMPLE 3   **ONE WAY OF STARTING THE STATEMENT OF FACTS IN THE APPELLEE'S BRIEF**

At about 9:30 a.m. on June 25, 2019, **Zachary Dillon** called 911 and reported that Peter Josephy was involved in selling drugs that had been brought into the United States from Canada. Two hours later, **ATF agents** searched Mr. Josephy's car and found four kilos of marijuana in the wheel well (ER 49).

EXAMPLE 4   **ANOTHER WAY OF STARTING THE STATEMENT OF FACTS IN THE APPELLEE'S BRIEF**

At 10:00 a.m., **the Bellingham Police Department** received a tip that Peter Josephy was involved in selling marijuana that had been brought into the United States from Canada (ER 30). During the 911 call, which was recorded, the **caller** identified himself as Zachary Dillon (ER 31). Although Mr. Dillon did not know where Josephy lived, **he** said that Josephy was currently at the Travel House Inn, a local motel (ER 32).

---

d. Emphasize Those Facts That Support Your Theory of the Case and De-emphasize Those That Do Not

In addition to presenting the facts from the client's point of view, good advocates emphasize those facts that support their theory of the case and de-emphasize those that do not. They do this by using one or more of the following techniques.

1. Airtime

As you learned in Chapter 6, try to give favorable facts more airtime and unfavorable facts less airtime. For example, in *United States v. Josephy*, Ms. Elder wants to emphasize the facts that support her argument that the tip should be treated as an anonymous tip because the person called the 911 operator from a public pay telephone and, other than giving the operator a name, the person making the call did not provide the operator with information that the agents could use to locate the caller. The facts that Ms. Elder has emphasized by giving them airtime are in bold. In contrast, Ms. Elder wants to de-emphasize the fact that the caller told the 911 operator that Mr. Josephy was selling drugs that had been brought into the United States from Canada. Thus, Ms. Elder gives these facts, which are underlined, very little airtime.

EXAMPLE 1   EXCERPT FROM THE APPELLANT'S BRIEF

Agent Bhasin had gone to the Travel House Inn after **receiving a phone call from a 911 operator who reported that she had received a call from a public pay telephone located in the Bellis Fair Mall**, which is about a five-minute drive from the Travel House Inn (ER 30, 34). <u>The informant claimed that a Mr. Josephy was at the Travel House Inn to sell drugs to a man named Oliver</u> (ER 30). In addition, the informant told the 911 operator that, if the police wanted to catch Mr. Josephy, they should go the Travel House Inn soon because Mr. Josephy would be there for only another hour or two (ER 32-33).

When asked to describe Mr. Josephy, the informant told the 911 operator that Mr. Josephy was a Native American with black hair in his mid- to late twenties and that he was driving a blue Chevy Blazer (ER 32). When asked about Oliver's last name, the informant said that he did not know Oliver's last name. When pushed for a description, the informant told the 911 operator that Oliver was about six feet tall, that he had brown hair and a beard, and that he was in his thirties (ER 32).

The 911 operator then asked the informant for his name, address, and a phone number so that the police or ATF agents could re-contact him. Although the informant told the 911 operator that his name was Zachary Dillon, he then became uncooperative and refused to give the 911 operator his address, his home telephone number, or a cell phone number (ER 32, 35).

In contrast, the prosecutor wants to de-emphasize the fact that the 911 call came from a pay phone, that the caller did not provide the 911 operator with any information about himself other than his name, and that Agent Bhasin was not able to locate anyone by the name of Zachary Dillon in the databases that he checked. Therefore, the prosecutor gives these facts very little airtime. Instead, he gives airtime to the facts that support the government's position: that Mr. Dillon gave the operator his name, that he gave the 911 operator a description of both Mr. Josephy and Oliver, and that the call was made from a phone that was very close to the Travel House Inn. The facts that the prosecutor has emphasized are in bold and the facts that he has de-emphasized are underlined.

EXAMPLE 2   **EXCERPT FROM THE APPELLEE'S BRIEF**

During the 911 call, which was recorded, Mr. Dillon told the operator that Mr. Josephy was at the Travel House Inn to meet with, and deliver marijuana to, a man named Oliver (ER 30-31). <u>While Mr. Dillon declined to give the 911 operator his address or phone number</u>, **Mr. Dillon did tell the 911 operator that Mr. Josephy was a Native American, that Josephy had black hair, and that Josephy was in his mid- to late twenties (ER 32). Mr. Dillon also told the operator that Mr. Josephy owned and was driving a blue Chevy Blazer (ER 32). Although Mr. Dillon did not know Oliver's last name, he described Oliver as being in his thirties and about six feet tall with brown hair and a beard (ER 32). Finally, Mr. Dillon told the police not to wait too long because Mr. Josephy would be leaving the motel in the next hour or two (ER 33).**

The 911 operator relayed the information from Mr. Dillon to Agent Bhasin, an ATF agent with more than ten years of service (ER 4). <u>Not finding anyone by the name of Zachary Dillon in the ATF databases</u>, Agent Bhasin drove to the Travel House Inn in an unmarked car to determine whether there was a blue Chevy Blazer in the parking lot (ER 35, 40). **When he arrived at the motel at approximately 10:15 a.m., Agent Bhasin located a blue Chevy Blazer in the parking lot; when he ran the license plates, dispatch told him the Blazer was registered to Peter Jason Josephy (ER 43).**

---

2. Detail

One way to give favorable facts more airtime is through the use of detail. In setting out favorable facts, include relevant details and, when appropriate, include adjectives and adverbs that help the judges "see" what happened. In contrast, if you want to de-emphasize a particular fact, use generic language in describing those facts. In the following examples, compare the ways in which the attorneys describe Ms. Whitefish's and Mr. Martin's statements during voir dire.

| EXAMPLE 1 | **EXCERPT FROM THE APPELLANT'S STATEMENT OF FACTS** |

Later, the prosecutor asked if anyone had ever had negative experiences with law enforcement personnel (ER 119). Ms. Whitefish, a Native American who was a junior majoring in history at Western Washington University, responded that each time she crossed the border she had been pulled over for questioning (ER 119). When the prosecutor asked if this bothered her, Ms. Whitefish stated that the fact that she was pulled aside for additional questioning did not bother her because she knew that the border agents were more suspicious of younger people than they were of older individuals (ER 119).

Similarly, Mr. Martin, a white man with long hair, told the prosecutor that he had had a number of negative experiences with police officers (ER 119-20). For example, Mr. Martin told the prosecutor that on one occasion a police officer had stopped him because one of his taillights was out, but the police had not stopped other individuals who had one of their taillights out (ER 120). In addition, Mr. Martin told the prosecutor that on two occasions he had been given tickets for jaywalking when other individuals on the same street who had short hair jaywalked but did not get tickets (ER 120). When the prosecutor asked whether he was bothered by the police officers' actions, Mr. Martin said, "You bet I am." (ER 121).

| EXAMPLE 2 | **EXCERPT FROM THE APPELLEE'S STATEMENT OF FACTS** |

During voir dire, the prosecutor asked the members of the jury panel whether anyone had had a negative experience with a law enforcement officer (ER 119). Juror No. 5, a young Native American, responded that she had negative experiences each time she crossed the border between the United States and Canada (ER 119). Although Juror No. 5 stated that she was not bothered by her experiences at the border, she also stated that she had been pulled aside for additional questioning every time that she had crossed the border (ER 119).

In contrast, Juror No. 11, Mr. Martin, a white man in his forties with long hair, told the prosecutor that he had been stopped by the police on one occasion because he had a taillight out and on two other occasions because he was jaywalking (ER 120). Although Mr. Martin said that he was bothered by the fact that he had been stopped by the police, he also said he felt that police officers tended to stop people with long hair more often than people with short hair (ER 120).

Note that in her statement of facts, Ms. Elder goes into detail in describing Ms. Whitefish: Ms. Elder tells the court that Ms. Whitefish is a Native American, Ms. Elder refers to Ms. Whitefish by name and not by her jury number, and Ms. Elder tells the court that Ms. Whitefish is a junior majoring in history at Western Washington University. In contrast, the prosecutor refers to Ms. Whitefish by her jury number, Juror No. 5, and only tells the court that Juror No. 5 is a young Native American. Also note that while Ms. Elder goes into very little detail in describing Ms. Whitefish's experiences at the border, the prosecutor does just the opposite. Because Ms. Elder does not want to emphasize that Ms. Whitefish had negative experiences crossing the border, she describes Ms. Whitefish's experiences at the border more generally and in fewer words. In contrast, the prosecutor emphasizes these facts, specifically stating that Juror No. 5 had been "pulled aside for additional questioning every time that she had crossed the border." Finally, note that although Ms. Elder goes into detail in describing Mr. Martin's negative experiences with the police, the prosecutor does not go into detail. Thus, although both Ms. Elder and the prosecutor have included all of the legally significant facts (for example, that Ms. Whitefish is a Native American and that Mr. Martin is white), when possible, they have described more favorable facts in more detail and less favorable facts in less detail.

Another way to provide detail is by quoting a party's trial transcript. Take another look at Example 1, above. In it, Ms. Elder quotes Mr. Martin as testifying "You bet I am." This quote provides both detail and color to Ms. Elder's statement of facts.

PRACTICE POINTER	If you include a quote, you must include a citation to the record.

3. Positions of Emphasis

Another technique is to place favorable facts in positions of emphasis. Because readers remember better those things that they read first and last, favorable facts should be placed at the beginning and end of the statement of facts, at the beginning and end of paragraphs, and at the beginning and end of sentences. Unfavorable facts should be "buried" in the middle: in the middle of the statement of facts, in the middle of a paragraph, and in the middle of a sentence.

Look again at the examples from *Patterson* set out in section 4.32. In the first example, defense counsel wanted to emphasize that the victim, Beatrice Martinez, told the police that her assailant was in his forties but that Mr. Patterson was only twenty-two. Thus, she puts that fact at the end of the paragraph. In addition, defense counsel juxtaposes this fact with the fact that Mr. Patterson is twenty-two. In contrast, the prosecutor put the fact that Ms. Martinez told the police that her assailant was in his forties in the middle of a paragraph, burying the age between the other, more accurate, portions of Ms. Martinez's description.

EXAMPLE 1   **EXCERPT FROM THE DEFENDANT'S BRIEF IN**
              PATTERSON

Because she was upset, Ms. Martinez was able to give the police only a general description of her assailant. She described him as being a short, white male with blondish-brown hair who was wearing glasses and a dark jacket. **In addition, she told police that her assailant was in his early forties. Mr. Patterson is twenty-two.**

EXAMPLE 2   **EXCERPT FROM THE STATE'S BRIEF IN**
              PATTERSON

Ms. Martinez told the police that her assailant was a white male who was about 5'7" tall, that her assailant had wavy blondish-brown hair, **that her assailant appeared to be in his early forties**, and that at the time of the assault, her assailant was wearing a dark jacket and wire-rim glasses.

In *United States v. Josephy*, the attorneys also use the positions of emphasis to emphasize favorable facts. For instance, Ms. Elder puts some of the facts that favor her client in the first paragraph of her statement of facts. In addition, in constructing that opening paragraph, she puts the most favorable fact—that the ATF agents pulled behind and in front of Mr. Josephy's car, preventing him from leaving—at the very end of the paragraph.

EXAMPLE 3   **EXAMPLE FROM THE APPELLANT'S BRIEF**

At 10:45 a.m. on June 25, 2019, Peter Josephy left his room at the Travel House Inn in Bellingham, Washington; checked out; and, after talking to a friend for three or four minutes, walked to his car and got in (ER 22, 43). As Mr. Josephy started his car, Agent Bhasin, an Alcohol, Tobacco, and Firearms (ATF) agent, pulled behind Mr. Josephy's car, and another ATF agent, Agent O'Brien, pulled in front (ER 44). As a result, Mr. Josephy could not move his car (ER 44).

Similarly, in the following example, Ms. Elder places the quote, which is a favorable fact, at the end of the paragraph.

EXAMPLE 4   **EXCERPT FROM APPELLANT'S BRIEF**

Mr. Martin told the prosecutor that on one occasion a police officer had stopped him because one of his taillights was out, but the police had not stopped other individuals who had one of their taillights out (ER 120). In addition, Mr. Martin told the prosecutor that on two occasions he had been given tickets for jaywalking when other individuals on the same street who had short hair jaywalked but did not get tickets (ER 120). When the prosecutor asked whether he was bothered by the police officers' actions, Mr. Martin said, "You bet I am." (ER 121).

The prosecutor also uses the positions of emphasis to his advantage. He puts some of the facts that favor the government in the opening paragraph of his statement of facts, and he puts the most favorable fact from that group of facts—that the police found four kilos of marijuana in the wheel well of Mr. Josephy's car—in the last sentence.

EXAMPLE 5 EXCERPT FROM THE APPELLEE'S BRIEF

At about 9:30 a.m. on June 25, 2019, Zachary Dillon called 911 and reported that Peter Josephy was involved in selling drugs that had been brought into the United States from Canada (ER 30). Two hours later, Alcohol, Tobacco, and Firearms (ATF) agents searched Mr. Josephy's car and found four kilos of marijuana in the wheel well (ER 49).

---

4. Sentence and Paragraph Length

Because readers tend to remember information placed in shorter sentences better than information placed in longer sentences, good advocates place favorable facts in shorter sentences. Similarly, because readers tend to remember information placed in shorter paragraphs better than information placed in longer paragraphs, when they can, good advocates place their most favorable facts in shorter paragraphs. In contrast, when they can, good advocates try to bury unfavorable facts in longer sentences and in longer paragraphs.

In the next example, Ms. Elder places a favorable fact—that the agents parked their vehicles in such a way that Mr. Josephy could not move his car—in a short sentence in a position of emphasis. The favorable fact is in bold.

EXAMPLE 1 EXCERPT FROM APPELLANT'S BRIEF

At 10:45 a.m. on June 25, 2019, Peter Josephy left his room at the Travel House Inn in Bellingham, Washington; checked out; and, after talking to a friend for three or four minutes, walked to his car and got in (ER 22, 43). As Mr. Josephy started his car, Agent Bhasin, an Alcohol, Tobacco, and Firearms (ATF) agent, pulled behind Mr. Josephy's car, and another ATF agent, Agent O'Brien, pulled in front (ER 44). **As a result, Mr. Josephy could not move his car** (ER 44).

In contrast, in the following example, the prosecutor buried an unfavorable fact—that Mr. Dillon would not give the 911 operator his address or phone number—in a long sentence in the middle of a long paragraph. The unfavorable fact is underlined.

EXAMPLE 2   **EXCERPT FROM THE APPELLEE'S BRIEF**

During the 911 call, which was recorded, Mr. Dillon told the operator that Mr. Josephy was at the Travel House Inn to meet with, and deliver marijuana to, a man named Oliver (ER 30-31). <u>While Mr. Dillon declined to give the 911 operator his address or phone number</u>, Mr. Dillon did tell the 911 operator that Mr. Josephy was a Native American, that Josephy had black hair, and that Josephy was in his mid- to late twenties (ER 32). Mr. Dillon also told the operator that Mr. Josephy owned, and was driving, a blue Chevy Blazer (ER 32). Although Mr. Dillon did not know Oliver's last name, he described Oliver as in his thirties and about six feet tall with brown hair and a beard (ER 32). Finally, Mr. Dillon told the police not to wait too long because Mr. Josephy would be leaving the motel in the next hour or two (ER 33).

---

5. Sentence Construction

Because information that is placed in a main or independent clause is more likely to be remembered than information that is placed in a subordinate clause or dependent clause, try to put favorable facts in the main clause and unfavorable ones in a subordinate clause. For example, in the next sample paragraph, Ms. Elder makes two points in the second sentence: (1) that the caller gave the 911 operator his name and (2) that the caller would not give the 911 operator his address or a telephone number. Because the fact that the caller gave the 911 operator his name is an unfavorable fact, Ms. Elder puts that fact in a subordinate clause. In contrast, because the facts that the caller would not give the 911 operator his address or his phone number are favorable facts, Ms. Elder sets out those facts in the main clause and gives them a fair amount of airtime. Note also how Ms. Elder buries the unfavorable fact in the middle of the paragraph and how she uses airtime and detail to emphasize the favorable facts. The unfavorable facts are underlined and the favorable facts are in bold.

EXAMPLE 1   **EXCERPT FROM THE APPELLANT'S BRIEF**

The 911 operator then asked the informant for his name, address, and a phone number so that the police or ATF agents could re-contact him. <u>Although the informant told the 911 operator that his name was Zachary Dillon</u>, **he then became uncooperative and refused to give the 911 operator his address, his home telephone number, or his cell phone number** (ER 32, 35).

If the prosecutor wanted to make the same two points, he would flip the order, putting the fact that the caller did not give the operator his address or phone number in the dependent clause and the fact that he did give the operator his name in the main clause. Also note that the prosecutor would not set out the unfavorable facts in any detail and that he would choose his words carefully. Once again, the unfavorable facts are under-lined and the favorable fact is in bold.

EXAMPLE 2   **HOW THE APPELLEE WOULD PRESENT THE SAME FACTS**

<u>Although the caller did not give the 911 operator his address or phone num-ber</u>, **he did give her his name** (ER 32).

PRACTICE POINTER   Putting favorable facts in the main clause often allows you to take advantage of the positions of emphasis: While the unfavorable fact is in a dependent clause in the middle of the paragraph, the favorable fact is in the main clause at the end of the paragraph.

6. Active and Passive Voice

Finally, use active voice when you want to emphasize who did the action and passive voice when you want to draw the reader's attention away from who performed an action. For instance, in setting out the facts relating to the *Batson* challenge, Ms. Elder uses active voice to describe the prosecu-tor's use of his peremptory challenges to strike the only Native Americans in the jury pool.

EXAMPLE 1   **EXCERPT FROM THE APPELLANT'S BRIEF**

The government used two of its peremptory challenges to remove the only two Native Americans in the jury pool.

If the prosecutor were to make the same point, he would use passive rather than active voice.

EXAMPLE 2   **HOW THE PROSECUTOR MIGHT MAKE THE SAME POINT**

Both Native Americans were excused.

Furthermore, more likely than not, the prosecutor would combine the use of passive voice with another persuasive technique. For example, the prosecutor might put the fact that he used his peremptory challenges to excuse the only Native Americans in the jury pool in a subordinate clause and the more favorable fact in the main clause. In the following example, the subordinate clause is written using passive voice, and the main clause is written using active voice. The subordinate clause, which uses passive voice, is underlined, and the main clause, which uses active voice, is in bold.

EXAMPLE 3   HOW THE PROSECUTOR MIGHT USE ACTIVE AND PASSIVE VOICE IN CONJUNCTION WITH THE MAIN AND DEPENDENT CLAUSES

<u>Although both Native Americans were excused</u>, **the prosecutor also excused a white juror who had similar commitments.**

---

e. Choose Words Carefully

Because words create powerful images, select your words carefully. In addition to selecting the word that conveys the right meaning, select the word that creates the right image. Look, for example, at words that Ms. Elder uses in the following examples.

EXAMPLE 1   EXCERPT FROM THE APPELLANT'S BRIEF

Agent Bhasin had gone to the Travel House Inn after receiving a phone call from a 911 operator who reported that she had received a call from a public pay telephone located in the Bellis Fair Mall, which is about a five-minute drive from the Travel House Inn (ER 30, 34). The informant **claimed** that a Mr. Josephy was at the Travel House Inn to sell drugs to a man named Oliver (ER 30). In addition, the informant told the 911 operator that, if the police wanted to catch Mr. Josephy, they should go to the Travel House soon because Mr. Josephy would be there for only another hour or two (ER 32-33).

Instead of using "claimed," which suggests that the caller might be lying, Ms. Elder could have used "stated," which is neutral, or "advised," "informed," "notified," or "reported," which suggest that the caller was a credible source telling the truth. Similarly, in the following example, the prosecutor chooses his words carefully. For example, while the prosecutor could have said that Mr. Dillon "refused" to give the operator his address or phone number, the prosecutor uses the word "declined," which has a softer feel and a more positive connotation.

EXAMPLE 2 **EXCERPT FROM THE APPELLEE'S BRIEF**

During the 911 call, which was recorded, Mr. Dillon told the operator that Mr. Josephy was at the Travel House Inn to meet with, and deliver marijuana to, a man named Oliver (ER 30-31). While Mr. Dillon **declined** to give the 911 operator his address or phone number, Mr. Dillon did tell the 911 operator that Mr. Josephy was a Native American, that Josephy had black hair, and that Josephy was in his mid- to late twenties (ER 32). Mr. Dillon also told the operator that Mr. Josephy owned, and was driving, a blue Chevy Blazer (ER 32). Although Mr. Dillon did not know Oliver's last name, he described Oliver as being in his thirties, about six feet tall, and with brown hair and a beard (ER 32). Finally, Mr. Dillon told the police not to wait too long because Mr. Josephy would be leaving the motel in the next hour or two (ER 33).

PRACTICE POINTER If you are having trouble coming up with just the right word, use a thesaurus. Most popular word processing programs include an electronic thesaurus. Do, however, make sure that the words that you choose have both the right denotation and connotation.

f. Be Subtly Persuasive

Many beginning attorneys make one of two mistakes. They either present the facts objectively, or in an attempt to be persuasive, they go over the line, including arguments in their statement of facts; setting out facts that are not supported by the record; or using "purple prose," that is, flowery language that draws attention to itself.

EXAMPLE **EXCERPT FROM AN APPELLEE'S BRIEF WITH NOVICE MISTAKES**

Based on this reliable tip, Agent Bhasin drove to the Travel House Inn, where he immediately located a blue Chevy Blazer in the parking lot (ER 40, 42). Not surprisingly, when Agent Bhasin ran the plates, he discovered that the Blazer belonged to Peter Josephy (ER 42). Expecting trouble, Agent Bhasin immediately called for backup (ER 43).

In this example, the writer makes a number of serious mistakes. First, in the opening sentence, the writer sets out a legal conclusion: that the tip was reliable. Although the writer might want to include this statement in his argument, he should not set out legal conclusions or arguments in the statement of facts. Second, in drafting the second sentence, the writer sets out his own "take" on the facts when he says "not surprisingly." Finally, in the last sentence, the writer misrepresents the testimony. There is nothing in the record that indicates that Agent Bhasin called for backup because he was "expecting trouble."

§ 14.4 Identifying Persuasive Techniques: Exercise

Reread the opening paragraphs from Cowdery's and the City's briefs, identifying the persuasive techniques that the attorneys used. Then take a step back. If you were the judge, would you find the statements persuasive? Why or why not?

EXAMPLE 1   COWDERY'S STATEMENT OF FACTS

Before joining the Seattle Police Department, Officer Cowdery served as an Army medic for six years; in this role, he participated in the Gulf War. Cowdery Decl. ¶4-5. After leaving the Army, Officer Cowdery began serving Seattle as a police officer for nearly five years. During his five years of service, Officer Cowdery received many commendations and awards. Cowdery Decl. ¶3.

On November 27, 2018, a chain of events began that would alter Officer Daniel Cowdery's career as a police officer. On that day, a bus crashed off of the Aurora Bridge, creating the first link in a tragic series of events. Within minutes of the department's radio call, Officer Cowdery and his partner arrived at the scene. Expecting to encounter a twisted wreck of steel and glass, Officer Cowdery put on two pairs of the latex gloves the police department had provided.

However, the flimsy gloves proved to be inadequate for the chaos and tore quickly. Officer Cowdery continued to re-glove until all of the available gloves had been used. Cowdery Decl. ¶7. Still wearing the torn gloves, the glass and debris cut Officer Cowdery's hands; his knees became cut.

One of the victims that Officer Cowdery tended to was a man with a badly mangled leg. Although the man was bleeding profusely and Officer Cowdery was wearing his last pair of badly torn gloves, Officer Cowdery used his training as a medic to assist him. Compl. ¶3.3-3.4. In helping him, Officer Cowdery cut his hands and his knees, and his uniform became so saturated with the man's blood that he was required to dispose of it as bio-hazardous waste. Cowdery Decl. ¶10.

❈ ❈ ❈

EXAMPLE 2   DEFENDANT'S STATEMENT OF FACTS

Plaintiff Daniel Cowdery was hired as a police officer with the Seattle Police Department in 2015. Between December 3, 2018, and September 23, 2019, plaintiff filed five workers' compensation claims.

Plaintiff filed his first claim on December 3, 2018. In this claim, the plaintiff listed his injury as "blood exposure." Ex. 3, Self-Insurer Accident Report

W 311422. Although the plaintiff was exposed to blood while assisting at the scene of a bus accident, he never contracted HIV or hepatitis. Compl. ¶3.5; Ex. 5, ER Notes and Report. Accordingly, his claim was denied. Ex. 4, Order and Notice Denying Claim W 311422.

On January 8, 2019, plaintiff filed a second claim for injuries sustained during a demonstration held in downtown Seattle. In this claim, the plaintiff listed his injury as "pneumonitis." Ex. 9, Self-Insurer Accident Report W 341766. Plaintiff's second claim was approved. *See* Ex. 13, Order and Notice Allowing Claim W 341766.

On March 25, 2019, plaintiff filed a third claim, once again, for pneumonitis. *See* Ex. 12, Self-Insurer Accident Report W 311703. This claim was combined with the second claim. *See* Ex. 14, Order and Notice stating that Claim W 311703 Duplicates Claim W 341766.

On September 23, 2019, plaintiff filed a fourth claim. In this claim, the plaintiff claimed a back injury after he fell off his bike while on a routine patrol. *See* Ex. 10, Self-Insurer Report W 342968. This claim was denied because plaintiff failed to provide a licensed physician's report or medical proof of the injury. *See* Ex. 11, Order and Notice denying Claim W 343968.

That same day, plaintiff filed a fifth claim, this time for depression. *See* Ex. 6, Self-Insurer Report W 342948. The Department of Labor and Industries determined that this fifth claim was a duplicate of his first claim and denied the claim. *See* Ex. 7, Order and Notice Stating that Claim W 342948 Duplicates Claim No. W 311422.

❋ ❋ ❋

For a checklist for critiquing the statement of facts, see section 4.4.

Drafting the Summary of the Argument and Argumentative Headings

§ 15.1 Drafting the Summary of the Argument

The summary of the argument is just what the title implies: a summary of the advocate's argument. Although some courts do not require a summary of the argument, the federal rules require "a summary of the argument, which must contain a succinct, clear, and accurate statement of the arguments made in the body of the brief, and which must not merely repeat the argument headings . . . ." Fed. R. App. P. 28(a)(8).

However, even when the rules do not require a summary of the argument, consider including one. For those judges who read the entire brief, such a summary provides an overview of the arguments; for those judges who do not read everything, it sets out the key points.

You might want to write two drafts of your summary of the argument. By preparing a first draft before you write the argument section, you will force yourself to identify the most important points in your argument. If you truly understand your arguments, you should be able to set out each of them in a paragraph or two. If you can't, more thinking, charting, outlining, or writing is needed.

Preparing a second draft after you have written the argument section is equally useful. This version can serve as a check on your arguments: When read together, the opening sentences of your paragraphs or paragraph blocks should provide the judges with a summary of the argument. If they don't, it is the argument section itself, and not the summary, that needs work.

The most common problem attorneys have with the summary of the argument is length. They write too much. The summary of the argument should be no more than one or two pages long, with one or two paragraphs for each argument. Citations to authority should also be kept to a minimum. Although you might want to refer to key cases and statutes, the focus should be on the arguments, not the citations. Another common problem is that attorneys do not make clear the connections between their arguments. Use transitions to make clear when one argument is a continuation of another argument and when an argument is an alternative argument. For examples of summaries of the argument, see the sample briefs in Chapter 18.

PRACTICE POINTER Some jurisdictions have replaced the summary of argument with an introductory section that is the first thing that judges read. See, for example, Rule 10.3 from the Washington Rules on Appeal. In addition to providing the judge with a summary of the law, these introductions should engage the judges and prime them to view the sections that follow in a light favorable to your client. For more on introductory sections, see Chapter 3.

Rules of Appellate Procedure

RAP 10.3

CONTENT OF BRIEF

(a) Brief of Appellant or Petitioner. The brief of the appellant or petitioner should contain under appropriate headings and in the order here indicated:

(1) Title Page. A title page, which is the cover.

(2) Tables. A table of contents, with page references, and a table of cases (alphabetically arranged), statutes and other authorities cited, with references to the pages of the brief where cited.

(3) Introduction. A concise introduction. This section is optional. The introduction need not contain citations to the record for authority.

(4) Assignments of Error. A separate concise statement of each error a party contends was made by the trial court, together with the issues pertaining to the assignments of error.

(5) Statement of the Case. A fair statement of the facts and procedure relevant to the issues presented for review, without argument. Reference to the record must be included for each factual statement.

(6) Argument. The argument in support of the issues presented for review, together with citations to legal authority and references to relevant

parts of the record. The argument may be preceded by a summary. The court ordinarily encourages a concise statement of the standard of review as to each issue.

(7) Conclusion. A short conclusion stating the precise relief sought.

§ 15.2 Drafting the Argumentative Headings

Argumentative headings serve two functions in an appellate brief. They provide the court with an outline of the argument, and they help to persuade the judges.

§ 15.2.1 Use the Argumentative Headings to Outline the Argument for the Court

When properly drafted, the argumentative headings provide the court with an outline of the arguments. By reading the headings set out in the table of contents, the judges can see your assertions, your support for those assertions, and the relationships between your various assertions and arguments.

Argumentative headings also serve several other purposes. They help the judges by dividing the argument into manageable sections. In addition, they help the writer. Because attorneys like Ms. Elder seldom have large blocks of time available for writing, the brief must usually be written in sections. By drafting the headings first, an attorney can write one section or subsection at a time, putting the pieces together at the end.

PRACTICE POINTER Although you might write your argumentative headings before the related arguments, do not let the headings lock you in to an analytical approach. The content of the arguments should drive the organization, and thus, the focus of the headings. Be willing to revise.

§ 15.2.2 Use the Argumentative Headings to Persuade

Good attorneys use argumentative headings in the same way good politicians use sound bites—to catch their reader's attention and to help their reader see the issue as they see it.

Most good argumentative headings have four characteristics: (1) they are framed as positive assertions, (2) they set out both the assertion and the support for that assertion, (3) they are specific, and (4) they are easy to read and understand. In addition, good argumentative headings use the same persuasive techniques that are used in drafting the issue statements and statement of facts.

a. Make a Positive Assertion

In general, a heading is easier to understand and more persuasive if it is in the form of a positive assertion. For example, instead of writing, "The district court did not act properly when it denied Mr. Josephy's *Batson* challenge," Ms. Elder would write, "The district court erred when it denied Mr. Josephy's *Batson* challenge." The following example sets out the appellant's main headings and subheadings. Note first that each heading contains an assertion. Second, note that although Ms. Elder begins each of the subheadings relating to the motion to suppress with the same assertion, she does not use this technique in the subheadings relating to the *Batson* issue. Although the technique works for the first set of headings, it does not work for the second set. Third, note that Ms. Elder uses dovetailing to make it clear how the subheadings are related to the main headings. For example, she ends her first main heading with the phrase "did not have a particularized objective suspicion that Mr. Josephy was engaged in criminal activity" and then uses that same phrase in the assertion that begins each of the subheadings. For more on dovetailing, see section 4.3.1 in *Just Writing, Fifth Edition.*
In the following examples, the assertions are in bold.

EXAMPLE 1   **ARGUMENTATIVE HEADINGS FROM THE APPELLANT'S BRIEF**

A. **The ATF agents violated Mr. Josephy's Fourth Amendment rights** because they did not have a particularized suspicion that Mr. Josephy was engaged in criminal activity.

   1. <u>**The ATF agents did not have a particularized objective suspicion that Mr. Josephy was engaged in criminal activity**</u> <u>because the tip came from an unknown informant: Although the informant gave the 911 operator his name, he refused to give her his address or phone number.</u>

   2. <u>**The ATF agents did not have a particularized objective suspicion that Mr. Josephy was engaged in criminal activity**</u> <u>because the tip included only general physical descriptions, it omitted any description of clothing, and the only action it predicted was that Mr. Josephy would be leaving a motel shortly before checkout time.</u>

   3. <u>**The ATF agents did not have a particularized objective suspicion that Mr. Josephy was engaged in criminal activity**</u> <u>because the police corroborated only innocuous details—for example, Mr. Josephy's physical appearance, his car, and his departure from a motel shortly before checkout time.</u>

B. **The district court erred in denying Mr. Josephy's *Batson* chal-lenge** because the prosecutor struck the only two Native Americans in the jury pool, and because the court's entire ruling consisted of a single sentence.

  1. <u>**The reasons the prosecutor gave for striking the only two Native Americans in the jury pool were a pretext for discrimi-nation** because they were not supported by the record and the prosecutor did not excuse white jurors who had similar obliga-tions and experiences.</u>

  2. <u>In the alternative, **the district court erred by not conducting the required sensitive inquiry and by not stating its reasoning on the record.**</u>

Likewise, the government sets out its positive assertions. The assertions are in bold.

EXAMPLE 2   ARGUMENTATIVE HEADINGS FROM THE APPELLEE'S BRIEF

A. **The *Terry* stop was permissible** because the ATF agents had a rea-sonable suspicion that Mr. Josephy was involved in criminal activity.

B. **The district court properly exercised its discretion in overruling Mr. Josephy's *Batson* objection.**

  1. <u>**Mr. Josephy has not met his burden of proving that the rea-sons that the prosecutor gave for the peremptory challenges were a pretext for purposeful discrimination.**</u>

  2. <u>**The record establishes that the district court conducted the required sensitive inquiry** because the court ensured that both parties had the opportunity to respond at each of the three steps in the *Batson* analysis.</u>

PRACTICE POINTER   The typefaces that attorneys use reflect the changes in technology. Historically, briefs were prepared using a typewriter, where the only fonts that were available were upper and lower case and, with the introduction of the IBM Selectric typewriter, underlining. As a consequence, attorneys used all caps for main headings, underlining for subheadings, and nothing for sub-subheadings. Today, attorneys have many more options and, because headings written using all capital letters are hard to read, most now use bold for the main headings. We talk more about typefaces in section 15.2.3.

b. Provide Support for Your Assertions

By itself an assertion is not persuasive. Therefore, in most instances, you will want to support your assertions. One way to provide this support is to add a "because" clause.

Assertion   +   because   +   support for assertion

For example, instead of just stating that the ATF agents violated Mr. Josephy's Fourth Amendment rights, Ms. Elder should include the reason why. Similarly, instead of just saying that the *Terry* stop was permissible, the prosecutor needs to add the support for that assertion. In the following examples, the support for each assertion is set out in bold.

EXAMPLE 1   APPELLANT'S ASSERTION FOLLOWED BY A "BECAUSE" CLAUSE

A. The ATF agents violated Mr. Josephy's Fourth Amendment rights **because they did not have a particularized suspicion that Mr. Josephy was engaged in criminal activity.**

   1. <u>The ATF agents did not have a particularized objective suspicion that Mr. Josephy was engaged in criminal activity</u> **the tip came from an unknown informant: Although the informant gave the 911 operator his name, he refused to give his address or phone number.**

   2. <u>The ATF agents did not have a particularized objective suspicion that Mr. Josephy was engaged in criminal activity</u> **because the tip included only general physical descriptions, it omitted any description of clothing, and the only action it predicted was that Mr. Josephy would be leaving a motel shortly before checkout time.**

   3. <u>The ATF agents did not have a particularized objective suspicion that Mr. Josephy was engaged in criminal activity</u> **because the police corroborated only innocuous details — for example, Mr. Josephy's physical appearance, his car, and his departure from a motel shortly before checkout time.**

You do not, however, always need to include a "because" clause. In some instances, it might work better to set out your assertion in the main heading and then the support for that assertion in the subheadings. In other instances, it might work better to save the support for the argument. For instance, in the following example, look at the second subheading. Because Ms. Elder thought that emphasizing the fact that the argument was an alternative argument was more important than setting out the facts, she sets out her assertion without using a "because" clause.

EXAMPLE 2   HEADINGS FROM THE APPELLANT'S BRIEF

B. The district court erred in denying Mr. Josephy's *Batson* challenge **because the prosecutor struck the only two Native Americans in the jury pool, and because the court's entire ruling consisted of a single sentence.**

    1. <u>The reasons the prosecutor gave for striking the only two Native Americans in the jury pool were a pretext for discrimination</u> **because they were not supported by the record and the prosecutor did not excuse white jurors who had similar obligations and experiences.**

    2. <u>In the alternative, the district court erred by not conducting the required sensitive inquiry and by not stating its reasoning on the record.</u>

---

c. Make Sure That Your Headings Are Neither Too Specific Nor Too General

As a general rule, make your headings specific to the case at hand. Instead of writing statements that are so broad that they could apply to a number of different cases, write statements that talk specifically about the parties and facts in your case. Do not, however, be so specific that the headings are not broad enough to cover all of the points that you make in that section. Compare the following examples. The headings set out in Example 1 are too broad because they could apply equally to any number of cases. In contrast, the headings set out in Example 2 are too narrow because they cover only one of the government's two peremptory challenges.

EXAMPLE 1   HEADINGS ARE TOO GENERAL

The trial court erred.
The trial court properly overruled the defendant's *Batson* objection.

EXAMPLE 2   HEADINGS ARE TOO SPECIFIC

The district court erred when it denied the defendant's *Batson* challenge because the prosecutor dismissed a Native American juror who had had negative experiences with law enforcement officers but not a white juror who had had similar experiences.

The district court properly overruled the defendant's *Batson* objection because the government excused both a Native American juror and a white juror who had work commitments.

---

d. Make Your Headings Readable

A heading that is not readable is not persuasive. For example, even though the following heading is in the proper form, it is not persuasive because it is so long that very few judges would read it.

EXAMPLE 1   **ARGUMENTATIVE HEADING THAT IS DIFFICULT TO READ**

A. THE DISTRICT COURT ERRED IN DENYING MR. JOSEPHY'S *BATSON* CHALLENGE BECAUSE (1) THE PROSECUTOR EXCUSED A NATIVE AMERICAN JUROR WHO HAD HAD A NEGATIVE EXPERIENCE WITH LAW ENFORCEMENT OFFICERS BUT DID NOT EXCUSE A WHITE JUROR WHO HAD HAD SIMILAR NEGATIVE EXPERIENCES AND (2) THE PROSECUTOR EXCUSED A NATIVE AMERICAN JUROR WHO HAD A TRIBAL COUNCIL MEETING AT THE END OF THE WEEK BUT WHO WAS WILLING TO MISS THAT MEETING BUT DID NOT EXCUSE A WHITE JUROR WHO MIGHT HAVE TO GO OUT OF TOWN TO CARE FOR HIS MOTHER WHO WAS IN THE HOSPITAL.

Thus, in drafting your headings, you need to balance two competing pieces of advice: making your headings fact specific and keeping your headings short. Ideally your headings would be both fact specific and short, but sometimes that is not possible, in which case you will have to choose between a longer, fact-specific heading and a shorter, more general heading. Compare the following two examples. In Example 2, Ms. Elder has chosen to write a longer heading that is fact specific. In contrast, in Example 3, the prosecutor has chosen to write a shorter heading that is more general.

EXAMPLE 2   **SUBHEADING FROM THE APPELLANT'S BRIEF THAT IS LONGER BUT MORE FACT SPECIFIC**

1. <u>The reasons the prosecutor gave for striking the only two Native Americans in the jury pool were a pretext for discrimination because they were not supported by the record and the prosecutor did not excuse white jurors who had similar obligations and experiences.</u>

EXAMPLE 3 **SUBHEADING FROM THE APPELLEE'S BRIEF THAT IS SHORTER BUT MORE GENERAL**

1. <u>Mr. Josephy has not met his burden of proving that the reasons that the prosecutor gave for the peremptory challenges were a pretext for purposeful discrimination.</u>

When you choose to write a longer heading, use sentence constructions that make the headings easier to read. Use parallel constructions (see section 8.7 in *Just Writing, Fifth Edition*) and, when appropriate, repeat the words that highlight the parallel structure (for example, "that" or "because"). Finally, when appropriate, use commas, semicolons, and colons to divide the sentence into more manageable units of meaning. See Chapter 9 in *Just Writing, Fifth Edition*.

e. Use the Same Persuasive Techniques You Used in Drafting the Issue Statements and Statement of Facts

In drafting argumentative headings, good advocates use many of the same persuasive techniques that they used in drafting their issue statements and statements of facts: When possible, they create a favorable context, set out the facts from the client's point of view, give more airtime to favorable facts than to unfavorable facts, describe favorable facts in more detail than unfavorable facts, take advantage of the positions of emphasis, and choose words carefully. In Example 1 below, the writer has set out her assertion and her support for that assertion, but she has not emphasized the favorable facts. In contrast, in Example 2, the writer has emphasized the favorable facts: She has said that "the prosecutor struck all of the Native Americans in the jury pool"; she has used the phrase "*Batson* challenge" rather than "*Batson* objection"; she has used the harsher word, "struck," rather than the softer word, "excused"; and instead of saying that the district court did not go into detail in explaining its reasoning, she states that the court's entire ruling consisted of a single sentence.

EXAMPLE 1 **APPELLANT HAS NOT USED PERSUASIVE TECHNIQUES**

A. The district court erred in denying Mr. Josephy's *Batson* objection because the prosecutor excused two Native American jurors and the district court did not go into detail in explaining its reasoning.

EXAMPLE 2   **APPELLANT HAS USED PERSUASIVE TECHNIQUES**

A. The district court erred in denying Mr. Josephy's *Batson* challenge because the prosecutor struck all the Native Americans in the jury pool and because the court's reasoning consisted of a single sentence.

---

§ 15.2.3 Use Conventional Formats for Headings

Although seldom set out in the court rules, in most jurisdictions there are conventions governing the number, type, and typeface for argumentative headings. For example, as we noted in section 5.1.2, convention dictates that you should have a main heading for each of your issue statements. Consequently, if you have one issue, you should have one main heading; if you have two issues, two main headings; and so on. The issue sets out the question, and the heading gives your answer to that question.

In addition to main headings, you can also use subheadings, sub-sub-headings, and, rarely, sub-sub-subheadings. There are, however, some things to keep in mind if you use additional headings. First, if you include one subheading, you need to have at least two headings at that same level. As a consequence, if you find that you have only one subheading in a section, either delete that heading or add at least one additional heading. Second, although you are not required to put text between the main heading and the first subheading, it is usually a good idea to do so: Use this space to set out the general rule and a succinct roadmap for that section of your brief. Finally, keep in mind the typefaces that attorneys use for the various levels of headings. These typefaces provide judges with signals about where they are in the argument.

The following example shows one way of using headings. The main headings are set out using bold, the subheadings are underlined, and the sub-subheadings are set out using regular typeface.

EXAMPLE   **CONVENTIONAL FORMATS FOR ARGUMENTATIVE HEADINGS**

Argument

A. **First Main Heading** [corresponds to first issue statement]

   [Introduce and set out the general rule.]

   [Provide your reader with a roadmap for your argument.]

   1. <u>First subheading</u>

      [Introduce and set out the specific rules.]

      a. First sub-subheading

         [Set out your argument.]

    b. Second sub-subheading

       [Set out your argument.]

  2. <u>Second subheading</u>

    [Set out your argument.]

  3. <u>Third subheading</u>

    [Set out your argument.]

B. **Second Main Heading** [corresponds to second issue statement]

[Introduce and set out the general rule.]

[Provide your reader with a roadmap for your argument.]

  1. <u>First subheading</u>

    [Set out your argument.]

  2. <u>Second subheading</u>

    [Set out specific rules.]

    a. First sub-subheading

       [Set out your argument.]

    b. Second sub-subheading

       [Set out your argument.]

See section 5.1.4 for a checklist for critiquing the argumentative headings.

Drafting the Arguments

Although it is relatively easy to tell someone how to draft the statement of the case, the statement of facts, the issue statements, and the argumentative headings, it is very difficult to tell someone how to draft the arguments. Although experienced attorneys can offer newer attorneys some general advice, by necessity, that advice is just that—general advice. Because the law and facts of each case are different, the arguments are also different, and there is no foolproof recipe for how to draft a persuasive argument.

At a minimum, you must have mastered the facts of your case, you must have a solid understanding of the governing law, and you must be able to write clearly and concisely. Although this mastery, understanding, and ability are necessary, they alone are not enough. Writing a persuasive brief also requires some things that are much harder to describe and are impossible to teach: insight, creativity, and confidence. Thus, although this chapter can get you started, it cannot give you all of the answers. Instead, we will remind you of the overriding question when it comes to any argument: Is it persuasive? When in doubt, use that question as your touchstone for determining what is and is not an effective argument.

§ 16.1 Knowing What You Need, and Want, to Argue

One of the first steps in drafting an argument is knowing what you need, and want, to argue. You cannot just throw out a number of assertions, rules, and cases and hope that the court will make sense of them for you.

As a consequence, before you begin to write, determine what type of argument you are making. For example, are you arguing an issue of first impression—that is, are you asking the appellate court to make new law by adopting a new rule or test—or are you arguing that the trial court improperly applied existing law, that the trial court abused its discretion when it ruled on a motion or objection, or that there is insufficient evidence to support the jury's verdict?

§ 16.2 Selecting an Organizational Scheme

Once you have determined what type of argument you want to make, select the organizational scheme that will work best for that argument.

If you are arguing an issue of first impression, you will usually use a version of the template set out in Example 1 below. You will start by establishing that there is no existing rule or test. You will then want to persuade the court that the rule or test you are proposing is "better" than the rule or test being proposed by your opponent. Finally, you will end by applying your proposed rule or test to the facts of your case. In addition, sometimes you will argue in the alternative: Even if the court adopts the rule or test being advocated by opposing counsel, you still win under that test.

EXAMPLE 1   ORGANIZATIONAL SCHEME FOR ISSUES OF FIRST IMPRESSION

A. MAIN HEADING
    Introduction establishing that the issue is one of first impression
    1. <u>Subheading setting out first assertion</u>
        - Paragraph setting out the rule that you want the court to adopt
        - Arguments relating to why the court should adopt your proposed rule rather than the rule being proposed by your opponent
        - Application of your proposed rule to the facts of your case
    2. <u>Subheading setting out additional or alternative argument(s)</u>
        - If appropriate, argue that even under the rule being proposed by your opponent your client wins

---

In contrast, if you are arguing that the trial court incorrectly applied the existing law, you have more options. For example, if your case involves an elements analysis or a multi-part test, you will usually want to include an introductory section in which you set out the general rules—that is, the standard of review and the applicable statutory language, the applicable regulations, the applicable court rule, or the applicable common law rule. However, once you begin your discussion of the elements or the multi-part test, you can start with an assertion, a statement of the rule, the facts of your case, or even an analogous case. The following examples show some of the options for an issue involving an elements analysis.

EXAMPLE 2   **ELEMENTS ANALYSIS IN WHICH THE AUTHOR BEGINS THE DISCUSSION OF EACH ELEMENT WITH AN ASSERTION**

A. MAIN HEADING

Paragraph setting out the standard of review, the applicable statutory language, regulations, court rule, or common law rule, and listing or identifying the elements

1. <u>Argumentative heading for first element</u>
    • Assertion
    • Statement of the rule
    • Descriptions of analogous cases
    • Your argument, including your response to your opponent's arguments
    • Conclusion

2. <u>Argumentative heading for second element</u>
    • Assertion
    • Statement of the rule
    • Descriptions of analogous cases
    • Your argument, including your response to your opponent's arguments
    • Conclusion

3. <u>Argumentative heading for third element</u>
    • Assertion
    • Statement of the rule
    • Descriptions of analogous cases
    • Your argument, including your response to your opponent's arguments
    • Conclusion

If appropriate, a more general conclusion for this issue.

| EXAMPLE 3 | ELEMENTS ANALYSIS IN WHICH THE AUTHOR BEGINS THE DISCUSSION WITH A FAVORABLE STATEMENT OF THE RULE |

A. MAIN HEADING
   Paragraph setting out a favorable statement, the standard of review, and the applicable statutory language, regulations, court rule or rules, or common law rule, and listing or identifying the elements
   1. Argumentative heading for first element
      • Favorable statement of the rule
      • Descriptions of analogous cases
      • Your argument, including your response to your opponent's arguments
      • Conclusion
   2. Argumentative heading for second element
      • Favorable statement of the rule
      • Descriptions of analogous cases
      • Your argument, including your response to your opponent's arguments
      • Conclusion
   3. Argumentative heading for third element
      • Favorable statement of the rule
      • Descriptions of analogous cases
      • Your argument, including your response to your opponent's arguments
      • Conclusion

   If appropriate, a more general conclusion for this issue.

| EXAMPLE 4 | ELEMENTS ANALYSIS IN WHICH THE AUTHOR STARTS THE DISCUSSION WITH A FAVORABLE STATEMENT OF THE FACTS |

A. MAIN HEADING
   Paragraph setting out the standard of review and the applicable statutory language, regulations, court rule or rules, or common law rule, and listing or identifying the elements
   1. Argumentative heading for first element
      • Statement of the facts
      • Statement of the rule
      • Descriptions of analogous cases
      • Your argument, including your response to your opponent's arguments
      • Conclusion
   2. Argumentative heading for second element
      • Statement of the facts
      • Statement of the rule

- Descriptions of analogous cases
- Your argument, including your response to your opponent's arguments
- Conclusion

3. <u>Argumentative heading for third element</u>
   - Statement of the facts
   - Statement of the rule
   - Descriptions of analogous cases
   - Your argument, including your response to your opponent's arguments
   - Conclusion

If appropriate, a more general conclusion for this issue.

EXAMPLE 5　**ELEMENTS ANALYSIS IN WHICH THE AUTHOR STARTS THE DISCUSSION WITH A FAVORABLE DESCRIPTION OF THE ANALOGOUS CASES**

A. MAIN HEADING
   Paragraph setting out the standard of review and the applicable statutory language, regulations, court rule or rules, or common law rule, and listing or identifying the elements.
   1. <u>Argumentative heading for first element</u>
      - Description of the analogous cases
      - Statement of the rule
      - Your argument, including the application of the law to your facts and your response to your opponent's arguments
      - Conclusion
   2. <u>Argumentative heading for second element</u>
      - Description of the analogous cases
      - Statement of the rule
      - Your argument, including an application of the law to your facts and your response to your opponent's arguments
      - Conclusion
   3. <u>Argumentative heading for third element</u>
      - Description of the analogous cases
      - Statement of the rule
      - Your argument, including your response to your opponent's arguments
      - Conclusion

If appropriate, a more general conclusion for this issue.

In selecting one of these organizational schemes, keep the following points in mind. First, you do not need to use the same organizational scheme for each element. For instance, it might work best to start your discussion of one element with an assertion, your discussion of another element with the facts, and your discussion of yet another element with a rule.

Second, in selecting an organizational scheme for a particular element, make sure that you pick a scheme that will work not only for you but also for the judges who will be reading your brief. Thus, select an organizational scheme that highlights your theory of the case and allows you to set out your points clearly and concisely.

Third, make sure that you don't get into a rut. Although there is always a temptation to use the organizational scheme with which you are most comfortable, as an advocate this is a temptation you need to resist. If you are to persuade the court, you need to pick the scheme that allows you to emphasize the strongest parts of your argument. For example, if the rule strongly favors your client, you will usually want to select an organizational scheme that allows you to put the rule at the beginning, in the position of emphasis. Conversely, if the facts are very favorable, you will usually want to use an organizational scheme that allows you to put them at the beginning. At other times, when there are a number of steps to the analysis, it works best to select an organizational scheme that allows you to begin your argument with your assertions, which can then act as a roadmap for the rest of the argument. Fourth, keep in mind that you are not bound by your opponent's organizational scheme. Instead, use the organizational scheme that allows you to make your points effectively.

Finally, make sure that you do not make one of the most common errors that attorneys make in writing briefs: setting out one case and then comparing the facts in that case to the facts in your case, setting out a second case and then comparing the facts in that second case to the facts in your case, and so on. Instead of organizing your arguments around individual cases, organize them around assertions.

EXAMPLE 6   POOR WAY OF ORGANIZING THE ARGUMENTS

  A. MAIN HEADING
     Statement of rule
       Description of Case A
         Comparison of the facts in your case to the facts in Case A
       Description of Case B
         Comparison of the same facts in your case to the facts in Case B
       Description of Case C
         Comparison of the same facts in your case to the facts in Case C
       Description of Case D
         Comparison of the same facts in your case to the facts in Case D
     Conclusion

EXAMPLE 7   **BETTER WAY OF ORGANIZING THE ARGUMENTS**

A.   MAIN HEADING
     Statement of rule
        Assertion 1
           • Principle
           • Description of Case A
           • Description of Case B
           • Argument using Case A and Case B
        Assertion 2
           • Principle
           • Description of Case C
           • Description of Case D
           • Argument using Case C and Case D
     Conclusion

---

§ 16.3 Presenting the Rules, Descriptions of Analogous Cases, and Arguments in the Light Most Favorable to Your Client

Although the organizational schemes for the argument section in a brief are similar to the organizational schemes for the discussion section in an objective memorandum, the method of presentation is different. While in an objective memorandum you present the rules, cases, and arguments objectively, in a brief you present them persuasively.

§ 16.3.1 Presenting the Rules

Good advocacy begins with a favorable statement of the rule. Although you do not want to misstate a rule, quote a rule out of context, or mislead the court, you do want to present the rule in such a way that it favors your client. There are a number of ways to do this: You can present the rule in a favorable context, you can state the rule broadly or narrowly, you can state the rule so that it suggests the conclusion you want the court to reach, and you can emphasize or de-emphasize who has the burden of proof.

The following example sets out an objective statement of a rule.

EXAMPLE 1   **OBJECTIVE STATEMENT OF THE RULE**

To determine if a *Batson* violation has occurred, courts engage in a three-step analysis. First, the defendant must make out a prima facie case "by showing that the totality of the relevant facts gives rise to an inference of discriminatory purpose." *Batson v. Kentucky*, 476 U.S. 79, 93-94 (citing *Washington v. Davis*, 426 U.S. 229, 239-42 (1976)). Second, if the defendant has made out a prima facie case, the "burden shifts to the Government to explain adequately the racial exclusion" by offering permissible race-neutral justifications for the strikes. *Batson*, 476 U.S. at 93-94. Third, "[i]f a race-neutral explanation is tendered, the trial court must then decide . . . whether the opponent of the strike has proved purposeful racial discrimination." *Johnson v. California*, 125 U.S. 2410, 2416 (2007). In a recent decision, the United States Supreme Court reaffirmed this rule. *Flowers v. Mississippi*, 139 S. Ct. 2228, 2242 (2019).

In the next example, Ms. Elder has rewritten the objective statement of the rule so that the rule is presented in a way that highlights her theory of the case and that is favorable to her client. Instead of beginning with the rule itself, she begins by creating a favorable context: In the first paragraph Ms. Elder reminds the court that the United States Supreme Court has "consistently and repeatedly . . . reaffirmed that racial discrimination by the State in jury selection offends the Equal Protection Clause." Then, in setting out the three-step test, Ms. Elder sets out the rules so that they suggest the conclusions that Ms. Elder wants the court to reach. For example, in setting out the test, Ms. Elder de-emphasizes the defendant's burden of proof and emphasizes the government's burden: "the defendant need only establish a prima facie case of purposeful discrimination," "the burden shifts to the government," and "the government must provide a race-neutral reason . . . ." In addition, Ms. Elder uses language that suggests that Mr. Josephy will be able to meet his burden: "once the defendant establishes a prima facie case." Finally, Ms. Elder sets up her "sensitive analysis" argument by using that language in the rule section.

| EXAMPLE 2 | **EXCERPT FROM THE APPELLANT'S BRIEF WITH PERSUASIVE PRESENTATION OF THE RULES** |

For more than a century, the United States Supreme Court has "consistently and repeatedly . . . reaffirmed that racial discrimination by the State in jury selection offends the Equal Protection Clause." *Miller-El v. Dretke*, 125 U.S. 2317, 2324 (2005) (quoting *Georgia v. McCollum*, 505 U.S. 42 (1992)). Racial discrimination in jury selection denies defendants their right to a jury trial, denies jurors the right to participate in public life, and undermines public confidence in the fairness of our justice system. *Batson v. Kentucky*, 476 U.S. 79, 86-87 (1986); *Williams v. Runnels*, 432 F.3d 1102, 1108 (9th Cir. 2006). "In the eyes of the Constitution, one racially discriminatory peremptory strike is one too many." *Flowers v. Mississippi*, 139 S. Ct. 2228, 2241 (2019).

In *Batson*, the Court developed a three-step test to uncover discrimination masked by peremptory challenges. 476 U.S. at 96-97. Under the first step of the test, the defendant need only establish a prima facie case of purposeful discrimination by showing that the prosecutor has struck a member of a cognizable class and that the circumstances raise an inference of discrimination. *Id.* at 96. Once the defendant establishes a prima facie case, the burden shifts to the government: The government must provide a race-neutral explanation for striking a member of a cognizable class. *Id.* at 97. If the government does meet its burden, the court must do a sensitive analysis to determine whether the government has engaged in purposeful discrimination. *See Johnson v. California*, 545 U.S. 162, 169 (2005).

Similarly, the prosecutor has rewritten the objective statement of the rule so that the rules are presented in a light that is more favorable to the government's position. In the following example, the prosecutor starts his statement of the rule by creating a favorable context: He reminds the court that peremptory challenges are an important tool available to both prosecutors and defense counsel. In the second sentence, the prosecutor de-emphasizes the United States Supreme Court's statements about the difficulty of balancing the need to protect constitutional rights with the proper use of peremptory challenges by placing that point in a dependent clause in the middle of a relatively long paragraph. The prosecutor then ends the paragraph with a favorable point: that the United States Supreme Court has not indicated a willingness to deprive parties of their right to use peremptory challenges or to change the *Batson* test.

EXAMPLE 3   **EXCERPT FROM THE APPELLEE'S BRIEF WITH PERSUASIVE PRESENTATION OF THE RULES**

Peremptory challenges are an important trial tool that permits both parties' counsel to use their professional judgment and educated hunches about individual jurors to select a fair and impartial jury. *United States v. Bauer*, 84 F.3d 1549, 1555 (9th Cir. 1996). While the Supreme Court has acknowledged difficulties in balancing the need to protect constitutional rights with the proper use of peremptory challenges, the Court has not indicated a willingness to deprive the parties of their right to use peremptory challenges. *See Miller-El v. Dretke*, 545 U.S. 231, 239 (2005). Indeed, Justice Breyer's concurrence, in which he posited that the Court should reconsider the *Batson* test and the peremptory system as a whole, failed to garner a single co-signer. *Id.* at 266-67 (Breyer, J. concurring).

Thus, courts continue to apply the three-step test set out in *Batson*. *Flowers v. Mississippi*, 139 S. Ct. 2228, 2241 (2019). Under the test, a defendant's rights are not violated unless (1) the defendant establishes a prima facie case of purposeful discrimination in the government's use of peremptory challenges by showing that the challenged juror is a member of a cognizable class and that the circumstances raise an inference of discrimination; and (2) the government fails to meet its burden to provide a race-neutral explanation for its strike; or (3) the government offers a race-neutral reason, but the defendant meets his burden of showing that a review of all relevant circumstances shows purposeful discrimination. *See Johnson v. California*, 545 U.S. 162, 169 (2005); *Batson*, 746 U.S. at 89, 96-98.

For additional examples, see section 6.3.3.

§ 16.3.2 Presenting the Cases

In drafting your brief, you will use cases in two ways: (1) as citations for rules, for example, as a citation for a common law rule or rules that courts have created in interpreting statutes, regulations, or court rules; and (2) as illustrations of how the courts have applied statutes, regulations, court rules, or common law rules in cases that are factually analogous to your case. What you do not want to do is to set out case descriptions just to set out case descriptions. Therefore, before you include a case description, consider the following questions.

- Does the case illustrate how courts have applied a statute, regulation, court rule, or common law rule in a case that is factually analogous to your case?
- Does the case or a group of cases illustrate how a particular rule has developed or is developing?
- Do you need to distinguish the case because the other side has relied on it or is likely to rely on it?
- As an officer of the court, are you obligated to bring the case to the court's attention?

Unless you have answered "yes" to one or more of these questions, do not include the case description in your brief.

> **PRACTICE POINTER**   Remember that you can use a case as authority for a rule without setting out its facts, holdings, and rationale.

When you do include descriptions of analogous cases, be clear about why you have included those descriptions. One way to do this is to set out the principle that you are using the case or cases to illustrate and to then describe the cases. The following example illustrates this type of "principle-based" analysis, that is, analysis in which the cases are used to illustrate how courts have applied a rule or principle. The principle-based topic sentences are in bold.

EXAMPLE 1   EXCERPT FROM APPELLANT'S BRIEF DEMONSTRATING PRINCIPLE-BASED ANALYSIS

2. <u>The ATF agents did not have a particularized objective suspicion that Mr. Josephy was engaged in criminal activity because the tip included only general physical descriptions, it omitted any description of clothing, and the only action it predicted was that Mr. Josephy would be leaving a motel.</u>   Subheading

A tip from an unknown informant that does no more than describe an individual's readily observable location and appearance does not have sufficient indicia of reliability to support a stop. *Florida v. J.L.*, 529 U.S. 266, 272 (2000). Although such a tip may help the police identify the person whom the informant means to accuse, such a tip does not establish that the informant has knowledge of concealed criminal activity. *Id.* at 272.

In the cases in which courts have held that the tip lacked sufficient indicia of reliability, the tip lacked predictive information and included only a general description of the defendant and his location, and the informant did not explain how he had acquired the information. *See, e.g., Florida v. J.L.*, 529 U.S. at 272. For instance, in *J.L.*, an anonymous caller reported to police that "a young black male standing at a particular bus stop and wearing a plaid shirt was carrying a gun." *Id.* at 269. In concluding that this tip was not sufficient to establish a reasonable suspicion of criminal activity, the Court said that "[t]he anonymous call concerning J.L. provided no predictive information and therefore left the police without means to test the informant's knowledge or credibility." *Id.* at 270. The Court went on to say that the fact that the allegation about the gun turned out to be true did not establish a reasonable basis for suspecting J.L. of engaging in unlawful conduct:

> The reasonableness of official suspicion must be measured by what the officers knew before they conducted their search. All the police had to go on in this case was the bare report of an unknown, unaccountable informant who neither explained how he knew about the gun nor supplied any basis for believing he had inside information about J.L.

Id. at 271.

In contrast, in most of the cases in which courts have held that the tips had sufficient indicia of reliability to support a *Terry* stop, the callers were reporting what they had recently seen or experienced, *see, e.g., United States v. Terry-Crespo*, 356 F.3d 1170, 1172 (9th Cir. 2004), **or the callers provided the police with not only details about the defendant and his or her current location but also information about what the defendant was about to do,** *see, e.g., United States v. Fernandez-Castillo*, 324 F.3d 1114, 1119 (9th Cir. 2003). For example, in *Terry-Crespo*, the court held that a 911 call contained sufficient indicia of reliability for four reasons: (1) the call was not anonymous because the caller provided the 911 operator with his name and the call was recorded; (2) the caller was the victim of a crime, and the police must be able to take seriously, and respond promptly to, emergency 911 calls; (3) the caller jeopardized any anonymity he might have had by calling 911 and providing his

---

Sidebar annotations:

Rules

Principle that Ms. Elder has drawn from the cases in which courts have held the tips lacked sufficient indicia of reliability

Description of case that illustrates the principle and illustrates the types of cases in which courts have held that the tips lacked sufficient indicia of reliability

Principle that Ms. Elder has drawn from the cases in which courts have held that the tips had sufficient indicia of reliability followed by descriptions of cases that illustrate that principle

name to an operator during a recorded call; and (4) the caller was giving first-hand information about an event that had just occurred. *Terry-Crespo* at 356 F.3d at 1172-77. Similarly, in *Fernandez-Castillo*, the court held that a tip had sufficient reliability because it came from a Montana Department of Transportation (MDOT) employee and there are relatively few MDOT employees; the MDOT employee who reported the erratic driving not only provided the dispatcher with the make and model of the car but also told the dispatcher that the car had North Dakota license plates; the MDOT employee made the report almost immediately after he observed the defendant driving erratically; and the report contained predictive information—that the car was driving eastbound near milepost 116. *Fernandez-Castillo*, 324 F.3d at 1119.

Although most of the time you will want to start your case description or descriptions by setting out the principle that you are using the case or cases to illustrate, there are times when it works to start with a citation to the case. For example, in the following excerpt, which is taken from the appellee's brief, the prosecutor starts the paragraph with a cite to *Alabama v. White*. In this instance, starting with a citation to a case is effective because it allows the prosecutor to emphasize that *Alabama v. White* is a United States Supreme Court case. When you use this technique, it usually works best to set out the court's holding in the topic sentence.

EXAMPLE 2   **EXCERPT FROM APPELLEE'S BRIEF IN WHICH THE PROSECUTOR HAS STARTED A PARAGRAPH WITH A CITATION TO A CASE**

Similarly, in *Alabama v. White*, 496 U.S. 325, 330 (1990), the United States Supreme Court held that the police had a reasonable suspicion that the defendant, White, was engaged in criminal activity. In *White*, an anonymous caller phoned 911 and told the operator that Vanessa White would be leaving the Lynnwood Terrace Apartments at a particular time in a brown Plymouth station wagon with a broken taillight to go to Dobey's Motel. *Id.* at 327. In addition, the caller told the 911 operator that White would have about "an ounce of cocaine inside a brown brief case." *Id.* Although the two police officers who went to the apartment complex saw White get into a brown Plymouth station wagon with a broken taillight, they did not see anything in White's hands. *Id.* Moreover, although White appeared to be driving to Dobey's Motel, the officers had a patrol unit stop the vehicle before it reached the motel. *Id.* The Court held that the officers had a reasonable suspicion despite failing to verify White's predicted destination.

Another way to make clear why you have included a particular case description is to state explicitly that the facts in the analogous case are similar to the facts in your case or to say that facts in the analogous case can be distinguished from the facts in your case. Example 3 shows how Ms. Elder sets up a case description by stating that the case can be distinguished. In reading this example, note the order in which Ms. Elder sets out information. Instead of putting the description of the analogous case between the rules and the arguments, Ms. Elder sets out the rules, her arguments based on those rules, and then the description of the case, which she then distinguishes.

EXAMPLE 3 **EXCERPT FROM APPELLANT'S BRIEF DEMONSTRATING DISTINGUISHING A CASE**

1. <u>The ATF agents did not have a particularized objective suspicion that Mr. Josephy was engaged in criminal activity because the tip came from an unknown informant; although the informant gave the 911 operator his name, he refused to give his address or phone number.</u>   Subheading

When an informant declines to be identified, there is a risk the tip has been fabricated, undercutting its reliability. *Florida v. J.L.*, 529 U.S. 266, 269-70, 272 (2000). The unknown informant's reputation cannot be accessed, nor can the informant be held responsible for a false accusation. *Id.* Consequently, the possibility that the informant might be lying outweighs the value of the information provided unless there are other factors that establish that the informant is reliable—for example, the informant provides law enforcement officers with information about the suspect's future actions, which law enforcement officers then independently verify. *United States v. Morales*, 252 F.3d 1070, 1075 (9th Cir. 2001).   Rules

In *State v. Josephy*, this Court should treat the tip as a tip from an unknown informant. Although the informant gave the 911 operator a name, "Zachary Dillon," he called from a public pay phone in a large mall, and he refused to give the 911 operator his address or phone number (ER 32, 35). In addition, when Agent Bhasin tried to locate an individual by the name of Zachary Dillon in his databases, he was not able to find anyone by that name in the greater Bellingham area (ER 42). Consequently, neither Agent Bhasin nor any other law enforcement officer was able to contact Zachary Dillon to determine how he obtained the information that he gave to the 911 operator or to hold him accountable if the statements that he made turned out to be false.   Argument

Accordingly, the facts in this case can be distinguished from the facts in *United States v. Terry-Crespo*, 356 F.3d 1170, 1172 (9th Cir. 2004), a case in which the court held that information provided by an individual who had called 911 to report that the defendant had threatened him with a firearm was sufficient to support a *Terry* stop even though the police were not able to   Case description locate anyone by the caller's name in their databases. Unlike the caller in *Terry-Crespo*, who was the victim of a crime, in this case the informant, "Dillon," was not the victim of a crime. In addition, unlike the caller in *Terry-Crespo*, who made the call from the scene of the crime, in this case "Dillon" made the call from a mall five minutes from the motel where the drug buy was allegedly occurring. Finally, while in *Terry-Crespo* the caller did not give the 911 operator his phone number because he did not know the number of the cell phone that he had borrowed to make the emergency call, in this case "Dillon" refused to give the operator his address, home phone number, or a cell phone number. Consequently, while in *Terry-Crespo* the facts supported the court's conclusion that the caller was not trying to hide his identity, in this case the facts suggest just the opposite.

Argument

Thus, because "Dillon" appears to have taken steps to hide his identity, this Court should treat his tip as a tip from an unknown informant. However, even if this Court does not treat the tip as coming from an unknown informant, the tip is not reliable because it lacks sufficient indicia of reliability.

Conclusion

Just as there are a number of techniques that you can use to present a rule in a light favorable to your client, there are also a number of techniques you can use to present a case in a light favorable to your client. You can set out the court's holding more broadly in cases that support your client's position and more narrowly in cases that support the other side's position; you can emphasize or de-emphasize particular facts or rules through the use of airtime, detail, the positions of emphasis, sentence length, and sentence construction; and you can choose words not only for their denotation but also for their connotation.

For instance, in the following example, the prosecutor uses detail, the positions of emphasis, and word choices to set out his description of *United States v. Terry-Crespo* in a light favorable to the government.

EXAMPLE 4   **EXCERPT FROM THE APPELLEE'S BRIEF SHOWING FAVORABLE PRESENTATION OF A CASE**

In determining whether a *Terry* stop was permissible, courts conduct a *de novo* review, looking at the totality of the circumstances and considering all relevant factors, including those factors that "in a different context, might be entirely innocuous." *Florida v. J.L.*, 529 U.S. at 277-78; *accord United States v. Terry-Crespo*, 356 F.3d 1170, 1172 (9th Cir. 2004). For example, in *Terry-Crespo*, this Court held that the informant's preliminary phone call was, by itself,

The prosecutor begins the paragraph by setting out the rule that he is using *Terry-Crespo* to illustrate.

sufficient to establish a reasonable suspicion that the defendant, Terry-Crespo, was engaged in criminal activity. *Id.* at 1172. In doing so, this Court rejected Terry-Crespo's argument that the informant, Mr. Domingis, should be treated as an anonymous informant because he was not able to provide the 911 operator with the number of the phone from which he placed the call; he changed the subject when the operator asked him to provide another number; and, when asked for his location, he gave the operator a nonexistent intersection. *Id.* at 1174-75. As this Court stated in its opinion:

> During the course of the 911 call, the operator asked Mr. Domingis for his telephone number. Mr. Domingis explained that he did not know the return number because he was calling from someone else's cellular telephone. When the operator asked if there was another number where she could reach him, he did not answer her question but returned to discussing the subject of the suspect's location. The operator asked Mr. Domingis for his location. Initially, he responded by providing a nonexistent intersection on Portland's grid system and then stammeringly told the operator that "I don't want . . . I don't want . . . I don't want. . . ." Although not certain, it appears that Mr. Domingis did not want police contact.

Id. at 1172.

This Court then went on to note that the police tried to locate Mr. Domingis in a number of different databases, including the Yahoo! databases, but that they were not able to locate anyone by that name. *Id.* However, this Court concluded that the tip had sufficient indicia of reliability because Mr. Domingis was reporting that he had just been the victim of a crime and because Mr. Domingis risked any anonymity that he might have enjoyed by giving the 911 operator his name during a recorded call. *Id.* at 1174-76. As this Court stated, "Merely calling 911 and having a recorded telephone conversation risks the possibility that the police could trace the call or identify Mr. Domingis by his voice." *Id.* at

The prosecutor uses active voice and the phrase, "this Court" to emphasize that *Terry-Crespo* is a Ninth Circuit case. In addition, by using the phrase "this Court rejected Terry-Crespo's argument" the prosecutor suggests that the court should do the same thing in this case.

By setting out the facts in detail and using a quotation, the prosecutor emphasizes the facts in *Terry-Crespo*.

Instead of putting the fact that the police tried to locate Mr. Domingis in a number of different databases in the same paragraph as the quote, the prosecutor starts a new paragraph, which allows him to emphasize this fact by putting it in a position of emphasis.

The prosecutor buries an unfavorable fact, that Mr. Domingis was the victim of a crime, in the middle of the paragraph.

1176. Thus, this Court held that, under the totality of the circumstances, the tip was sufficient to support a finding that Terry-Crespo was engaged in criminal activity even though the police did not independently verify any of the information contained in the tip.

By putting the dependent clause at the end of the sentence rather than at the beginning, the prosecutor is able to put a favorable fact, that the police did not independently verify any of the information in the tip, in a position of emphasis.

Although you will want to include full descriptions of the most important cases, avoid the temptation to describe all, or even most, of the cases that you found while researching the issue. By being selective, you will keep your brief shorter, something that will please almost every judge, and your preparation for oral argument will be easier. (Remember, for every case you cite, you need to know that case, inside and out, for oral argument.) When it is important to cite more than a few cases, set out the best case or cases in text and then reference the other cases using parentheticals.

EXAMPLE 5   **EXCERPT FROM APPELLANT'S BRIEF DEMONSTRATING FULL CASE DESCRIPTION AND USE OF A PARENTHETICAL**

Under this comparative analysis, a defendant meets his burden of proving the reason the prosecutor gave for striking a juror was a pretext for discrimination when the reason given applies equally to a juror of another race, but the prosecutor strikes only one of the jurors. *McClain v. Prunty,* 217 F.3d 1209, 1221 (9th Cir. 2000). For instance, in *McClain,* this Court concluded that the reason the prosecutor gave for striking a black juror was a pretext for discrimination when the reason given applied equally to a white juror, but the prosecutor did not strike the white juror. *Id.* at 1222. Although the prosecutor stated that he had struck a black juror because the juror lacked experience making decisions, the prosecutor did not strike a white juror who also lacked decision-making experience. *Id.* As this Court stated, the fact that the prosecutor did not treat jurors of different races in the same way "fatally undermine[d] the credibility of the prosecutor's stated justification." *Id.*; *see also United States v. Chinchilla,* 874 F.2d 695 (9th Cir. 1989) (reversing a conviction because the prosecutor's stated reason for striking a Hispanic juror—that the juror lived in La Mesa—applied equally to a juror who was not Hispanic and who was not struck).

Principle that Ms. Elder wants to illustrate

Full description of first case

Description of second case using a parenthetical

Finally, remember that if you describe a case you need to use that case in your argument. Do not describe a case and then leave the judge to figure out why you included a description of that case in your brief.

> **PRACTICE POINTER**   In choosing cases on which to rely, keep in mind your jurisdiction's rule on citing to unpublished opinions. In December 2006, the United States Supreme Court amended Fed. R. App. P. 32.1 to allow citation to unpublished federal opinions issued on or after January 1, 2007. However, some state jurisdictions still prohibit citations to most unpublished cases. *See, e.g.,* Cal. Rules of Court, 8.1105.

§ 16.3.3 Constructing and Presenting the Arguments

For many attorneys, the most enjoyable part of drafting the brief is constructing and presenting the arguments: It is in constructing and presenting the arguments that attorneys get to use their insights and creativity to pull together, into a coherent and persuasive package, the facts, rules, and cases that they have set out in the earlier sections of their brief.

In constructing the arguments, think first about the standard types of arguments: factual arguments in which you apply the plain language of a statute, regulation, court rule, or common law rule to the facts of your case; analogous case arguments in which you compare and contrast the facts in your case to the facts in analogous cases; and policy arguments.

While factual arguments are very common in trial briefs, they are less common in appellate briefs. In most instances, the appellate courts defer to the trial court's findings of fact or the jury's verdict, only overturning a finding or the verdict if it is not supported by the evidence. There are, however, times when you can make an effective factual argument, either letting that factual argument stand by itself or combining it with an analogous case or policy argument.

For example, in *United States v. Josephy*, Ms. Elder makes a factual argument that the tip is from an unknown rather than a known informant. In reading the following example, examine the way in which Ms. Elder uses the facts to support her assertion that the court should treat the tip as a tip from an unknown informant. Ms. Elder puts unfavorable facts—for example, the fact that the informant gave the 911 operator a name—in a dependent clause; she uses the phrase "gave the operator a name" rather than the phrase "gave the operator his name" to suggest that the informant might not have given the operator his real name. In addition, she places her strongest argument, that neither Agent Bhasin nor any other law enforcement officer was able to contact the informant to determine how he obtained the information or to hold him accountable if the statements turned out to be false, in a position of emphasis at the end of the paragraph.

EXAMPLE 1	**EXCERPT FROM THE APPELLANT'S BRIEF SHOWING HOW TO PRESENT A FACTUAL ARGUMENT**

When an informant declines to be identified, there is a risk the tip has been fabricated, undercutting its reliability. *Florida v. J.L.*, 529 U.S. 266, 269-70, 272 (2000). The unknown informant's reputation cannot be assessed, nor can the informant be held responsible for a false accusation. *Id.* This possibility that the informant may be lying outweighs the value of the information provided unless there are other factors that establish that the informant is reliable—for example, the informant provides law enforcement officers with information about the suspect's future actions, which law enforcement officers then independently verify. *United States v. Morales*, 252 F.3d 1070, 1075 (9th Cir. 2001).

Rules

In this case, the Court should treat the tip as a tip from an unknown informant. Although the informant gave the 911 operator a name, "Zachary Dillon," he called from a public pay phone in a large mall, and he refused to give the 911 operator his address or phone number (ER 32, 35). In addition, when Agent Bhasin tried to locate an individual by the name of Zachary Dillon in his databases, he was not able to find anyone by that name in the greater Bellingham area (ER 42). Consequently, neither Agent Bhasin nor any other law enforcement officer was able to contact Zachary Dillon to determine how he obtained the information that he gave to the 911 operator or to hold him accountable if the statements that he made turned out to be false.

Assertion

Factual argument

If a factual argument is the least common type of argument in appellate briefs, the most common type is an analogous case argument—that is, an argument in which a party either compares its case to analogous cases or distinguishes its case from the cases that the other side says are analogous.

In constructing and presenting analogous case arguments, keep five things in mind. First, as a general rule, begin your argument by stating your assertion. Second, be explicit in making the comparisons. Third, in addition to making comparisons, explain why those comparisons are legally significant. Fourth, make sure that you compare like things; for example, make sure that you compare cases to cases, people to other people, and facts to facts. (See section 6.1.5 in *Just Writing, Fifth Edition*.) Finally, keep in mind that you can do more than just compare and contrast facts: You can also compare and contrast the arguments that the parties make and the courts' reasoning.

In the following excerpt from the appellant's brief, Ms. Elder begins her analogous case argument by setting out her assertion: Like the tip in *J.L.*, the tip in this case lacks the required indicia of reliability. Ms. Elder is then explicit in comparing the facts in *J.L.* to the facts in her case: "In *J.L.*, the informant called from a borrowed cell phone and did not give the 911 operator either his own phone number or his own address. Similarly, in this case 'Dillon' called from a public pay telephone and refused to give the operator his phone number or his address (ER 30)." Ms. Elder however, does more than just tell the judge how the cases are similar. She also explains why that similarity is important: Because neither of the informants provided the 911 operator with contact information, law enforcement officers were not able to contact either informant to determine the basis for the allegations or to hold them accountable if the information that they provided turned out to be false. Finally, Ms. Elder is precise in comparing the analogous case and her case. In the first sentence, she compares a tip to a tip, a case to a case, and facts to facts. In addition, in the second sentence, Ms. Elder compares a case to a case: *J.L.* to *United States v. Josephy*.

EXAMPLE 2   **EXCERPT FROM THE APPELLANT'S BRIEF SHOWING AN ANALOGOUS CASE ARGUMENT**

Like the tip in *J.L.*, the tip in this case lacked the required indicia of reliability. In *J.L.*, the informant called from a borrowed cell phone and did not give the 911 operator either his own phone number or his own address. Similarly, in this case "Dillon" called from a public pay telephone and refused to give the operator his phone number or his address (ER 30). As a consequence, in both cases, law enforcement officers were not able to contact the informants to determine the basis for their allegations or to hold them accountable if the information that they provided turned out to be false.

PRACTICE POINTER   When you italicize a name, you are telling your reader that you are citing to a case. In contrast, when you do not italicize a name, you are telling your reader that you are referring to the party or person. "*J.L.*" is a reference to *Florida v. J.L.*, but "J.L." is a reference to the defendant, a juvenile with the initials J and L.

Although you might incorporate policy statements into your presentation of the rules and your descriptions of analogous cases on a fairly regular basis, typically you will not make a policy argument unless you are asking the court to modify an existing rule or adopt a new rule. Our example case, *United States v. Josephy*, illustrates this point. If Ms. Elder had argued that the court should eliminate peremptory challenges because they can mask discrimination, her primary argument would have been a policy argument, and the government's primary argument would have been a policy argument. Ms. Elder would have argued that, as a matter of public policy, courts should eliminate peremptory challenges, and the government would have argued that, as a matter of public policy, courts should not deprive parties of their right to use such challenges. However, given the fact that the United States Supreme Court rejected a request to eliminate peremptory challenges in a relatively recent opinion, *see Miller-El v. Dretke*, 545 U.S. 231, 239-40 (2005), Ms. Elder decided not to pursue this line of argument. As a consequence, although both Ms. Elder and the prosecutor refer to policy in their statements of the rules and their descriptions of the cases, neither Ms. Elder nor the prosecutor makes a policy argument in their brief.

§ 16.3.4 Using Quotations

While some attorneys and judges will tell you that you should not include quotations, and particularly long quotations, in your brief, other attorneys and judges will tell you that quotations are one of the advocate's most valuable tools. Both groups have legitimate points.

In drafting your brief, do not use quotations as a crutch. For example, do not use a quotation to cover up the fact that you do not understand a rule or a court's holding or reasoning. Instead, take the time to figure out the rule and the court's decision. Similarly, do not use a quotation because you lack confidence in your writing skills or because you do not want to take the time to construct your own language.

Do, however, use quotations in the following circumstances. First, as a general rule, quote the relevant portions of governing statutes, regulations, and court rules, and quote applicable sections of contracts, wills, and similar documents. Second, as a general rule, quote from the record when the specific language that the judge, attorney, witness, or juror used is important. In addition, feel free to use quotations to emphasize favorable facts, rules, and cases.

The following example illustrates an effective use of quotations from the record. Because Ms. Elder wants to emphasize that Ms. Whitefish was not bothered by the fact that she was subjected to additional scrutiny at the border but that Mr. Williams was bothered by the fact that police officers seemed to target him, Ms. Elder quotes from the record and places most of those quotations at the end of a paragraph in a position of emphasis.

EXAMPLE 1   **EXCERPT FROM THE APPELLANT'S BRIEF SHOWING USE OF QUOTATIONS FROM THE RECORD TO EMPHASIZE FAVORABLE FACTS**

Later, the prosecutor asked if anyone had ever had negative experiences with law enforcement personnel (ER 119). Ms. Whitefish, a Native American who was a junior majoring in history at Western Washington University, responded that each time she crossed the border she had been "pulled aside for additional questions" (ER 119). However, when the prosecutor asked Ms. Whitefish whether she was bothered by the fact that she had been pulled over for additional questions, she stated, "Not particularly. I am a college student, and all of us have had similar experiences. They seem to stop young people more . . . ." (ER 119-20).

Similarly, Mr. Martin, a white man with long hair, told the prosecutor that he had had a number of negative experiences with police officers (ER 120). For example, Mr. Martin told the prosecutor that on one occasion a police officer had stopped him because one of his taillights was out but that the police had not

stopped other individuals who had one of their taillights out (ER 120). In addition, Mr. Martin told the prosecutor that on two occasions he had been given
tickets for jaywalking when other individuals on the same street who had
short hair jaywalked but did not get tickets (ER 120). When the prosecutor
asked whether he was bothered by the police officers' actions, Mr. Martin
said, "You bet I am." (ER 121).

When you are using quotations for emphasis, you will usually want to begin
by making the point using your own language. You can then use the quotation
to give that point more airtime or to give that point additional emphasis through
the use of detail. The following example illustrates this use of a quotation.
Ms. Elder makes her points using her own language, and then she emphasizes
those points by quoting from the court's opinion. Although the quotation is
longer than Ms. Elder would have liked, she uses the quotation because it
was not possible to edit it without losing coherence and key content, and the
point that she uses the quotation to illustrate is an important one.

EXAMPLE 2   EXCERPT FROM THE APPELLANT'S BRIEF SHOWING USE OF A QUOTATION

Even though the tip contained a number of details, the United States
Supreme Court held that the tip was not, by itself, sufficient to justify a *Terry*
stop. *White*, 496 U.S. at 329. According to the Court, it became reasonable to
think that the information was reliable only after the police verified not only easily
obtained facts but also future actions that are not easily predicted. *Id.* at 332.

> We think it also important that, as in *Gates*, "the anonymous [tip] con-
> tained a range of details relating not just to easily obtained facts and con-
> ditions existing at the time of the tip, but to future actions of third parties
> ordinarily not easily predicted." [462 U.S. at 245.] The fact that the offi-
> cers found a car precisely matching the caller's description in front of the
> 235 building is an example of the former. Anyone could have "pre-
> dicted" that fact because it was a condition presumably existing at the
> time of the call. What was important was the caller's ability to predict
> respondent's *future behavior*, because it demonstrated inside informa-
> tion—a special familiarity with respondent's affairs. The general public
> would have had no way of knowing that respondent would shortly leave
> the building, get in the described car, and drive the most direct route to
> Dobey's Motel. Because only a small number of people are generally
> privy to an individual's itinerary, it is reasonable for police to believe
> that a person with access to such information is likely to also have access
> to reliable information about that individual's illegal activities. *See ibid.*
> When significant aspects of the caller's predictions were verified,
> there was reason to believe not only that the caller was honest but
> also that he was well informed, at least well enough to justify the stop.

Id. (emphasis in original).

Although ultimately the Court concluded that the anonymous tip, as corroborated, was sufficient to justify the *Terry* stop, the Court labeled the case as a "close case." *Id*.

| PRACTICE POINTER | Remember to include a citation to authority for every quotation. If the quotation is from the record, the citation to authority should be to the record; if the quotation is from a statute, the citation to authority should be to the statute; and if the quotation is from a case, the citation should be to the case, including the specific page on which the quotation appears. |

§ 16.3.5 Responding to the Other Side's Arguments

In addition to setting out your own arguments, you need to respond to the other side's arguments. If you are the appellee, you do not have a choice about where to set out these responses: You need to set them out in your opening brief. However, when you are the appellant, you do have a choice: You can either anticipate what the appellee is going to argue and try to preempt its arguments by setting out your responses in your opening brief, or you can wait to see if the appellee makes the argument and then, if it does, respond in your reply brief. Even though there are pros and cons to both of these approaches, the conventional wisdom is that if you are relatively certain that the appellee will make an argument, you should anticipate and respond to that argument in your opening brief. In contrast, if there is a good possibility that the appellee will not make a particular point, you should wait for the appellee's brief.

The same considerations apply to deciding when to address cases on which the appellee relies. Although both parties have an ethical obligation to bring to the court's attention a case that is controlling, an appellant can choose to preempt a key, but not controlling, case the other side will likely rely on for support by distinguishing it in the opening brief. If the appellant is not sure the appellee will rely on the case, or the appellant believes the case is not critical to the analysis, the appellant might choose to wait until the reply brief to distinguish cases in the appellee's brief.

In responding to the other side's arguments, avoid repeating the other side's argument. Instead of repeating your opponent's arguments, make your own affirmative arguments.

Example 1 below sets out one of the appellant's arguments: that there was purposeful discrimination because the prosecutor excused Native Americans who had had a particular experience or commitment but did not excuse white jurors who had similar experiences or commitments. Example 2 is from a weak appellee's brief. By repeating the appellant's argument, the prosecutor gives the appellant's arguments additional airtime. In addition, instead of attacking the argument, the prosecutor attacks defense counsel when he states that she has misstated the law. Example 3 is a rewrite of Example 2, in which the prosecutor does a more effective job of responding to the appellant's argument without repeating the appellant's argument and without attacking defense counsel.

EXAMPLE 1   EXCERPT FROM THE APPELLANT'S BRIEF THAT SETS UP ARGUMENT TO WHICH APPELLEE MUST RESPOND

Moreover, the government cannot lawfully exercise peremptory challenges "against potential jurors of one race unless potential jurors of another race with comparable characteristics are also challenged." *United States v. You*, 382 F.3d 958, 969 (9th Cir. 2004) (quoting *Turner*, 121 F.3d at 1252). Accordingly, a "comparative analysis of jurors struck and those remaining is a well-established tool for exploring the possibility that facially race-neutral reasons are a pretext for discrimination." *McClain v. Prunty*, 217 F.3d 1209, 1220-21 (9th Cir. 2000).

Under this comparative analysis, a defendant meets his burden of proving the reason the prosecutor gave for striking a juror was a pretext for discrimination when the reason given applies equally to a juror of another race, but the prosecutor strikes only one of the jurors. *McClain*, 217 F.3d at 1221. For instance, in *McClain*, this Court concluded that the reason the prosecutor gave for striking a black juror was a pretext for discrimination when the reason given applied equally to a white juror, but the prosecutor did not strike the white juror. Although the prosecutor stated that he had struck a black juror because the juror lacked experience making decisions, the prosecutor did not strike a white juror who also lacked decision-making experience. As this Court stated, the fact that the prosecutor did not treat jurors of different races in the same way "fatally undermine[d] the credibility of the prosecutor's stated justification." *Id.* at 1221-22; *see also United States v. Chinchilla*, 874 F.2d 695 (9th Cir. 1989) (reversing a conviction because the prosecutor's stated reason for striking a Hispanic juror—that the juror lived in La Mesa—applied equally to a juror who was not Hispanic and who was not struck).

In *United States v. Josephy*, the reason the prosecutor gave for striking Mr. Williams, a Native American, was a pretext for discrimination because the reason applied equally to Mr. Woods, who is white. In explaining why he struck Mr. Williams, the prosecutor said that Mr. Williams would have difficulty focusing on the facts of the case because he had a meeting scheduled for the following week (ER 125). However, the prosecutor did not strike Mr. Woods, who told the court that his mother was seriously ill and in the hospital, and that he might have to go out of town (ER 117-18).

In addition, the reason that the prosecutor gave for striking Ms. Whitefish, a Native American, was a pretext for discrimination because the prosecutor did not strike a white juror who had had similar experiences with law enforcement personnel. When the judge asked the prosecutor why he had struck Ms. Whitefish, the prosecutor responded that he did not think Ms. Whitefish would be able "to judge this case fairly and impartially" based on her experiences crossing the border (ER 125). However, although Ms. Whitefish stated that she had been "pulled aside for additional questions," (ER 19), when asked whether this bothered her, Ms. Whitefish replied, "Not particularly. I am a college student, and all of us have had similar experiences. They seem to stop young people more . . . ." (ER 119).

In contrast, Mr. Martin believed he had been targeted by police officers because he had long hair (ER 120). He was stopped for having a taillight that was out; others were not. He was ticketed for jaywalking; others, who had short hair, were not (ER 119-20). When asked whether he was bothered by his experiences with police officers, he said, "You bet I am." (ER 121).

Although in one case this Court concluded that the reasons a prosecutor gave were not pretextual even though a black and white juror gave similar responses to a question and only the black juror was struck, the court noted, "While subjective factors may play a legitimate role in the exercise of challenges, reliance on such factors alone cannot overcome strong objective indicia of discrimination such as a clear and sustained pattern of strikes against minority jurors." *Burks v. Borg*, 27 F.3d 1424, 1429 (9th Cir. 1994).

In our case, there are objective indicia of discrimination stemming from a clear and sustained pattern of strikes against minority jurors. The prosecutor used two of his peremptory challenges to strike the only two Native American potential jurors. He struck Mr. Williams, who said he had a meeting scheduled after the trial was expected to end, despite the fact that Mr. Williams expressed willingness to serve even if it meant missing the meeting. In addition, he struck Ms. Whitefish based on her experiences at the border even though Ms. Whitefish assured the court that her experiences at the border did not bother her.

Because the prosecutor did not excuse white jurors who had similar experiences to the Native Americans whom he did strike, the district court erred in denying Mr. Josephy's *Batson* challenge. Such an erroneous denial is presumed to be prejudicial. *See Gray v. Mississippi*, 481 U.S. 648, 668 (1987). Therefore, this Court should reverse and remand the case for a new trial.

EXAMPLE 2   POOR RESPONSE BY THE APPELLEE

In her brief, defense counsel argues that a "comparative analysis of jurors struck and those remaining is a well-established tool for exploring the possibility that facially race-neutral reasons are a pretext for discrimination." *McClain v. Prunty*, 217 F.3d 1209, 1220-21 (9th Cir. 2000). In addition, defense counsel argues that a defendant meets his burden of proving the reason the prosecutor gave for striking a juror was a pretext for discrimination when the reason given applies equally to a juror of another race, but the prosecutor strikes only one of the jurors. *Id.* at 1221. Based on these rules, defense counsel argues that the appellant has met his burden of proving purposeful discrimination because the prosecutor excused Ms. Whitefish, a Native American, because she had problems crossing the border, but the prosecutor did not excuse Mr. Woods, who is white, even though Mr. Woods said that he believed that the police targeted him because he had long hair. In addition, defense counsel argues that the appellant has met his burden of proving purposeful discrimination because the prosecutor excused a Native American who had a tribal council meeting scheduled for the end of the week but did not excuse a white juror who said that he might have to go out of town to care for his mother.

Defense counsel misstates the law when she states that *Batson* is violated whenever prospective jurors of different races provide similar responses and one is excused while the other is not. *See Burks v. Borg*, 27 F.3d 1424, 1429 (9th Cir. 1994). For example, in *Burks*, this Court held that there was not purposeful discrimination in spite of the fact that a minority juror who was struck shared characteristics with a nonminority juror who was not struck. *Id.* The prosecutor told the court that he had stricken the minority jurors "because they were 'squishy' on the death penalty, expressed a reluctance to serve, and/or lacked certain life experiences." *Id.* In concluding that there was no purposeful discrimination, the court reaffirmed that "[t]rial counsel is entitled to exercise his full professional judgment in pursuing his client's 'legitimate interest in using [peremptory] challenges . . . to secure a fair and impartial jury.'" *Id.* (quoting *J.E.B. v. Alabama ex rel. T.B.*, 511 U.S. 127, 137 (1994)). Thus, in using his or her peremptory challenges, trial counsel is entitled to take into account "tone, demeanor, facial expression, emphasis—all those factors that make the words uttered by the prospective juror convincing or not." *Burks*, 27 F.3d at 1429.

EXAMPLE 3   BETTER RESPONSE BY APPELLEE

Furthermore, case law does not support the notion that *Batson* is violated whenever prospective jurors of different races provide similar responses and one is excused while the other is not. *Burks v. Borg*, 27 F.3d 1424, 1429 (9th Cir. 1994). For example, in *Burks*, this Court held that there was not purposeful discrimination in spite of the fact that a minority juror who was struck shared characteristics with a nonminority juror who was not struck. *Id.* The prosecutor told the court that he had stricken the minority jurors "because they were 'squishy' on the death penalty, expressed a reluctance to serve, and/or lacked certain life experiences." *Id.* In concluding that there was no purposeful discrimination, the court reaffirmed that "[t]rial counsel is entitled to exercise his full professional judgment in pursuing his client's 'legitimate interest in using [peremptory] challenges . . . to secure a fair and impartial jury.'" *Id.* (quoting *J.E.B. v. Alabama ex rel. T.B.*, 511 U.S. 127, 137 (1994)). Thus, in using his or her peremptory challenges, trial counsel is entitled to take into account "tone, demeanor, facial expression, emphasis—all those factors that make the words uttered by the prospective juror convincing or not." *Burks*, 27 F.3d at 1429.

---

§ 16.3.6 Avoiding the Common Problem of Neglecting to Make Explicit Connections

One of the most common mistakes that attorneys make in writing a brief is that they do not explicitly "connect" the parts of their argument. They set out an assertion but do not connect that assertion to a rule; they set out the rule but do not connect it to the descriptions of analogous cases; or they set out descriptions of analogous cases but do not connect the facts and holdings in those analogous cases to their case. For instance, in the following example, the attorney describes a case, *McClain*, but she does not make it clear that she is using the case to illustrate how courts have applied the rule that she set out in the first sentence of the paragraph. In addition, although the attorney states that the facts in *McClain* are similar to the facts in her case, she does not explain how they are similar.

EXAMPLE 1   POOR EXAMPLE BECAUSE OF LACK OF EXPLICIT CONNECTIONS

A court may conclude that the prosecutor's reasons are pretextual when the reason that the prosecutor gives for striking a juror applies equally to a juror of a different race who was not stricken. *McClain*, 217 F.3d at 1220. In *McClain*, the reason that the prosecutor gave for excusing a black juror was that she lacked decision-making experience. *Id.* at 1216. However, the prosecutor did not excuse a similar white juror. *Id.* at 1221. Thus, the court concluded that the prosecution's explanations were pretextual. *Id.* Similarly, in our case, the prosecutor excused Mr. Williams, a Native American, but she did not excuse Mr. Woods.

The following example is better because it uses a variety of ways to create connections and coherence. First, the attorney has gone into more detail in setting out the rules, the cases, and her arguments. The extra detail gives the attorney the raw material she needs to make the connections. Second, the author has used topic sentences to set up each paragraph. Third, the attorney has used transitions such as "for example" and "in addition" to make it clear how the information in one sentence is related to the information in the preceding or following sentence. Finally, to create coherence, the attorney has repeated key terms. For example, she has used the word "reason" and a version of the phrase "not supported by the record" in the statement of the rule, in the description of the analogous case, and in the argument. In the following example, the transitions are in all capital letters, the word "reason" is in bold, and the versions of the phrase "not supported by the record" are underlined.

EXAMPLE 2   BETTER EXAMPLE BECAUSE OF CONNECTIONS AND COHERENCE

When the **reasons** that a prosecutor gives for striking a juror are <u>not supported by the record</u>, "serious questions about the legitimacy of a prosecutor's reasons for exercising peremptory challenges are raised." *McClain v. Prunty*, 217 F.3d 1209, 1221 (9th Cir. 2000). FOR EXAMPLE, in *McClain*, this Court determined that the first **reason** that the prosecutor gave for striking a black juror—that the juror mistrusted the system and had been treated unfairly—<u>was not supported by the record</u>. *Id.* at 1222. Instead of saying that she mistrusted the system and had been treated badly, the juror stated that she did not trust the public defender and, although she initially believed that her son had been treated unfairly, she had changed her mind. *Id.* at 1221. IN ADDITION, this Court determined that there was <u>nothing in the record to support</u> the prosecutor's second **reason**, that the juror must have lied about being a stewardess because she was heavyset. *Id.* The juror did not state that she was a stewardess; what she said was that she worked in airline maintenance. *Id.* Because the <u>record did not support</u> the **reasons** that the prosecutor gave, this Court held that the **reasons** that the prosecutor gave were a pretext for discrimination. *Id.*

As in *McClain*, in this case <u>the record does not support</u> the **reasons** that the prosecutor gave for excusing Mr. Williams and Ms. Whitefish. Although the prosecutor stated that he excused Mr. Williams because Mr. Williams would not be able to focus on the case because he had "other obligations next week" (ER 125), Mr. Williams told the court that he was willing to miss his tribal council meeting should the trial be extended (ER 117). SIMILARLY, although the prosecutor stated that he excused Ms. Whitefish because her experiences at the border would make it difficult for her "to judge this case fairly and impartially" (ER 125), Ms. Whitefish's response to the prosecutor's question about whether she was bothered by the fact that she had been "pulled aside for additional questions" was the following: "Not particularly. I am a college student, and all of us have had similar experiences. They seem to stop young people more . . . ." (ER 119).

THUS, just as the *McClain* court held that the trial court erred when it concluded that the **reasons** that the prosecutor gave were not a pretext for discrimination, this Court should decide that the district court erred when it concluded that the prosecutor's **reasons** were not a pretext for discrimination. "When there is **reason** to believe that there is a racial motivation for the challenge, [this Court is not] bound to accept at face value a list of neutral **reasons** that are either <u>unsupported in the record</u> or refuted by it. Any other approach leaves *Batson* a dead letter." *Johnson v. Vasquez*, 3 F.3d 1327, 1331 (9th Cir. 1993).

§ 16.3.7 Avoiding the Common Problem of Not Dealing with Weaknesses

Another error that attorneys commonly make is that they do not deal with the "weaknesses" in their argument. Although this strategy might work occasionally, more often it does not. Even if the opposing party does not notice the problems, the court will.

Look again at the last example. The writer does not deal with an important weakness: Courts do not always find it a pretext for discrimination when a prosecutor gives a reason for excusing a juror, prospective jurors of different races provide similar responses, and one is excused while the other is not. By not confronting contrary authority, the attorney allows the other side to make the following argument.

EXAMPLE 1   **EXCERPT FROM APPELLEE'S BRIEF TAKING ADVANTAGE OF AN UNADDRESSED WEAKNESS**

Furthermore, case law does not support the notion that *Batson* is violated whenever prospective jurors of different races provide similar responses and one is excused while the other is not. *Burks v. Borg*, 27 F.3d 1424, 1429 (9th Cir. 1994). For example, in *Burks*, this Court held that there was not purposeful discrimination in spite of the fact that a minority juror who was struck shared characteristics with a nonminority juror who was not struck. *Id.* The prosecutor told the court that he had stricken the minority jurors "because they were 'squishy' on the death penalty, expressed a reluctance to serve, and/or lacked certain life experiences." *Id.* In concluding that there was no purposeful discrimination, the court reaffirmed that "[t]rial counsel is entitled to exercise his full professional judgment in pursuing his client's 'legitimate interest in using [peremptory] challenges . . . to secure a fair and impartial jury.'" *Id.* (quoting *J.E.B. v. Alabama ex rel. T.B.*, 511 U.S. 127, 137 (1994)). Thus, in using his or her peremptory challenges, trial counsel is entitled to take into account "tone, demeanor, facial expression, emphasis—all those factors that make the words uttered by the prospective juror convincing or not." *Burks*, 27 F.3d at 1429.

Instead of ignoring problems, the better strategy is to anticipate and respond to arguments that you know the other side will make. In Example 2, Ms. Elder anticipated the government's argument and included the following paragraph.

EXAMPLE 2   **EXCERPT FROM THE APPELLANT'S BRIEF ANTICIPATING OPPONENT'S ARGUMENT**

While in *United States v. Burks*, 27 F.3d 1424, 1429 (9th Cir. 1994), this Court concluded that the subjective reasons prosecutors gave for excusing minority jurors were not pretextual even though prospective jurors of different races provided similar responses and one was excused while the other was not. In doing so this Court made the following statement: "While subjective factors may play a legitimate role in the exercise of challenges, reliance on such factors alone cannot overcome strong objective indicia of discrimination such as a clear and sustained pattern of strikes against minority jurors." *United States v. Burks*, 27 F.3d 1424, 1429 (9th Cir. 1994).

---

§ 16.3.8 Avoiding the Mistake of Overlooking Good Arguments

Finally, sometimes attorneys become so enthusiastic about one argument that they overlook other persuasive arguments. For example, in *United States v. Josephy*, Ms. Elder's strongest arguments are that the prosecutor's reasons are not supported by the record and that a comparative analysis of the Native American jurors who were struck and white jurors who were not reveals that the prosecutor's reasons were a pretext for discrimination. However, Ms. Elder can also argue that a *Batson* violation occurred because the district court failed to do the required sensitive inquiry before ruling on the *Batson* objection.

EXAMPLE 1 **EXCERPT FROM THE APPELLANT'S BRIEF SHOWING AN ADDITIONAL ARGUMENT**

2. <u>In addition, the district court erred by not conducting the required sensitive inquiry and by not stating its reasoning on the record.</u>

A trial court commits reversible error if it fails to do the required "sensitive inquiry" of the defendant's *Batson* challenge or if the trial court's decision is made in haste or is imprecise. *Jordan v. Lefevre*, 206 F.3d 196, 198 (2d Cir. 2006). For example, in *Jordan* the trial judge attempted to save "an awful lot of time" by ruling on the defendant's *Batson* challenge without considering all of the facts and arguments and without setting out its analysis in the record. *Id.* at 199. As a result, the reviewing court concluded that the trial court had violated the defendant's right to equal protection by making a hasty decision and not stating on the record its analysis of why the reasons that the prosecutor gave for striking jurors were not a pretext for discrimination. *Id.*

As in *Jordan*, in this case the court made a hasty decision and did not state on the record why the reasons that the prosecutor gave were not a pretext for discrimination. In fact, the record consists of a single sentence: "Your objection is noted, Counsel, but the Court finds no purposeful discrimination here" (ER 126).

The "duty of assessing the credibility of the prosecutor's race-neutral reasons [embodies] the 'decisive question' in the *Batson* analysis." *Id.* at 200. Although the lack of a reasoned analysis does not seem to stem from a blatant impatience with the proceedings as it did in *Jordan*, the result and the violation are the same: This Court is left with a record devoid of the reasoned credibility analysis regarding each challenged juror that due process requires.

Because the district court's erroneous denial of Mr. Josephy's *Batson* challenge is presumed to be prejudicial, *see Gray*, 481 U.S. at 668, this Court should reverse and remand the case for a new trial.

Although adding the additional argument makes the brief a bit longer, in this instance including it was a good choice. Because both of her arguments are legally sound, Ms. Elder increases her chances of getting a reversal.

See section 6.4 for a checklist for critiquing the argument section.

CHAPTER

17

Finishing the Appellate Brief: Drafting the Final Sections and Revising, Editing, and Proofreading

§ 17.1 Drafting the Final Sections of the Brief

§ 17.1.1 Conclusion or Prayer for Relief

The final section of the brief is the conclusion or the prayer for relief. In most jurisdictions, this section is short. Unlike the conclusion in an objective memorandum, you do not summarize the arguments. Instead, simply set out the relief you are requesting. *See, e.g.*, Fed. R. App. P. 28(a)(10). For example, as the appellant you usually ask the court to reverse or reverse and remand, and if you are the respondent you usually ask the court to affirm or remand. Sometimes you will ask for a single type of relief; at other times you will ask for different types of relief for different errors or for alternative forms of relief. To determine what type of relief you can request, read cases that have decided the same or similar issues and look to see what type of relief the parties requested and what type of relief the court granted.

In *United States v. Josephy*, Ms. Elder wants the court to reverse or, in the alternative, to remand the case for a new trial. Although it is possible that the court would reverse and dismiss, holding that the ATF agents did not have probable cause to arrest Mr. Josephy, the court could also remand the case and leave the decision to the prosecutor as to whether the case is to be retried without the suppressed evidence. However, if the court reverses on the *Batson* issue, it would remand for a new trial. In contrast, the prosecution wants the appellate court to affirm the district court's decision.

EXAMPLE   **THE APPELLANT'S CONCLUSION**

The district court erred in denying Mr. Josephy's motion to suppress evidence obtained during a warrantless seizure unsupported by probable cause. Therefore, this Court should reverse his conviction.

In the alternative, the district court erred in denying Mr. Josephy's *Batson* challenge because the prosecution's reasons for striking the only two Native American jurors on the panel were a pretext for purposeful discrimination. Therefore, this Court should reverse his conviction and remand the case for a new trial.

---

§ 17.1.2 Preparing the Signature Block

Before submitting your brief to the court, you must sign it, listing your name and, in most jurisdictions, your bar number. The format typically used is as follows:

Dated: _____

Respectfully submitted,

_____
Name of attorney
Bar Number
Attorney for [Appellant or Respondent]
Address

§ 17.1.3 Preparing the Appendix

Most jurisdictions allow the parties to attach one or more appendices to their briefs. Such appendices should not be used to avoid the page limits. Instead, use appendices to set out information that a judge would find useful but that might not be readily available. For example, if you are arguing there was an instructional error, include a copy of the court's instructions to the jury. Likewise, if one of your issues requires the court to interpret the language in a particular statute or set of statutes, set out the text of the statute or statutes in an appendix.

Under Fed. R. App. P. 30(a)(1), an appendix containing specifically listed content is required. In contrast, under the Ninth Circuit local rules, an appendix need not be included, but excerpts of the record must be filed. Ninth Cir. R. 30-1.1(a).

§ 17.2 Revising, Editing, and Proofreading

It is impossible to state strongly enough the importance of revising, editing, and proofreading your brief. You do not want to waste a judge's time by making the judge read and reread a confusing sentence or by taking two pages to make a point that you could make in one page. In addition, you want the judges to focus on your arguments and not on grammar, punctuation, citation, or proofreading errors.

Because she wants to do the best that she can for her clients, Ms. Elder spends as much time revising, editing, and proofreading her brief as she does researching the issues and preparing the first draft. After completing the first draft, she sets it aside for a day or two while she works on other projects. When she comes back to the brief, she looks first at the arguments she has made, asking herself the following questions: Have I identified all of the issues? For each issue, have I made clear my position and what relief I am requesting? Have I provided the best support for each of my assertions? Have I included issues, arguments, or support that is unnecessary?

When she is happy with the content, Ms. Elder then rereads her brief, trying to read it as a judge would read it. Is the material presented in a logical order? Has she made clear the connections between arguments and parts of arguments? Is each argument, paragraph block, paragraph, and sentence easy to read and understand? At this stage, Ms. Elder also works more on writing persuasively. She checks to make sure that she has presented the rules, cases, and facts in a light favorable to her client and that she has used persuasive devices effectively.

Ms. Elder then tries to put the brief aside for at least a short period of time so that she can, once again, come back to it with "fresh eyes." This time, she works primarily on two things. She begins by looking at her writing style. Are there places where she could make her writing more eloquent? See Chapter 7 in *Just Writing, Fifth Edition*. She then goes back through the brief, revising for conciseness and precision and making sure that her writing is correct. See Chapters 7, 9, and 10 in *Just Writing, Fifth Edition*. In particular, she looks for the types of mistakes that she knows she has a tendency to make. Finally, she goes back through her brief, checking her citations and adding the page numbers to her table of contents and table of authorities.

Although this process is time-consuming, and thus expensive, Ms. Elder finds that the process pays off in a number of ways. First, and most important, she does a good job of representing her client. Because her briefs are well written, her clients get a fair hearing from the court. Second, because she has worked at it, through the years she has become both a better and a faster writer. Finally, she has protected and enhanced one of her most important assets: her reputation. Because her briefs are well written, judges tend to take them, and her, more seriously.

Sample Briefs

In this chapter we set out an appellant's brief and an appellee's brief.

§ 18.1 Appellant's Brief

EXAMPLE 1   **APPELLANT'S BRIEF**

No. 19-12345

UNITED STATES COURT OF APPEALS

FOR THE NINTH CIRCUIT

UNITED STATES OF AMERICA,

Plaintiff-Appellee,

v.

PETER JASON JOSEPHY,

Defendant-Appellant.

On Appeal from the United States District Court
for the Western District of Washington

APPELLANT'S OPENING BRIEF

Susan Elder
Federal Public Defender
Westlake Center Office Tower
1601 Fifth Avenue, Suite 700
Seattle, WA 98101
Tel: (206) 555-4321
Counsel for Appellant

TABLE OF CONTENTS

I.   STATEMENT OF JURISDICTION 1

II.   BAIL STATUS 1

III.   STATEMENT OF THE ISSUES 1

IV.   STATEMENT OF THE CASE 2

V.   STATEMENT OF THE FACTS 2

VI.   SUMMARY OF THE ARGUMENT 6

VII.   ARGUMENT 7

        A.   The ATF agents violated Mr. Josephy's Fourth
              Amendment rights because they did not have
              a particularized objective suspicion that
              Mr. Josephy was engaged in criminal activity. 7

              1.   The ATF agents did not have a particularized objective
                   suspicion that Mr. Josephy was engaged in criminal
                   activity because the tip came from an unknown
                   informant; although the informant gave the 911
                   operator a name, he refused to give his address or
                   phone number. 8

              2.   The ATF agents did not have a particularized objective
                   suspicion that Mr. Josephy was engaged in criminal
                   activity because the tip included only general physical
                   descriptions, it omitted any description of clothing,
                   and the only action it predicted was that Mr. Josephy
                   would be leaving a motel shortly before checkout time. 10

              3.   The ATF agents did not have a particularized objective
                   suspicion that Mr. Josephy was engaged in criminal
                   activity because the police corroborated only innocuous
                   details, for example, Mr. Josephy's physical appearance,
                   his vehicle, and his departure from a motel shortly
                   before checkout time. 13

B.   The district court erred in denying Mr. Josephy's *Batson* challenge because the prosecutor struck the only Native Americans in the jury pool, and the court's entire ruling consisted of a single sentence. 15

1.   The reasons the prosecutor gave for striking the only two Native Americans in the jury pool were a pretext for discrimination because they were not supported by the record and the prosecutor did not excuse white jurors who had similar obligations and experiences. 16

2.   In addition, the district court erred by not conducting the required sensitive inquiry and by not stating its reasoning on the record. 20

VIII.   CONCLUSION 22

STATEMENT OF RELATED CASES 23

TABLE OF AUTHORITIES

A. Table of Cases

Alabama v. White, 496 U.S. 325 (1990) 8, 13, 14, 15

Batson v. Kentucky, 476 U.S. 79 (1986) 1, 7, 15, 16, 20

Burks v. Borg, 27 F.3d 1424 (9th Cir. 1994) 20

Florida v. J.L., 529 U.S. 266 (2000) 8, 10, 11, 12

Flowers v. Mississippi, 139 S. Ct. 2228 (2019) 16

Georgia v. McCollum, 505 U.S. 42 (1992) 15

Gray v. Mississippi, 481 U.S. 648 (1987) 20, 21

Hernandez v. New York, 500 U.S. 352 (1991) 21

Johnson v. California, 545 U.S. 162 (2005) 16

Johnson v. Vasquez, 3 F.3d 1327 (9th Cir. 1993) 18

Jordan v. Lefevre, 206 F.3d 196 (2d Cir. 2000) 21

Illinois v. Gates, 462 U.S. 213 (1983) 8

McClain v. Prunty, 217 F.3d 1209 (9th Cir. 2000) 16, 17, 18

Miller-El v. Dretke, 125 U.S. 2317 (2005) 15

Ornelos v. United States, 517 U.S. 690 (1996) 8

Turner v. Marshall, 121 F.3d 1248 (9th Cir. 1997) 18

United States v. Alanis, 335 F.3d 965 (9th Cir. 2003) 20

United States v. Chinchilla, 874 F.2d 695 (9th Cir. 1989) 18, 19

United States v. Fernandez-Castillo, 324 F.3d 1114 (9th Cir. 2003) 8, 11, 12

United States v. Jimenez-Medina, 173 F.3d 752 (9th Cir. 1999) 8

United States v. Morales, 252 F.3d 1070 (9th Cir. 2001) 8

United States v. Terry-Crespo, 356 F.3d 1170 (9th Cir. 2004) 9, 10, 11

United States v. Thomas, 211 F.3d 1186 (9th Cir. 1999) 8

United States v. Vasquez-Lopez, 22 F.3d 900 (9th Cir. 1992) 16

United States v. Velazco-Durazo, 372 F. Supp. 2d 520 (D. Ariz. 2005) 15

United States v. You, 382 F.3d 958 (9th Cir. 2004) 18

Williams v. Runnels, 432 F.3d 1102 (9th Cir. 2006) 15

B. Constitutional Provisions

U.S. Const. amend. IV 8

U.S. Const. amend. XIV 15

C. Statutes

8 U.S.C. §3231 (2018) 1

21 U.S.C. §841(a)(1) (2018) 1, 2

28 U.S.C. §1291 (2018) 1

D. Rules

Fed. R. App. P. 4(b) 1

I. STATEMENT OF JURISDICTION

The appellant, Peter Jason Josephy, appeals his conviction and sentence on one count of unlawful possession of a controlled substance with the intent to deliver in violation of 21 U.S.C. §841(a)(1) (2018). The district court asserted jurisdiction pursuant to 8 U.S.C. §3231 (2018) and entered judgment and commitment on January 17, 2019 (CR 34; ER 205).[1] Mr. Josephy filed his notice of appeal on January 24, 2019, within the ten-day period set out in Fed. R. App. P. 4(b) (CR 35). Therefore, this Court has jurisdiction to review Mr. Josephy's final judgment pursuant to 28 U.S.C. §1291 (2018).

II. BAIL STATUS

Mr. Josephy is currently serving his seventy-seven-month sentence at the Bureau of Prisons' Washington Correctional Institution.

III. STATEMENT OF THE ISSUES

A. Did the district court err in concluding that a telephone tip created an objective particularized suspicion when the informant refused to give more than a name; the informant called from a public pay phone and gave only a general physical description of Mr. Josephy, Mr. Josephy's vehicle, and Mr. Josephy's location; and the police merely corroborated that Mr. Josephy left a motel shortly before checkout time?

B. Did the district court err in denying Mr. Josephy's *Batson* challenge when the prosecutor used his peremptory challenges to excuse both Mr. Williams and Ms. Whitefish, the only Native Americans in the jury pool and when, in denying the challenge, the trial judge's only statement was, "Your objection is noted, Counsel, but the Court finds no purposeful discrimination here"?

---

[1] "CR" refers to the Clerk's Record and will be followed by the entry number of the cited document as it appears in the district court docket sheet. "ER" refers to the Excerpts of Record.

1

IV. STATEMENT OF THE CASE

On June 25, 2019, Peter Jason Josephy was charged with one count of Unlawful Possession of a Controlled Substance with the Intent to Deliver under 21 U.S.C. §841(a)(1) (2018) (CR 7). After an evidentiary hearing, the district court denied Mr. Josephy's motion to suppress evidence obtained during a warrantless search (CR 26; ER 30).

The case proceeded to jury trial, the Honorable Alesha J. Moore presiding (CR 28). During voir dire, Mr. Josephy challenged the government's use of two of its peremptory challenges to excuse the only Native Americans on the jury panel (ER 123-24). The district court concluded that although Mr. Josephy had established a prima facie case of discrimination, the reasons given by the government were race neutral and that Mr. Josephy had not established purposeful discrimination (ER 124). Thus, the court denied Mr. Josephy's *Batson* challenge.

V. STATEMENT OF FACTS

<u>Motion to Suppress</u>

At 10:45 a.m. on June 25, 2019, Peter Josephy left his room at the Travel House Inn in Bellingham, Washington; checked out; and, after talking to a friend for three or four minutes, walked to his car and got in (ER 22, 43). As Mr. Josephy started his car, Agent Bhasin, an Alcohol, Tobacco, and Firearms (ATF) agent, pulled behind Mr. Josephy's car, and another ATF agent, Agent O'Brien, pulled in front. As a result, Mr. Josephy could not move his car (ER 44).

Agent Bhasin had gone to the Travel House Inn after receiving a phone call from a 911 operator who reported that she had received a call from a public pay telephone located in the Bellis Fair Mall, which is about a five-minute drive from the Travel House Inn (ER 30, 34). The informant claimed that a Mr. Josephy was at the Travel House Inn to sell drugs to a man named Oliver (ER 30). In addition, the informant told the 911 operator that, if the police wanted to catch Mr.

Josephy, they should go to the Travel House Inn soon because Mr. Josephy would be there for only another hour or two (ER 32-33).

When asked to describe Mr. Josephy, the informant told the 911 operator that Mr. Josephy was a Native American with black hair, that he was in his mid to late twenties, and that he was driving a blue Chevy Blazer (ER 32). When asked about Oliver's last name, the informant said that he did not know Oliver's last name. When pushed for a description, the informant told the 911 operator that Oliver was about six feet tall, that he had brown hair and a beard, and that he was in his thirties (ER 32).

The 911 operator then asked the informant for his name, address, and a phone number so that the police or ATF agents could recontact him. Although the informant told the 911 operator that his name was Zachary Dillon, he then became uncooperative and refused to give the 911 operator his address, his home telephone number, or a cell phone number (ER 32, 35).

Despite the fact that he was not able to find anyone by the name of Zachary Dillon in his databases, Agent Bhasin went to the Travel House Inn (ER 42). When he arrived at the motel, Agent Bhasin searched the parking lot and located a blue Chevy Blazer registered to Peter Jason Josephy (ER 42). After being told by the motel desk clerk that Mr. Josephy was a registered guest, Agent Bhasin returned to his car and requested a backup unit with a dog from the K-9 unit.

At about 10:40 a.m., Agent O'Brien arrived with his dog. However, before Agent O'Brien could walk the dog around Mr. Josephy's vehicle, Mr. Josephy left his motel room with another man, went into the office and paid his bill, and walked to his car (ER 43). As soon as Mr. Josephy got in his car and started it, Agent Bhasin pulled in front of Mr. Josephy's car, and Agent O'Brien pulled in behind. Blocked, Mr. Josephy could not move his car (ER 44).

After blocking Mr. Josephy's car, Agent Bhasin got out of his vehicle and approached the driver's side of Mr. Josephy's Blazer. When Agent Bhasin asked Mr. Josephy to step out of his vehicle, Mr. Josephy readily complied (ER 46). Mr. Josephy did, however, decline Agent Bhasin's request to search the vehicle (ER 46-47). In response, Agent O'Brien took his dog out of his car and walked the dog around the Blazer (ER 47). When the dog alerted to the smell of marijuana, Agent Bhasin arrested Mr. Josephy. During a search incident to the arrest, Agent Bhasin found marijuana in the wheel well (ER 49).

At the suppression hearing, the district court agreed with Mr. Josephy that a seizure occurred when the agents blocked Mr. Josephy's vehicle with their own vehicles (CR 26; ER 52). However, the district court denied the motion to suppress on the grounds that, at the time they blocked Mr. Josephy's car, the agents had a reasonable suspicion that Mr. Josephy was engaged in criminal activity (CR 26-27; ER 52).

Voir Dire

Mr. Josephy is a Native American (ER 124). The government used two of its peremptory challenges to remove the only Native Americans in the jury pool (ER 123-24).

At the beginning of voir dire, a Monday, the trial judge told the jurors that the trial was scheduled to last for two or three days and asked the members of the venire whether this schedule would create a hardship. Two jurors responded (ER 116). Juror No. 12, Mr. Williams, a Native American, told the judge that he had a tribal council meeting scheduled for the end of the week but that he could miss the meeting if necessary (ER 117). Juror No. 18, Mr. Woods, who is white, told the judge that he might have to leave town the following week because his mother was ill and in the hospital (ER 117-18).

4

Later, the prosecutor asked if anyone had ever had negative experiences with law enforcement personnel (ER 119). Ms. Whitefish, a Native American who was a junior majoring in history at Western Washington University, responded that each time she crossed the border she had been "pulled aside for additional questions" (ER 119). However, when the prosecutor asked Ms. Whitefish whether she was bothered by the fact that she had been pulled over for additional questions, she stated, "Not particularly. I am a college student, and all of us have had similar experiences. They seem to stop young people more . . . ." (ER 119-20).

Similarly, Mr. Martin, a white man with long hair, told the prosecutor that he had had a number of negative experiences with police officers (ER 120). For example, Mr. Martin told the prosecutor that on one occasion a police officer had stopped him because one of his taillights was out but that the police had not stopped other individuals who had one of their taillights out (ER 120). In addition, Mr. Martin told the prosecutor that on two occasions he had been given tickets for jaywalking when other individuals on the same street who had short hair jaywalked but did not get tickets (ER 120). When the prosecutor asked whether he was bothered by the police officers' actions, Mr. Martin said, "You bet I am." (ER 121).

At the end of voir dire, the government used two of its peremptory challenges to remove Mr. Williams and Ms. Whitefish (ER 122). Because the prosecutor used his peremptory challenges to remove both of the Native Americans in the jury pool, Mr. Josephy made a *Batson* challenge to the exclusion of the two jurors based on race (ER 123). Concluding that Mr. Josephy had established a prima facie case of discrimination, the judge asked the prosecutor to provide reasons for his strikes. The prosecutor stated that he struck Juror No. 5, Ms. Whitefish, because he believed that Ms. Whitefish would have difficulty being impartial given her personal experiences at the border, which could lead her to have negative feelings about law enforcement personnel in general. He said that he struck Mr. Williams because Mr. Williams would have difficulty focusing on the facts of the case given his meeting scheduled for the end of the week (ER 125).

Mr. Josephy responded, stating that the reasons provided were not neutral and "are only a mask for unconstitutional race . . . discrimination" (ER 125). The trial judge's only statement was, "Your objection is noted, Counsel, but the Court finds no purposeful discrimination here" (ER 126).

VI. SUMMARY OF THE ARGUMENT

Mr. Josephy's conviction should be reversed for two reasons: (1) his Fourth Amendment rights were violated when the district court failed to suppress evidence obtained by police from an investigative detention unsupported by a reasonable suspicion of criminal activity, and (2) his constitutional right to equal protection was violated because the reasons that the prosecutor gave for using his peremptory challenges to excuse the only Native Americans in the jury pool were a pretext for discrimination.

First, the district court erred in failing to suppress evidence obtained by police following an illegal seizure. At the time that the ATF agents seized Mr. Josephy by pulling their vehicles in front of and behind his vehicle, the only information that the agents had came from a telephone tip made from a public pay telephone at a mall. Although the informant gave a name, the tip should be treated as being from an anonymous source: The informant gave no other identifying information, he ensured he could not be located by calling 911 from a public pay telephone at a shopping mall, and the police were unable to locate anyone with that name in the greater Bellingham area. Because there was no way to assess the caller's reputation or hold him responsible if the tip turned out to be a fabrication, the tip was less reliable than a tip from a known informant.

The tip also lacked sufficient indicia of reliability because it contained only a general description of Mr. Josephy, his location, and his vehicle. Although such information helped the police locate the person the caller accused, it did not show that the caller had information about hidden criminal activity. Moreover, police observations did no more than corroborate innocuous details, such as the time Mr. Josephy would check out of a motel. Because the agents did not have a reasonable suspicion of criminal activity, the investigatory detention was unconstitutional, and all evidence obtained should have been suppressed.

Second, Mr. Josephy's constitutional right to equal protection was violated when the prosecutor used his peremptory challenges to remove the only Native Americans from the jury pool. The reasons that the prosecutor gave for striking the only two Native Americans in the jury pool were a pretext for discrimination both because the reasons are not supported by the record and because a comparative analysis shows that the prosecutor did not excuse white jurors who had similar obligations and experiences. In addition, the district court erred by not doing the "sensitive analysis required" under *Batson* and by not setting out its reasoning on the record. In fact, the trial judge's ruling on this crucial third step of the analysis consisted of only one statement: "Your objection is noted, Counsel, but the Court finds no purposeful discrimination here."

VII. ARGUMENT

A. The ATF agents violated Mr. Josephy's Fourth Amendment rights because they did not have a particularized objective suspicion that Mr. Josephy was engaged in criminal activity.

The district court erred in denying Mr. Josephy's motion to suppress because, at the time that the ATF agents seized Mr. Josephy, they did not have a particularized objective suspicion that Mr. Josephy was engaged in criminal activity. This Court reviews a district court's determination of reasonable suspicion *de novo*. *Ornelos v. United States*, 517 U.S. 690, 699 (1996); *United States v. Fernandez-Castillo*, 324 F.3d 1114, 1117 (9th Cir. 2003).

"The Fourth Amendment allows government officials to conduct an investigatory stop of a vehicle only upon a showing of reasonable suspicion: 'a particularized and objective basis for suspecting the particular person stopped of criminal activity.'" *United States v. Thomas*, 211 F.3d 1186, 1189 (9th Cir. 1999) (quoting *United States v. Jimenez-Medina*, 173 F.3d 752, 754 (9th Cir. 1999)); *see* U.S. Const. amend. IV. In determining whether the government officials had a reasonable suspicion, courts look at the totality of the circumstances, including whether the informant was a known or unknown informant; whether the tip included sufficient indicia of reliability; and whether the law enforcement officer verified, through an independent investigation, details other than innocuous details. *See, e.g., Alabama v. White*, 496 U.S. 325, 330 (1990); *Illinois v. Gates*, 462 U.S. 213, 238-40 (1983).

1. <u>The ATF agents did not have a particularized objective suspicion that Mr. Josephy was engaged in criminal activity because the tip came from an unknown informant; although the informant gave the 911 operator a name, he refused to give his address or phone number.</u>

Where an informant refuses to be identified, there is a risk the tip has been fabricated, undercutting its reliability. *Florida v. J.L.*, 529 U.S. 266, 269-70, 272 (2000). The unknown informant's reputation cannot be accessed, nor can the informant be held responsible for a false accusation. *Id.* This possibility that the informant might be lying outweighs the value of the information provided unless there are other factors that establish that the informant is reliable, for example, the informant provides law enforcement officers with information about the suspect's future actions, which law enforcement officers then independently verify. *United States v. Morales*, 252 F.3d 1070, 1075 (9th Cir. 2001).

In *United States v. Josephy*, the Court should treat the tip as a tip from an unknown informant. Although the informant gave the 911 operator a name, "Zachary Dillon," he called from a public pay phone in a large mall, and he refused to give the 911 operator his address or phone number (ER 32, 35). In addition, when Agent Bhasin tried to locate an individual by the name of Zachary Dillon in his databases, he was not able to find anyone by that name in the greater Bellingham area (ER 42). Consequently, neither Agent Bhasin nor any other law enforcement officer was able to contact Zachary Dillon to determine how he obtained the information that he gave to the 911 operator or to hold him accountable if the statements that he made turned out to be false.

Thus, the facts in this case can be distinguished from the facts in *United States v. Terry-Crespo*, 356 F.3d 1170, 1172 (9th Cir. 2004), a case in which this Court held that information provided by an individual who had called 911 to report that the defendant had threatened him with a firearm was sufficient to support a *Terry* stop even though the police were not able to locate anyone by the caller's name in their databases. Unlike the caller in *Terry-Crespo*, who was the victim of a crime, *id.* at 1177, in this case the informant, "Dillon," was not the victim of a crime. In addition, unlike the caller in *Terry-Crespo*, who made the call from the scene of the crime, *id.* at 1176, in this case, "Dillon" made the call from a mall five minutes from the motel where the drug buy was allegedly occurring. Finally, in *Terry-Crespo*, the caller did not give the 911 operator his phone number because he did not know the number of the cell phone that he had borrowed to make the emergency call, *id.* at 1172, but in this case, "Dillon" refused to give the operator his address, home phone number, or a cell phone number. Consequently, in *Terry-Crespo*, the facts supported the court's conclusion that the caller was not trying to hide his identity, but in this case the facts suggest just the opposite.

9

Thus, because "Dillon" appears to have taken steps to hide his identity, this Court should treat his tip as a tip from an unknown informant. However, even if this Court does not treat the tip as coming from an unknown informant, the tip is not reliable because it lacks sufficient indicia of reliability.

2. <u>The ATF agents did not have a particularized objective suspicion that Mr. Josephy was engaged in criminal activity because the tip included only general physical descriptions, it omitted any description of clothing, and the only action it predicted was that Mr. Josephy would be leaving a motel shortly before checkout time.</u>

A tip from an unknown informant that does no more than describe an individual's readily observable location and appearance does not have sufficient indicia of reliability to support a stop. *Florida v. J.L.*, 529 U.S. 266, 272 (2000). Although such a tip might help the police identify the person whom the informant means to accuse, such a tip does not establish that the informant has knowledge of concealed criminal activity. *Id.* at 272.

In the cases in which courts have held that the tip lacked sufficient indicia of reliability, the tip lacked predictive information and included only a general description of the defendant and his location, and the informant did not explain how he had acquired the information. *See, e.g., J.L.*, 529 U.S. at 272. For instance, in *J.L.*, an anonymous caller reported to police that "a young black male standing at a particular bus stop and wearing a plaid shirt was carrying a gun." *Id.* at 269. In concluding that this tip was not sufficient to establish a reasonable suspicion of criminal activity, the Court said that "[t]he anonymous call concerning J.L. provided no predictive information and therefore left the police without means to test the informant's knowledge or credibility." *Id.* at 270. The Court went on to say that the fact that the allegation about the gun turned out to be true did not establish a reasonable basis for suspecting J.L. of engaging in unlawful conduct:

> The reasonableness of official suspicion must be measured by what the officers knew before they conducted their search. All the police had to go on in this case was the bare report of an unknown, unaccountable informant who neither explained how he knew about the gun nor supplied any basis for believing he had inside information about J.L.

Id. at 271.

In contrast, in most of the cases in which courts have held that the tips had sufficient indicia of reliability to support a *Terry* stop, the callers were reporting what they had recently seen or experienced, *see, e.g., United States v. Terry-Crespo*, 356 F.3d 1170, 1172 (9th Cir. 2004), or the callers provided the police with not only details about the defendant and his or her current location but also information about what the defendant was about to do, *see, e.g., United States v. Fernandez-Castillo*, 324 F.3d 1114, 1119 (9th Cir. 2003). For example, in *Terry-Crespo*, this Court held that a 911 call contained sufficient indicia of reliability for four reasons: (1) the call was not anonymous because the caller provided the 911 operator with his name and the call was recorded; (2) the caller was the victim of a crime, and the police must be able to take seriously, and respond promptly to, emergency 911 calls; (3) the caller jeopardized any anonymity he might have had by calling 911 and providing his name to an operator during a recorded call; and (4) the caller was giving first-hand information about an event that had just occurred. *Terry-Crespo*, 356 F.3d at 1172-77. Similarly, in *Fernandez-Castillo*, the court held that a tip had sufficient reliability because it came from a Montana Department of Transportation (MDOT) employee and there are relatively few MDOT employees; the MDOT employee who reported the erratic driving not only provided the dispatcher with the make and model of the car but also told the dispatcher that the car had North Dakota license plates; the MDOT employee made the report almost immediately after he observed the defendant driving erratically; and the report contained predictive

11

information: that the car was driving eastbound near milepost 116. *Fernandez-Castillo*, 324 F.3d at 1119.

In the case before this Court, the tip lacked the required indicia of reliability. Like the informant in *J.L.*, who called from a borrowed cell phone and did not give the 911 operator either his own phone number or his own address, Dillon called from a public pay telephone and refused to give the operator his phone number or his address (ER 30). As a consequence, in both cases, law enforcement officers were not able to contact the informants to determine the basis for their allegations or to hold them accountable if the information that they provided turned out to be false.

More important, though, Dillon's tip lacked sufficient indicia of reliability because he failed to give a description of Josephy's clothing, he failed to provide information based on first-hand observation, and he failed to give specific predictive information. First, in *J.L.*, the caller told the operator that the defendant was wearing a plaid jacket; in this case, Dillon did not describe either Mr. Josephy's or Oliver's clothing (ER 32), which suggests that Dillon had not seen Mr. Josephy or Oliver on the day of the call. Second, unlike *Terry-Crespo* and *Fernandez-Castillo*, in which it was clear that the callers were providing first-hand information, in this case, there is nothing to suggest that Dillon's statements were based on his own observations. At no time during the call did Dillon tell the operator how he knew that Mr. Josephy was at the motel or why he believed that Mr. Josephy was involved in illegal activity (ER 30-35). Third, unlike *Fernandez-Castillo*, in which the caller provided the operator with specific predictive information about the defendant's location and direction of travel, in this case, Dillon provided the operator with only general information: that Mr. Josephy was going to leave the motel shortly before checkout time (ER 32-33). While predicting where a car will be at a given time provides evidence

12

that the tip is reliable, predicting that a guest will check out of a motel at check-out time does not.

Thus, under the totality of the circumstances, the tip did not have the required indicia of reliability and was not, therefore, sufficient to support a *Terry* stop unless the police independently verified more than innocuous details.

3. <u>The ATF agents did not have a particularized objective suspicion that Mr. Josephy was engaged in criminal activity because the police corroborated only innocuous details, for example, Mr. Josephy's physical appearance, his vehicle, and his departure from a motel shortly before checkout time.</u>

When a tip lacks the required indicia of reliability, the tip is not sufficient to support a *Terry* stop unless law enforcement officers independently corroborate more than innocuous details. *See Alabama v. White,* than 496 U.S. 325, 330 (1990). As the Court noted in *White,* when a tip has a relatively low degree of reliability, more information will be required to establish the requisite quantum of suspicion than would be required if the tip were more reliable. *Id.*

In *White,* the police received an anonymous tip in which the caller stated that "Vanessa White would be leaving 235-C Lynnwood Terrace Apartments at a particular time in a brown Plymouth station wagon with the right taillight lens broken, that she would be going to Dobey's Motel, and that she would be in possession of about an ounce of cocaine inside a brown brief case." *Id.* at 327. After receiving this tip, two police officers went to the Lynnwood Terrace Apartments, where they located a brown Plymouth station wagon with a broken right taillight in the parking lot in front of the 235 building. *Id.* As the police officers sat in their vehicle, they observed the defendant leave the 235 building, carrying nothing in her hands, and enter the station wagon. *Id.* The officers followed the vehicle as it drove the most direct route to Dobey's Motel. When the vehicle reached the Mobile Highway, on which Dobey's Motel is located, the officers had a patrol unit stop the vehicle. *Id.*

13

Even though the tip contained a number of details, the United States Supreme Court held that the tip was not, by itself, sufficient to justify a *Terry* stop. *White*, 496 U.S. at 329. According to the Court, it became reasonable to think that the information was reliable only after the police verified not only easily obtained facts but also future actions that are not easily predicted. *Id.* at 332.

> We think it also important that, as in *Gates,* "the anonymous [tip] contained a range of details relating not just to easily obtained facts and conditions existing at the time of the tip, but to future actions of third parties ordinarily not easily predicted." [462 U.S. at 245.] The fact that the officers found a car precisely matching the caller's description in front of the 235 building is an example of the former. Anyone could have "predicted" that fact because it was a condition presumably existing at the time of the call. What was important was the caller's ability to predict respondent's *future behavior,* because it demonstrated inside information—a special familiarity with respondent's affairs.

Id. (emphasis in original).

Although ultimately the Court concluded that the anonymous tip, as corroborated, was sufficient to justify the *Terry* stop, the Court labeled the case as a "close case." *Id.*

If *White* was a close case, this case is an easy case. First, in *White*, the informant provided the police with far more details than Dillon gave the 911 operator. For example, in *White*, the informant provided the police with the defendant's apartment number and the fact that the car had a broken taillight, but in this case Dillon did not provide anything more than the name of the motel and the make and model of the vehicle (ER 32). Second, in *White*, the informant provided the police with information about the defendant's future actions that only someone who had a special familiarity with the defendant could know, but in this case, Dillon only predicted that Mr. Josephy would leave the motel shortly before checkout time (ER 32-33). Finally, in *White*, the police

14

independently verified most of the information that the informant had provided, including the fact that the defendant would leave the apartment at a particular time and drive to a particular motel; in this case, the police did not verify anything more than Mr. Josephy owned a vehicle and that he left the motel at checkout time (ER 42-43).

Although in this case the *Terry* stop might have been justified if Dillon had told the 911 operator that Mr. Josephy would leave the motel and drive to a particular house or restaurant at a particular time, and the ATF agents had verified these facts through their own surveillance, those facts are not the facts of this case. Under the facts of this case, the stop was not justified for three reasons: (1) the tip was, for all practical purposes, an anonymous tip; (2) the tip did not contain sufficient indicia of reliability; and (3) the ATF agents were not able to verify, through their own independent investigation, facts that established a "particularized and objective basis" for suspecting Mr. Josephy of criminal wrongdoing. *See United States v. Velazco-Durazo*, 372 F. Supp. 2d 520, 528 (D. Ariz. 2005).

B. The district court erred in denying Mr. Josephy's *Batson* challenge because the prosecutor struck the only Native Americans in the jury and pool and because the court's entire ruling consisted of a single sentence.

For more than a century, the United States Supreme Court has "consistently and repeatedly . . . reaffirmed that racial discrimination by the State in jury selection offends the Equal Protection Clause." *Miller-El v. Dretke*, 125 U.S. 2317, 2324 (2005) (quoting *Georgia v. McCollum*, 505 U.S. 42 (1992)); *see also* U.S. Const. amend. XIV. Racial discrimination in jury selection denies defendants their right to a jury trial, denies jurors the right to participate in public life, and undermines public confidence in the fairness of our justice system. *Batson v. Kentucky*, 476 U.S. 79, 86-87 (1986); *Williams v. Runnels*, 432 F.3d

15

1102, 1108 (9th Cir. 2006). "In the eyes of the Constitution, one racially discriminatory peremptory strike is one too many." *Flowers v. Mississippi*, 139 S. Ct. 2228, 2241 (2019).

In *Batson*, the Court developed a three-step test to uncover discrimination masked by peremptory challenges. 476 U.S. at 96-97. Under the first step of the test, the defendant need only establish a prima facie case of purposeful discrimination by showing that the prosecutor has struck a member of a cognizable class and that the circumstances raise an inference of discrimination. *Id.* at 96. Once the defendant establishes a prima facie case, the burden shifts to the government: The government must provide a race-neutral explanation for striking a member of a cognizable class. *Id.* at 97. If the government does meet its burden, the court must do a sensitive analysis to determine whether the government has engaged in purposeful discrimination. *See Johnson v. California*, 545 U.S. 162, 169 (2005).

In this case, the district court's decision was clearly erroneous. *See Flowers v. Mississippi*, 139 S. Ct. 2228, 2266 (2019). First, the district court erred when it concluded that the reasons that the prosecutor gave were not a pretext for discrimination (ER 126). Second, the district court erred by not doing the "sensitive analysis required" under *Batson* and by not setting out its reasoning on the record (ER 126).

    1. <u>The reasons the prosecutor gave for striking the only Native Americans in the jury pool were a pretext for discrimination because they were not supported by the record and the prosecutor did not excuse white jurors who had similar obligations and experiences.</u>

When a prosecutor misstates the record in explaining a strike, that misstatement can be another clue showing discriminatory intent. *Flowers*, 139 S. Ct. at 2250. For example, in *McClain v. Prunty*, 217 F.3d 1209, 1221 (9th Cir. 2000), this Court determined that the first reason that the prosecutor gave for striking

16

a black juror, that the juror mistrusted the system and had been treated unfairly, was not supported by the record. *Id.* at 1222. Instead of saying that she mistrusted the system and had been treated badly, the juror stated that she did not trust the public defender and, although she initially believed that her son had been treated unfairly, she had changed her mind. *Id.* at 1221. In addition, this Court determined that there was nothing in the record to support the prosecutor's second reason, that the juror must have lied about being a stewardess because she was heavyset. *Id.* The juror did not state that she was a stewardess; what she said was that she worked in airline maintenance. *Id.* Because the record did not support the reasons that the prosecutor gave, this Court held that the reasons that the prosecutor gave were a pretext for discrimination. *Id.*

As in *McClain*, in this case, the record does not support the reasons that the prosecutor gave for excusing Mr. Williams and Ms. Whitefish. Although the prosecutor stated that he excused Mr. Williams because Mr. Williams would not be able to focus on the case because he had "other obligations next week" (ER 125), Mr. Williams told the court that he was willing to miss his tribal council meeting should the trial be extended (ER 117). Similarly, although the prosecutor stated that he excused Ms. Whitefish because her experiences at the border would make it difficult for her "to judge this case fairly and impartially" (ER 125), Ms. Whitefish's response to the prosecutor's question about whether she was bothered by the fact that she had been "pulled aside for additional questions" was the following: "Not particularly. I am a college student, and all of us have had similar experiences. They seem to stop young people more . . . ." (ER 119).

Thus, just as the *McClain* court held that the trial court erred when it concluded that the reasons that the prosecutor gave were not a pretext for discrimination, this Court should decide that the district court erred when it concluded that the

17

prosecutor's reasons were not a pretext for discrimination. "When there is reason to believe that there is a racial motivation for the challenge, [this Court is not] bound to accept at face value a list of neutral reasons that are either unsupported in the record or refuted by it. Any other approach leaves *Batson* a dead letter." *Johnson v. Vasquez*, 3 F.3d 1327, 1331 (9th Cir. 1993).

Moreover, the government cannot lawfully exercise peremptory challenges "against potential jurors of one race unless potential jurors of another race with comparable characteristics are also challenged." *United States v. You*, 382 F.3d 958, 969 (2004) (quoting *Turner v. Marshall*, 121 F.3d 1248, 1252 (9th Cir. 1997)). Accordingly, a "comparative analysis of jurors struck and those remaining is a well-established tool for exploring the possibility that facially race-neutral reasons are a pretext for discrimination." *McClain*, 217 F.3d at 1220-21.

Under this comparative analysis, a defendant meets his burden of proving the reason the prosecutor gave for striking a juror was a pretext for discrimination when the reason given applies equally to a juror of another race, but the prosecutor strikes only one of the jurors. *McClain v. Prunty*, 217 F.3d 1209, 1221 (9th Cir. 2000). For instance, in *McClain*, this Court concluded that the reason the prosecutor gave for striking a black juror was a pretext for discrimination when the reason given applied equally to a white juror, but the prosecutor did not strike the white juror. Although the prosecutor stated that he had struck a black juror because the juror lacked experience making decisions, the prosecutor did not strike a white juror who also lacked decision-making experience. *Id.* at 1221-22. As this Court stated, the fact that the prosecutor did not treat jurors of different races in the same way "fatally undermine[d] the credibility of the prosecutor's stated justification." *Id.* at 1222; *see also United States v. Chinchilla*, 874 F.2d 695 (9th Cir. 1989) (reversing a conviction because the

18

prosecutor's stated reason for striking a Hispanic juror—that the juror lived in La Mesa—applied equally to a juror who was not Hispanic and who was not struck).

In *United States v. Josephy*, the reason the prosecutor gave for striking Mr. Williams, a Native American, was a pretext for discrimination because the reason applied equally to Mr. Woods, who is white. In explaining why he struck Mr. Williams, the prosecutor said that Mr. Williams would have difficulty focusing on the facts of the case because he had a meeting scheduled for the end of the week (ER 125). However, the prosecutor did not strike Mr. Woods, who told the court that his mother was seriously ill and that he might have to go out of town (ER 117-18).

In addition, the reason that the prosecutor gave for striking Ms. Whitefish, a Native American, was a pretext for discrimination because the prosecutor did not strike a white juror who had had similar experiences with law enforcement personnel. When the judge asked the prosecutor why he had struck Ms. Whitefish, the prosecutor responded that he did not think Ms. Whitefish would be able "to judge this case fairly and impartially" based on her experiences crossing the border (ER 125). However, although Ms. Whitefish stated that she had been "pulled aside for additional questions" (ER 19), when asked whether this bothered her, Ms. Whitefish replied, "Not particularly. I am a college student, and all of us have had similar experiences. They seem to stop young people more . . . ." (ER 119).

In contrast, Mr. Martin believed he had been targeted by police officers because he had long hair (ER 120). He was stopped for having a taillight that was out; others were not. He was ticketed for jaywalking; others, who had short hair, were not (ER 119-20). When asked whether he was bothered by his experiences with police officers, he said, "You bet I am." (ER 121).

In some cases, courts have concluded that the subjective reasons prosecutors gave for excusing minority jurors were not pretextual even though prospective jurors of different races provided similar responses and one was excused but the other was not. *Burks v. Borg*, 27 F.3d 1424, 1429 (9th Cir. 1994). However, as this Court noted in *Burks,* "While subjective factors may play a legitimate role in the exercise of challenges, reliance on such factors alone cannot overcome strong objective indicia of discrimination such as a clear and sustained pattern of strikes against minority jurors." *Id.*

In our case, there are objective indicia of discrimination stemming from a clear and sustained pattern of strikes against minority jurors. The prosecutor used two of his peremptory challenges to strike the only two Native American potential jurors. He struck Mr. Williams, who said he had a meeting scheduled after the trial was expected to end, despite his expressed willingness to serve, even if it meant missing the meeting. He struck Ms. Whitefish based on her experiences at the border, even though Ms. Whitefish assured the Court that her experiences at the border did not bother her.

Because the prosecutor did not excuse white jurors who had similar experiences to the Native Americans whom he did strike, the district court erred in denying Mr. Josephy's *Batson* challenge. Such an erroneous denial is presumed to be prejudicial. *See Gray v. Mississippi*, 481 U.S. 648, 668 (1987). Therefore, this Court should reverse and remand the case for a new trial.

2. <u>In addition, the district court erred by not conducting the required sensitive inquiry and by not stating its reasoning on the record.</u>

A trial court commits an error if it fails to conduct "a sensitive inquiry into such circumstantial and direct evidence of intent as may be available," *Batson*, 476 U.S. at 93, or if it fails to show on the record that its decision was deliberate. *United States v. Alanis*, 335 F.3d 965, n.2 (9th Cir. 2003).

20

A trial court commits reversible error if it fails to do the required "sensitive inquiry" or if the trial court's decision is made in haste or is imprecise. *Jordan v. Lefevre*, 206 F.3d 196, 198 (2d Cir. 2006). In *Jordan*, the trial judge attempted to save "an awful lot of time" by ruling on the defendant's *Batson* challenge without considering all of the facts and arguments and without setting out its analysis in the record. *Id.* at 199. As a result, the reviewing court concluded that the trial court had violated the defendant's right to equal protection by making a hasty decision and not stating on the record its analysis of why the reasons that the prosecutor gave for striking jurors were not a pretext for discrimination. *Id.*

As in *Jordan*, in this case, the court made a hasty decision and did not state on the record its analysis of why the reasons that the prosecutor gave were not a pretext for discrimination. In fact, the record consists of a single sentence: "Your objection is noted, Counsel, but the Court finds no purposeful discrimination here" (ER 126).

The "duty of assessing the credibility of the prosecutor's race-neutral reasons [embodies] the 'decisive question' in the *Batson* analysis." *Jordan*, 206 F.3d at 200 (citing *Hernandez v. New York*, 500 U.S. 352, 365 (1991)). Although the lack of a reasoned analysis does not seem to stem from a blatant impatience with the proceedings as it did in *Jordan*, the result and the violation are the same: This Court is left with a record devoid of the reasoned credibility analysis regarding each challenged juror that due process requires.

Because the district court's erroneous denial of Mr. Josephy's *Batson* challenge is presumed to be prejudicial, *see Gray*, 481 U.S. at 668, this Court should reverse and remand the case for a new trial.

21

VIII. CONCLUSION

The district court erred in denying Mr. Josephy's motion to suppress evidence obtained during an investigatory stop unsupported by a reasonable suspicion of criminal activity. Therefore, this Court should reverse his conviction.

In the alternative, the district court erred in denying Mr. Josephy's *Batson* challenge because the prosecutor's reasons for striking the only Native Americans were a pretext for purposeful discrimination and because the district court failed to conduct the required sensitive inquiry or state its reasoning. Therefore, this Court should reverse his conviction and remand the case for a new trial.

Dated: _____

Respectfully submitted,

_____

Susan Elder
Federal Public Defender
Westlake Center Office Tower
1601 Fifth Avenue, Suite 700
Seattle, WA 98101

STATEMENT OF RELATED CASES

The appellant knows of no other related cases pending in this Court.

§ 18.2 Appellee's Brief

EXAMPLE 2   **APPELLEE'S BRIEF**

No. 19-12345

UNITED STATES COURT OF APPEALS

FOR THE NINTH CIRCUIT

UNITED STATES OF AMERICA,

Plaintiff-Appellee,

v.

PETER JASON JOSEPHY,

Defendant-Appellant.

On Appeal from the United States District Court
for the Western District of Washington

BRIEF OF APPELLEE

Andrew Froh
United States Attorney
Western District of Washington

James Jorgenson
Assistant United States
Attorney
700 Stewart Street
Seattle, WA 98101
Tel: (206) 555-1234
Counsel for Appellee

TABLE OF CONTENTS

I. STATEMENT OF JURISDICTION 1

II. STATEMENT OF THE ISSUES 1

III. STATEMENT OF THE CASE 1

IV. STATEMENT OF THE FACTS 1

V. SUMMARY OF THE ARGUMENT 5

VI. ARGUMENT 6

    A.   **The *Terry* stop was permissible because the ATF agents had a reasonable suspicion that Mr. Josephy was involved in criminal activity.** 6

    B.   **The district court properly exercised its discretion in overruling Mr. Josephy's *Batson* objection.** 12

        1.   Mr. Josephy has not met his burden of proving that the reasons that the prosecutor gave for the peremptory challenges were a pretext for purposeful discrimination. 13

        2.   The record establishes that the district court conducted the required sensitive inquiry because the court ensured that both parties had the opportunity to respond at each of the three steps of the *Batson* analysis. 16

VII. CONCLUSION 17

TABLE OF AUTHORITIES

A. Table of Cases

Alabama v. White, 496 U.S. 325 (1990) 8, 9, 10, 11

Batson v. Kentucky, 476 U.S. 79 (1986) 12

Burks v. Borg, 27 F.3d 1424 (9th Cir. 1994) 14, 15

Florida v. J.L., 529 U.S. 266 (2000) 7, 9, 10, 11

Flowers v. Mississippi, 139 S. Ct. 2228 (2019) 12

J.E.B. v. Alabama, 511 U.S. 127 (1994) 14

Johnson v. California, 545 U.S. 162 (2005) 12

Jordan v. Lefevre, 206 F.3d 196 (2d Cir. 2000) 16

McClain v. Prunty, 217 F.3d 1209 (9th Cir. 2000) 13

Miller-El v. Dretke, 545 U.S. 231 (2005) 12

United States v. Bauer, 84 F.3d 1549 (9th Cir. 1996) 12, 13

United States v. Fernandez-Castillo, 324 F.3d 1114 (9th Cir. 2003) 7

United States v. Terry-Crespo, 356 F.3d 1170 (9th Cir. 2004) 7, 8, 10

United States v. U.S. Gypsum Co., 333 U.S. 364 (1948) 13

I. STATEMENT OF JURISDICTION

The appellee agrees with the appellant's statement of jurisdiction.

II. STATEMENT OF THE ISSUES

A. Whether police had a reasonable articulable suspicion that Mr. Josephy was engaged in criminal activity when (1) Zachary Dillon called 911 to report that Mr. Josephy was in possession of drugs he planned to sell; (2) Mr. Dillon provided the 911 operator with descriptions of Mr. Josephy, Mr. Josephy's car, and Mr. Josephy's companion; (3) Mr. Dillon told the 911 operator that Mr. Josephy and his companion were at the Travel House Inn and that Mr. Josephy would soon leave the motel in a blue Chevy Blazer; and (4) ATF agents verified that the blue Blazer in the motel parking lot was registered to Mr. Josephy and observed men matching the descriptions Mr. Dillon had given leave the motel in the predicted time frame.

B. Whether Mr. Josephy failed to prove that the government engaged in purposeful discrimination when (1) the prosecutor excused a 21-year-old Native American juror who volunteered that she had experienced problems each time she had crossed from the United States into Canada and (2) the government excused both a Native American juror who told the judge that he had a tribal council meeting at the end of the week and a white juror who was worried about missing work.

III. STATEMENT OF THE CASE

The appellee agrees with the appellant's statement of the case.

IV. STATEMENT OF THE FACTS

Motion to Suppress

At about 9:30 a.m. on June 25, 2019, Zachary Dillon called 911 and reported that Peter Josephy was involved in selling drugs that had been brought into the

United States from Canada (ER 30). Two hours later, Alcohol, Tobacco, and Firearms (ATF) agents searched Mr. Josephy's vehicle and found four kilos of marijuana in the wheel well (ER 49).

During the 911 call, which was recorded, Mr. Dillon told the operator that Mr. Josephy was at the Travel House Inn to meet with and deliver marijuana to a man named Oliver (ER 30-31). Although Mr. Dillon declined to give the 911 operator his address or phone number, Mr. Dillon did tell the 911 operator that Mr. Josephy was a Native American, that Josephy had black hair, and that Josephy was in his mid to late twenties (ER 32). Mr. Dillon also told the operator that Mr. Josephy owned, and was driving, a blue Chevy Blazer (ER 32). Although Mr. Dillon did not know Oliver's last name, he described Oliver as being in his thirties, being about six feet tall, and having brown hair and a beard (ER 32). Finally, Mr. Dillon told the police not to wait too long because Mr. Josephy would be leaving the motel in the next hour or two (ER 33).

The 911 operator relayed the information from Mr. Dillon to Agent Bhasin, an ATF agent with more than ten years of service (ER 4). Not finding anyone by the name of Zachary Dillon in the ATF databases, Agent Bhasin drove to the Travel House Inn in an unmarked car to determine whether there was a blue Chevy Blazer in the parking lot (ER 35, 40). When he arrived at the motel at approximately 10:15 a.m., Agent Bhasin located a blue Chevy Blazer in the parking lot. When he ran the license plates, he learned that the Blazer was registered to Peter Jason Josephy (ER 42).

After confirming with the desk clerk not only that the blue Chevy Blazer in the parking lot was registered to Josephy but also that Josephy was a registered guest, Agent Bhasin called for backup and a K-9 unit (ER 43).

Agent O'Brien arrived with his dog in an unmarked car at about 10:40 a.m. (ER 43). However, before Agent O'Brien could walk his dog around the Blazer,

Agents Bhasin and O'Brien saw two men matching the descriptions of Josephy and Oliver come out of a motel room (ER 43). The man matching Oliver's description walked out of the parking lot (ER 44). The other man, who was later confirmed to be Peter Josephy, walked to the blue Blazer (ER 43).

Based on Dillon's tip and his own observations, Agent Bhasin believed Mr. Josephy had possession of a controlled substance with intent to deliver (ER 44). Therefore, when Mr. Josephy got into the Blazer and started the engine, Agent Bhasin pulled in front of Josephy's car, and Agent O'Brien pulled behind (ER 44). Although Josephy complied with Agent Bhasin's request to get out of the Blazer, Josephy refused the request for permission to search the Blazer. As a consequence, Agent O'Brien walked his dog around the Blazer (ER 46-7). After the dog alerted, Agent Bhasin arrested Mr. Josephy for possession of a controlled substance (ER 49). During a search incident to the arrest, Agent Bhasin found four kilos of marijuana in the wheel well (ER 49).

After a pretrial hearing, the district court denied Mr. Josephy's motion to suppress, concluding that the *Terry* stop was justified because Agent Bhasin had a reasonable suspicion that Mr. Josephy was engaged in criminal conduct (CR 26-27; ER 52).

<u>Voir Dire</u>

Out of a venire of twenty-four potential jurors, twelve jurors and one alternate were chosen by use of the Struck Jury Method (ER 130). After Judge Moore explained the selection process to the jurors (ER 113-15), she asked whether serving on the jury would create a hardship (ER 116). Juror No. 12, Mr. Williams, indicated that, although he could forgo attending a tribal council meeting scheduled for Thursday and Friday, he would prefer not to (ER 117). In addition, Juror No. 2, Mr. Feldman, told the judge that he was scheduled to go to Africa on the following Saturday and that his "boss would be unhappy if he did not finish some projects before he left" (ER 117). However, Mr. Feldman also told the judge that his boss would have to accept it if he was selected for the jury (ER 117). Finally, Juror No. 18, Mr. Woods, revealed that his mother had recently had a heart attack and that he was unsure whether he would have to go out of town the next week to attend to her (ER 117-18). None of these jurors were excused for cause (ER 118).

During voir dire, the prosecutor asked the members of the jury panel whether anyone had had a negative experience with a law enforcement officer (ER 119). Juror No. 5, a young Native American, responded that she had negative experiences each time she crossed the border between the United States and Canada (ER 119). Although Juror No. 5 stated that she was not bothered by her experiences at the border, she also stated that she had been pulled aside for additional questioning every time that she had crossed the border (ER 119).

In contrast, Juror No. 11, Mr. Martin, a white man in his forties with long hair, told the prosecutor that he had been stopped by the police on one occasion because he had a taillight out and on two other occasions because he was jay-walking (ER 120). Although Mr. Martin said that he was bothered by the fact that he had been stopped by the police, he also said he felt that police officers tended to stop people with long hair more often than people with short hair (ER 120).

After defense counsel questioned the jury, both the prosecutor and defense counsel were permitted to exercise their peremptory challenges (ER 122). The prosecutor excused Mr. Feldman, Ms. Whitefish, and Mr. Williams (ER 122).

At sidebar, defense counsel objected to the prosecutor's use of his peremptory challenges on the grounds that they were based on race, arguing that the prosecutor had excused Mr. Williams and Ms. Whitefish because they were Native Americans (ER 123). After a hearing outside the presence of the jury,

Judge Moore concluded that Mr. Josephy had established a prima facie case for racial discrimination and asked the prosecutor to explain why he had used his peremptory challenges to excuse Mr. Williams and Ms. Whitefish (ER 124). The prosecutor explained that he excused both Mr. Feldman and Mr. Williams because he thought they would be unable to keep their minds on the case because of their other obligations—namely, Feldman's trip to Africa and Williams's tribal council meeting (ER 125). The prosecutor then explained that he had excused Ms. Whitefish because her experiences at the border would make it difficult for her to remain impartial (ER 125).

The judge ruled that these explanations were race neutral and that Josephy had not met his burden of proving that the reasons that the prosecutor had given were a pretext for discrimination (ER 125). Thus, based on these facts and explanations, Judge Moore overruled the *Batson* objection (ER 126).

V. SUMMARY OF THE ARGUMENT

Mr. Josephy's conviction should be affirmed: The district court correctly concluded that the evidence obtained during an investigatory stop was admissible because Agent Bhasin had a reasonable suspicion that Mr. Josephy was involved in criminal activity, and the district court properly exercised its discretion in finding that Mr. Josephy did not meet his burden of establishing that the reasons that the prosecutor gave for using two of his peremptory challenges to excuse Mr. Williams and Ms. Whitefish were a pretext for discrimination.

First, the district court correctly concluded that, under the totality of the circumstances, the *Terry* stop was permissible because Agent Bhasin had a reasonable suspicion that Mr. Josephy was engaged in criminal activity. The informant, Zachary Dillon, gave the 911 operator his name; Mr. Dillon's 911 call was recorded and transcribed; Mr. Dillon provided the 911 operator not only with a description of Mr. Josephy, Mr. Josephy's car, and Mr. Josephy's companion but also with the name of the motel where Mr. Josephy was staying; Mr. Dillon

predicted when Mr. Josephy would leave the motel; and Agent Bhasin verified

that Mr. Josephy was staying at the motel, that the vehicle found in the parking

lot was registered to Mr. Josephy, and that men matching the descriptions given

by Mr. Dillon left the motel during the time frame that Mr. Dillon had predicted.

Second, the district court properly exercised its discretion in denying Mr.

Josephy's *Batson* objection based on a finding that Mr. Josephy failed to meet

his burden of showing discrimination in the prosecutor's use of peremptory chal-

lenges. Peremptory challenges are an important trial tool that permits both par-

ties' counsel to use their professional judgment and educated hunches about

individual jurors to ensure a fair and impartial jury. As a result, a *Batson* violation

is not established whenever prospective jurors of different races provide similar

responses and one is excused but the other is not. Thus, in this case, the district

court correctly found that the prosecutor's reasons for exercising peremptory

challenges were not a pretext for discrimination. The prosecutor excused one

juror because he was concerned that the juror would be distracted by his outside

obligations, and the prosecutor excused the second juror because he was con-

cerned that the juror's negative experiences when crossing the border would

affect her ability to judge the government's case fairly. In addition, the district

court did the required analysis, and the record supports its conclusion that no

Batson violation occurred. The court allowed Mr. Josephy to present his prima

facie case and then asked the prosecutor to explain his reasons for excusing

the jurors before stating that Mr. Josephy had not met his burden of proof.

VI. ARGUMENT

**A. The *Terry* stop was permissible because the ATF agents had a reason-
able suspicion that Mr. Josephy was involved in criminal activity.**

Both the United States Supreme Court and this Court have repeatedly held that law enforcement officers have the authority to conduct an investigatory stop anytime they have a reasonable suspicion that a suspect is engaged in criminal activity. *See, e.g., Florida v. J.L.*, 529 U.S. 266, 272 (2000); *United States v. Fernandez-Castillo*, 324 F.3d 1114, 1119 (9th Cir. 2003). In addition, both the United States Supreme Court and this Court have repeatedly held that evidence obtained during a permissible *Terry* stop is admissible. *J.L.*, 529 U.S. at 272; *Fernandez-Castillo*, 324 F.3d at 1119.

In determining whether a *Terry* stop was permissible, courts do a *de novo* review, looking at the totality of the circumstances and considering all relevant factors, including those factors that "in a different context, might be entirely innocuous." *Florida v. J.L.*, 529 U.S. at 277-78; *accord United States v. Terry-Crespo*, 356 F.3d 1170, 1172 (9th Cir. 2004). For example, in *Terry-Crespo*, this Court held that the informant's preliminary phone call was, by itself, sufficient to establish a reasonable suspicion that the defendant, Terry-Crespo, was engaged in criminal activity. *Id.* at 1172. In doing so, this Court rejected Terry-Crespo's argument that the informant, Mr. Domingis, should be treated as an anonymous informant because he was not able to provide the 911 operator with the number of the phone from which he placed the call; he changed the subject when the operator asked him to provide another number; and, when asked for his location, he gave the operator a nonexistent intersection. *Id.* at 1174-75. As this Court stated in its opinion:

> During the course of the 911 call, the operator asked Mr. Domingis for his telephone number. Mr. Domingis explained that he did not know the return number because he was calling from someone else's cellular telephone. When the operator asked if there was another number where she could reach him, he did not answer her question but returned to discussing the subject of the suspect's location. The operator asked Mr. Domingis for his location. Initially, he responded by providing a nonexistent intersection on Portland's grid system and then stammeringly told

the operator that "I don't want . . . . I don't want . . . . I don't want . . . ." While not certain, it appears that Mr. Domingis did not want police contact.

Id. at 1172.

The Court then went on to note that, although the police tried to locate Mr. Domingis in a number of different databases, including the Yahoo! databases, they were not able to locate anyone by that name. *Id.* However, the Court concluded that the tip had sufficient indicia of reliability because Mr. Domingis was reporting that he had just been the victim of a crime and because Mr. Domingis risked any anonymity that he might have enjoyed by giving the 911 operator his name during a recorded call. *Id.* at 1174-76. As the Court stated, "Merely calling 911 and having a recorded telephone conversation risks the possibility that the police could trace the call or identify Mr. Domingis by his voice." *Id.* at 1176. Thus, even though the police did not independently verify any of the information contained in the tip, this Court held that, under the totality of the circumstances, the tip was sufficient to support a finding that Terry-Crespo was engaged in criminal activity. *Id.* at 1177.

Similarly, in *Alabama v. White*, 496 U.S. 325, 330 (1990), the United States Supreme Court held that the police had a reasonable suspicion that the defendant, White, was engaged in criminal activity. In *White*, an anonymous caller phoned 911 and told the operator that Vanessa White would be leaving the Lynnwood Terrace Apartments at a particular time in a brown Plymouth station wagon with a broken taillight to go to Dobey's Motel. *Id.* at 327. In addition, the caller told the 911 operator that White would have about "an ounce of cocaine inside a brown brief case." *Id.* Although the two police officers who went to the apartment complex saw White get into a brown Plymouth station wagon with a broken taillight, they did not see anything in White's hands. *Id.* Moreover, although White appeared to be driving to Dobey's Motel, the officers had a patrol unit stop the vehicle before it reached the motel. *Id.* The Court held that the officers had a reasonable suspicion despite failing to verify White's predicted destination. *Id.* at 330.

In considering the totality of the circumstances, this Court noted that "the anonymous [tip] contained a range of details relating not just to easily obtained facts and conditions existing at the time of the tip, but to future actions of third parties ordinarily not easily predicted." As this Court stated:

> The general public would have had no way of knowing that respondent would shortly leave the building, get in the described car, and drive the most direct route to Dobey's Motel. Because only a small number of people are generally privy to an individual's itinerary, it is reasonable for police to believe that a person with access to such information is likely to also have access to reliable information about that individual's illegal activities. See *ibid.* When significant aspects of the caller's predictions were verified, there was reason to believe not only that the caller was honest but also that he was well informed, at least well enough to justify the stop.

Id. at 332.

In contrast, in *Florida v. J.L.,* the Court held that the officers did not have a reasonable suspicion that the defendant, a minor, was engaged in criminal activity. *Id.* at 271. In *J.L.*, the only information the officers had at the time they stopped J.L. was a tip from an anonymous caller reporting that a "young black male standing at a particular bus stop and wearing a plaid shirt was carrying a gun." *Id.* at 269. Two officers were dispatched to the bus stop and, when they arrived, they saw three black males, one of whom was wearing a plaid shirt. *Id.* The officers did not, however, see a firearm, and J.L. made no threatening or otherwise unusual movements. *Id.* In concluding that, under the totality of the circumstances, the officers did not have a reasonable suspicion that J.L. was involved in criminal conduct, the Court considered three factors: (1) that the tip came from an individual who did not give his name; (2) that the call

9

was not recorded; and (3) that the call did not contain any predictive information that would have allowed the police "to test the informant's knowledge or credibility." *Id.* at 270-72.

In contrast, in this case, under the totality of the circumstances, Agent Bhasin had a reasonable suspicion that Mr. Josephy was engaged in criminal activity.

First, like the caller in *Terry-Crespo*, in this case, the caller gave the 911 operator his name: Zachary Dillon (ER 30). Although the ATF agents were not able to locate anyone by that name in their databases (ER 42), the same was true in *Terry-Crespo*, and in *Terry-Crespo*, this Court concluded that a tip was not turned into an anonymous tip simply because the police officers were unable to find anyone by the informant's name in their databases.

Second, like the 911 call in *Terry-Crespo*, in this case, the 911 call was recorded and transcribed (ER 30). As a result, there is no risk that the tip was manufactured after the fact. *See id.* at 1175. In addition, the fact that Mr. Dillon gave his name in a recorded call subjected Mr. Dillon to the risk that the police could locate him and that, if he had provided false information, he would be subjected to criminal sanctions.

Third, like the caller in *White*, in this case, Mr. Dillon provided the 911 operator with a number of details. For example, Mr. Dillon provided the operator not only with a physical description of Josephy, but also with a physical description of the man Josephy was meeting (ER 32). Moreover, Mr. Dillon gave the operator the make, model, and color of Josephy's car and the name of the motel where Mr. Josephy was staying (ER 30, 32). Although there may be a number of individuals who could provide the police with a description of a particular individual and his car, only a small number of people are generally privy to an individual's itinerary.

Fourth, as in *White*, in which the caller predicted that White would be leaving the apartment complex at a particular time, in this case, Mr. Dillon predicted that Josephy would be leaving the motel within an hour or two (ER 33). That the time frame that Mr. Dillon provided coincides with the standard checkout time is not dispositive. Many motel guests check out long before the established checkout time, and many guests stay more than one night.

Finally, in this case, the ATF agents verified all of the information that Mr. Dillon provided. As a consequence, the facts in this case are stronger than the facts in *Terry-Crespo*, in which the officers did not independently verify any of the information in the tip, and they are stronger than the facts in *White*, in which the officers did not see White carrying a brown brief case and did not verify that she was in fact going to the motel.

Taken together, these factors establish that, under the totality of the circumstances, the tip was far more reliable than the tip in *J.L.*, in which the caller did not give his name, provided the police with only a general description of J.L., and did not provide the police with any predictive information. In fact, these factors establish that, under the totality of the circumstances, the tip is even more reliable than the tip in *Terry-Crespo*. In *Terry-Crespo*, Mr. Domingis reported that Terry-Crespo assaulted him, but the police did not independently verify this fact or any of the other information contained in the tip, and Mr. Domingis appears to have tried to hide from the police by changing the topic when asked for his phone number, by giving a nonexistent intersection as his location, and by making statements that suggested that he did not want the police to contact him. *Id.* at 1172.

Because the totality of the circumstances establish that Agent Bhasin had a reasonable suspicion to believe that Mr. Josephy was engaged in criminal

11

activity, the stop was permissible and the Court should affirm the district court's denial of Mr. Josephy's motion to suppress.

B. The district court properly exercised its discretion in overruling Mr. Josephy's *Batson* objection.

Peremptory challenges are an important trial tool that permits both parties' counsel to use their professional judgment and educated hunches about individual jurors to select a fair and impartial jury. *United States v. Bauer*, 84 F.3d 1549, 1555 (9th Cir. 1996). While the Supreme Court has acknowledged difficulties in balancing the need to protect constitutional rights with the proper use of peremptory challenges, the Court has not indicated a willingness to deprive the parties of their right to use peremptory challenges. *See Miller-El v. Dretke*, 545 U.S. 231, 239-40 (2005). Indeed, Justice Breyer's concurrence, in which he posited that the Court should reconsider the *Batson* test and the peremptory system as a whole, failed to garner a single co-signer. *Id.* at 266-67 (Breyer, J. concurring).

Thus, courts continue to apply the three-step test set out in *Batson*. 476 U.S. at 89, 96-98. Under the test, a defendant's rights are not violated unless (1) the defendant establishes a prima facie case of purposeful discrimination in the government's use of peremptory challenges by showing that the challenged juror is a member of a cognizable class and that the circumstances raise an inference of discrimination; and (2) the government fails to meet its burden to provide a race-neutral explanation for its strike; or (3) the government offers a race-neutral reason, but the defendant meets his burden of showing that a review of all relevant circumstances shows purposeful discrimination. *See Johnson v. California*, 545 U.S. 162, 169 (2005); *Batson v. Kentucky*, 476 U.S. 79, 89, 96-98 (1986). "[A] trial court's ruling on the issue of discriminatory intent must be sustained unless it is clearly erroneous." *Flowers v. Mississippi*, 139 S. Ct. 2244, 2262 (2019).

In the case before the Court, Mr. Josephy has not argued that the district court erred in deciding that the reasons the prosecutor gave for exercising the peremptory challenges were not facially neutral. Thus, the only issues before this Court are whether the district court properly concluded that Mr. Josephy had not met his burden of proving that the reasons the prosecutor gave for exercising the peremptory challenges were a pretext for discrimination and whether the record is adequate.

1. <u>Mr. Josephy has not met his burden of proving that the reasons that the prosecutor gave for the peremptory challenges were a pretext for purposeful discrimination.</u>

In reviewing the third step in the *Batson* analysis, appellate courts give great deference to the trial court's determination and reverse a trial court only when the appellate court has a "definite and firm conviction" that a mistake has been made. *United States v. U.S. Gypsum Co.*, 333 U.S. 364, 395 (1948); *Bauer*, 84 F.3d 1555. While such a mistake occurs when the record contradicts the prosecutor's stated reasoning, *see, e.g., McClain v. Prunty*, 217 F.3d 1209, 1220-21 (9th Cir. 2000), in this case, there is no such contradiction.

United States v. Josephy stands in stark contrast to *McClain*, where a review of the record revealed a clear contradiction in objectively verifiable facts. *Id.* In *McClain*, the first reason the prosecutor gave for excusing a black juror was that the juror had stated that she mistrusted the system and had been treated unfairly. *Id.* at 1221. In fact, what the juror said was that *her son* did not trust the public defender and that, although she initially believed that her son had been treated unfairly, this was no longer true. *Id.* In addition, the record contradicted the second reason the prosecutor gave for striking the juror. *Id.* Although the prosecutor stated that he was excusing the juror because she had lied about being a stewardess because she was heavyset, the juror had actually said she worked in airline maintenance. *Id.*

13

In contrast, in *United States v. Josephy*, the record supports the reasons that the prosecutor gave for excusing Mr. Williams and Ms. Whitefish. When asked why he had excused Mr. Williams, the prosecutor stated that he was concerned that, because Mr. Williams had a tribal council meeting scheduled for the end of the week, Mr. Williams might be distracted (ER 125). The record supports this explanation: Mr. Williams told the court that although he could forgo attending a tribal council meeting scheduled for the end of the week, he would prefer not to (ER 117). Similarly, the prosecutor excused Ms. Whitefish because the prosecutor believed she would be unable "to judge this case fairly and impartially" based on her prior experiences crossing the border (ER 125). The record supports the prosecutor's reason: Ms. Whitefish acknowledged that she had been subjected to additional questioning at the border (ER 119).

Furthermore, case law does not support the notion that *Batson* is violated whenever prospective jurors of different races provide similar responses and one is excused but the other is not. *Burks v. Borg*, 27 F.3d 1424, 1429 (9th Cir. 1994). For example, in *Burks*, this Court held that there was not purposeful discrimination in spite of the fact that a minority juror who was struck shared characteristics with a nonminority juror who was not struck. *Id.* The prosecutor told the court that he had stricken the minority jurors "because they were 'squishy' on the death penalty, expressed a reluctance to serve, and/or lacked certain life experiences." *Id.* In concluding that there was no purposeful discrimination, this Court reaffirmed that "[t]rial counsel is entitled to exercise his full professional judgment in pursuing his client's 'legitimate interest in using [peremptory] challenges . . . to secure a fair and impartial jury.'" *Id.* (quoting *J.E.B. v. Alabama*, 511 U.S. 127 (1994)). Thus, in using his or her peremptory challenges, trial counsel is entitled to take into account "tone, demeanor, facial

expression, emphasis—all those factors that make the words uttered by the prospective juror convincing or not." *Burks*, 27 F.3d at 1429.

In this case, such a comparison supports the district court's decision that
there was no purposeful discrimination. For example, in response to the trial
judge's question regarding other obligations, three jurors answered that they
had conflicts the following week, and all stated a willingness to still serve on
the jury (ER 117-18). The prosecutor used two of his peremptory challenges
against the two jurors who already had definite plans—one had a tribal council
meeting and the other was going to Africa (ER 117). In addition, the prosecutor
provided the same neutral reason for both strikes—that the jurors would be too
distracted to tend to the business of the jury (ER 125). Therefore, the prosecutor
acted consistently: He struck the two jurors who had definite plans for the following week, and he did not strike the one whose plans were not definite. Finally, in
making his decision, the prosecutor was allowed to consider factors that are difficult to discern from a paper record, for example, the demeanor of each of the
potential jurors.

Likewise, the district court did not err in concluding that the prosecutor had
not engaged in purposeful discrimination when he excused Ms. Whitefish but
not Mr. Martin. Although both Ms. Whitefish and Mr. Martin volunteered that
they had negative experiences with law enforcement personnel, there may
have been other factors that influenced the prosecutor in his decision about
how to use his peremptory challenges. For example, the prosecutor may have
taken into consideration Ms. Whitefish's young age or limited set of experiences.
Because this type of judgment call is not based on race, it falls well within the
purpose behind peremptory challenges of providing a "useful instrument for
molding a more impartial jury." *See Burks*, 27 F.3d at 1429.

15

2. <u>The record establishes that the district court conducted the required sensitive inquiry because the court ensured that both parties had the opportunity to respond at each of the three steps of the *Batson* analysis.</u>

Mr. Josephy's reliance on *Jordan v. Lefevre*, 206 F.3d 196, 198 (2d Cir. 2000), is misplaced: In this case, the district court did the required analysis, and the record is sufficient.

In *Jordan*, the defendant objected to the prosecutor's use of his peremptory challenges to strike several black jurors. *Id.* at 199. However, before the defendant could even make his prima facie case, the court cut him short "in order to save us an awful lot of time." *Id.* Instead, the trial court immediately asked the prosecutor for a "non-racial reason for exercising the challenges," prefacing the request with a statement that "I don't think it's necessary or required." *Id.*

The prosecutor gave neutral reasons, and the trial court summarily overruled the defendant's objection, stating only, "[T]o the extent there is any application [on] the *Batson*, I'm denying it. It seems to me there is some rational basis for the exercise of the challenge." *Id.* When defense counsel later tried to create a record, the trial judge told him, "You've already made your record." *Id.* When defense counsel made a second objection, arguing that "the record is not complete," the judge replied, "Do it very succinctly, because I'm not going to be spending more time in here listening to you." *Id.* Given this specific set of facts, the Court of Appeals agreed with the defendant that "the district court's conclusory statement that the prosecutor's explanations were race neutral did not satisfy *Batson*'s third step." *Id.* at 200.

In contrast, in this case, the district court allowed Mr. Josephy to present his prima facie case and then asked the prosecutor to explain why he had excused Mr. Williams and why he had excused Ms. Whitefish (ER 123-24). It was not until after the prosecutor had set out his reason that the district court judge stated that Mr. Josephy had not met his burden of proof (ER 125-26). Therefore, in this case,

16

the district court did the required analysis, and the record supports its conclusion.

VII. CONCLUSION

For the reasons set out above, the Government respectfully requests that the Court of Appeals affirm the district court. The district court properly denied the motion to suppress because the investigatory stop was supported by a reasonable suspicion that Mr. Josephy was involved in drug trafficking. In addition, the district court properly overruled the *Batson* objection because it properly found that Mr. Josephy failed to meet his burden of proving purposeful discrimination.

Dated: _____   Respectfully submitted,

_____

Andrew Froh
United States Attorney
Western District of Washington
James Jorgenson
Assistant United States Attorney
700 Stewart Street
Seattle, WA 98101
Tel: (206) 555-1234
Counsel for Appellee

Oral Advocacy

Oral argument. For some, it is the part of practice they most enjoy; for others, it is the part they most dread.

Whichever group you fall into, oral argument is probably not what you expect. It is not a speech, a debate, or a performance. Instead, when done right, it is a dialogue between the attorneys and the judges. The attorneys explain the issues, facts, and law, and the judges ask questions, not because they want to badger the attorney or because they want to see how much he or she knows, but because they want to make the right decision.

Preparing and Presenting an Effective Oral Argument

§ 19.1 Audience

In making an oral argument, who is your audience? At the trial court level, the audience is the trial judge who is hearing the motion; at the appellate level, it is the panel of judges hearing the appeal. In both instances, the audience is extremely sophisticated. Although an eloquent oral argument is more persuasive than an oral argument that is not eloquent, form seldom wins out over substance. If you do not have anything to say, it does not matter how well you say it.

At oral argument, the court can be either "hot" or "cold." The court is hot when the judges come prepared to the oral argument. The judges have studied the briefs and, at least in some appellate courts, have met in a pre–oral argument conference to discuss the case. In contrast, a cold court is not as prepared. The judge or judges are not familiar with the case, and if they have read the briefs, they have done so only quickly.

As a general rule, hot courts are more active than cold courts. Because they have studied the briefs, they often have their own agenda. They want to know more about point A, or they are concerned about how the rule being advocated might be applied in other cases. As a consequence, they often take more control over the argument, directing counsel to discuss certain issues and asking a number of questions. A cold court is usually comparatively passive. Because the judges are not as familiar with the case, most of their questions are informational. They want counsel to clarify the issue, supply a fact, or explain in more detail how the law should be applied.

§ 19.2 Purpose

In making your oral argument, you have two goals: to educate and to persuade. You want to explain the law and the facts in such a way that the court rules in your client's favor.

§ 19.3 Preparing for Oral Argument

The key to a good oral argument is preparation. You must know what you must argue to win; you must know the facts of your case and the applicable constitutional provisions, statutes, regulations, and cases; and you must have practiced both the text of your argument and your responses to the questions the court can reasonably be expected to ask.

§ 19.3.1 Deciding What to Argue

In making your argument, you will have only a limited amount of time. Depending on the case and the court, you will be granted ten, fifteen, or thirty minutes to make your points; answer the judge or judges' questions; and, if you are the appellant, to make your rebuttal. Because time is so limited, you will not be able to make every argument that you made in your brief. You must be selective.

> **PRACTICE POINTER** In selecting the issues and arguments that you will make, choose those that are essential to your case. Do not spend your time on the easy argument if, to get the relief you want, you must win on the hard one. Make the arguments that you must make in order to win.

Also anticipate the arguments that the other side is likely to make. Although you do not want to make the other side's arguments, try to integrate your responses into your argument. Similarly, anticipate the court's concerns and decide how they can best be handled.

§ 19.3.2 Preparing an Outline

Do not write out your argument. If you do, you will either read it or, perhaps worse yet, memorize and recite it. Neither is appropriate. A dialogue does not have a predetermined text. Instead, prepare either a list of the points you want to cover or create an outline.

Because it is difficult to predict how much of the oral argument time will be spent answering the court's questions, many advocates prepare two lists or outlines: a short version, in which they list only those points that they must make, and a long version, in which they list the points they would like to make if they have time. If the court is hot and asks a number of questions, they argue from the short list or outline; if the court is cold, they use the long one.

§ 19.3.3 Practicing the Argument

The next step is to practice, both by yourself and with colleagues. Working alone, practice your opening, your closing, your statements of the law, and the arguments themselves. Think carefully about the language you will use and about how you will move from one issue to the next and, within an issue, from argument to argument. Also list every question that you could reasonably expect a judge to ask and decide (1) how you will respond and (2) how you can move from the answer to another point in your argument.

Then, with colleagues, practice delivering the argument. Ask your colleagues to play the role of the judge, sometimes asking almost no questions and at other times asking many. As you deliver the argument, concentrate on "reading" the court, adjusting your argument to meet its concerns. You should also focus on responding to questions and on the transitions between issues and arguments. Before a major argument, you will want to go through your argument five to ten times, practicing in front of as many different people as you can.

§ 19.3.4 Reviewing the Facts and the Law

You will also want to review the facts of the case, the law, and both your brief and your opponent's brief. When you walk into the courtroom, you should know everything there is to know about your case.

| PRACTICE POINTER | In practice, months might pass between the writing of the brief and the oral argument. When this is the case, it is essential that you update your research, and, when appropriate, file a supplemental brief with the court. |

§ 19.3.5 Organizing Your Materials

Part of the preparation is getting your materials organized. You do not want to be flipping through your notes or searching the record during oral argument.

a. Notes or Outline

To avoid the "flipping-pages syndrome," limit yourself to two pages of notes: a one-page short list or outline, and a one-page long list or outline, which you can staple to the inside of a manila folder. Use colored markers to highlight the key portions of the argument.

b. The Briefs

You will want to take a copy of your brief and your opponent's brief with you to the podium, placing them on the inside shelf. Make sure that you know both what is in the briefs and where that information is located.

c. The Record

In arguing an appeal, you will usually want to have the relevant portions of the record in the courtroom, either on the podium shelf or on counsel table. You should also be fully familiar with the record, as with the briefs, knowing both what is in the record and where particular information can be found. Many attorneys tab the record or prepare a quick index so that they can locate information quickly.

d. The Law

Although you do not need to have copies of all of the law with you, you should be familiar with the constitutional provisions, statutes, regulations, cases, and court rules you cited in your brief and those on which your opponent's case is based. If you do bring cases with you, have them indexed and highlighted for quick reference.

§ 19.4 Courtroom Procedures and Etiquette

Like much of law, oral argument has its own set of conventions and procedures.

§ 19.4.1 Seating

In many jurisdictions, the moving party sits on the left (when facing the court) and the responding party sits on the right.

§ 19.4.2 Before the Case Is Called

If court is not in session, sit at counsel table, reviewing your notes or quietly conversing with co-counsel. If court is in session, sit in the audience until the prior case is completed. When your case is called, rise and move to counsel table.

§ 19.4.3 Courtroom Etiquette

Stand each time you are instructed to do so by the bailiff. For example, stand when the bailiff calls court into session and announces the judge or judges, and stand when court is recessed or adjourned. In the first instance, remain standing until the judges are seated, and in the latter instance, remain standing until the judges have left the courtroom.

Also stand each time you address the court, whether it be to tell the court that you are ready to proceed, to make your argument, or to respond to a question.

In addressing the court, you will want to use the phrases "Your Honor," "Your Honors," "this Court," "the Court," or, occasionally, the judge's name—for example, "Judge Brown" or "Justice Smith." Never use a judge's or justice's first name.

> **PRACTICE POINTER** The title judge or justice can vary depending on your jurisdiction and on whether you are in an intermediate court or the jurisdiction's highest court. Make sure that you are using the correct title to address the members of the bench.

Finally, during the argument, do not speak directly to opposing counsel. Instead, address all of your statements to the court. Also remember that you are always "on." While opposing counsel is arguing, sit attentively at counsel table, listening and, if appropriate, taking notes.

§ 19.4.4 Appropriate Dress

As a sign of respect, both for the court and the client, most attorneys wear suits. Men wear conservative suits and ties, and women wear suit coats and matching pants or skirts. The key is to look professional but not severe. During oral argument, the judge's attention should be focused on your argument, not on your attire.

§ 19.5 Making the Argument

Like the brief, the oral argument has a prescribed format. The following example sets out the typical outline for an oral argument.

| EXAMPLE 1 | **OUTLINE OF ORAL ARGUMENT** |

A. *Moving party* (party bringing the motion or, on appeal, the appellant)
1. Introductions
2. Opening
3. Statement of the issue(s)
4. Brief summary of the significant facts (when appropriate)
5. Argument
6. Conclusion and request for relief
B. *Responding party* (party opposing the motion or, on appeal, the respondent or appellee)
1. Introductions
2. Opening
3. Statement of position
4. Brief summary of significant facts (when appropriate)
5. Argument
6. Conclusion and request for relief
C. *Moving party's rebuttal*
D. *Sur-rebuttal* (when allowed)

§ 19.5.1 Introductions

Begin your oral argument by introducing yourself and your client. At the trial court level, the language is relatively informal. Most attorneys say, "Good morning, Your Honor," and then introduce themselves and the client. At the appellate level, the language is more formal. By convention, most attorneys begin by saying, "May it please the Court, my name is _____, and I represent the [appellant] [respondent], _____."

| PRACTICE POINTER | In many courts, the introduction is also used to reserve rebuttal time. The attorney for the moving party reserves rebuttal either before introducing himself or herself or immediately afterwards: |

"Your Honor, at this time, I would like to reserve _____ minutes for rebuttal." If you do not reserve rebuttal time, the court might not allow you to present a rebuttal.

§ 19.5.2 Opening

The first minute of your argument should be memorable. The opening sentences should catch the judge's attention, making the case's importance clear, establishing the theme, and creating the appropriate context for the argument that follows.

§ 19.5.3 Statement of the Issues

a. The Moving Party

If you are the moving party, you need to set out the issues. Sometimes this is best done as part of the opening. From the issue statement alone, the case's importance is clear: "In this case, the appellant asks the Court to overrule *Roe v. Wade*." At other times, such a strategy is not effective. For example, few trial judges would find the following opening memorable: "In this case, the defendant asks the court to suppress identification testimony." In such cases, the opening and the statement of the issues should not be combined.

As a general rule, the statement of the issues should precede the summary of the facts. Before hearing the facts, the court needs a context. There are times, however, when it is more effective to set out the issues after the summary of the facts.

Whenever they are presented, the issue statements must be tailored to oral argument. What is effective in writing might not be effective when spoken. For example, although the under-does-when format works well in a brief, it does not work well orally. In oral argument, the issue needs to be presented more simply: "In this case, the court is asked to decide whether . . ." or "This case presents two issues: first, whether . . . and second, whether . . . ." An issue statement can be even stronger if it is stated as a positive assertion, much like an argumentative heading: "This court should reverse because Mr. Josephy's constitutional rights were violated by the admission of evidence obtained from an unlawful search and by the prosecutor's purposeful discrimination in the use of its peremptory challenges to remove Native Americans from the jury. The search was unlawful because . . . ."

Even though they are streamlined, the issues should be presented in the light most favorable to the client. The questions should be framed as they were in the brief, and the significant and emotionally favorable facts should be included. See sections 5.1.3 and 13.2.3.

b. The Responding Party

As a general rule, the responding party does not restate the issue or issues. Instead, it states its position, either as part of its opening or as a lead-in to its arguments: "The trial court did not err in denying Mr. Josephy's motion to suppress because the officers had a particularized objective suspicion that the defendant was engaged in criminal activity."

§ 19.5.4 Summary of the Facts

a. The Moving Party

When arguing to a cold court, you will want to spend one to three minutes on a summary of the facts, telling the court what the case is about. You might also want to include a summary of the facts when arguing to a hot court. If the facts are particularly important, you will want to summarize them, refresh the court's memory, and present the facts in the light most favorable to the client. There will, however, be times when a separate summary of the facts is not the best use of limited time. In those instances, instead of presenting the facts in a separate summary at the beginning, integrate them into the argument.

b. The Responding Party

As the responding party, you do not want to use your time repeating what opposing counsel just said. Consequently, for you a summary of the facts is optional even if the court is cold. If opposing counsel has set out the facts accurately, the summary can be omitted. Just integrate the significant facts into the argument. You will, however, want to include a summary if opposing counsel has misstated key facts or has omitted facts that are important to your argument, or if you need to present the facts from your client's point of view.

> **PRACTICE POINTER** In presenting the facts, you will not, as a matter of course, include references to the record. You must, however, be able to provide such references if asked to do so by the court or if you are correcting a misstatement made by opposing counsel.

§ 19.5.5 The Argument

Unless the issues and arguments build on each other, start with your strongest issue and, in discussing that issue, start with your strongest argument. This allows you to take advantage of the positions of emphasis and ensures that you will have the opportunity to make your best, or most crucial, arguments. In addition, it usually results in better continuity. Because the moving party's strongest issue is usually the responding party's weakest, the moving party's final issue will often be the responding party's first, providing the responding party with an easy opening for his or her argument.

Moving Party	Responding Party
Issue 1 → Issue 2	Issue 2 → Issue 1

In presenting the arguments, do what you did in your brief but in abbreviated form. If you are the moving party, begin by stating the rule, presenting that rule in the light most favorable to your client (see sections 6.3.3 and 16.3.1). Then argue that rule, explaining why the court should reach the result that you advocate. If you are the responding party, do not repeat the rule unless your opponent has misstated the rule or you are arguing for a different rule. Instead, use your time to make your own affirmative arguments and to counter the arguments that your opponent has made.

In both instances, you must support your assertions. You can do so by making plain language arguments, by arguing legislative intent, by using analogous cases, or by making policy arguments. When appropriate, cite to the relevant portions of a statute or to a common law rule and, when using analogous cases, be specific: Explain the rule that the court applied, the significant facts, and the court's reasoning. Although you should have the full case citations available, you do not need to include them in your argument. A reference to the case name is usually sufficient.

Although you want to cite to the relevant authorities, you do not, as a general rule, want to quote them or your own brief. Reading more than a line is seldom effective. If it is important that the court have specific language before it, refer the judge or judges to the appropriate page in the brief or, better yet, prepare a visual aid.

There are several other things that you need to keep in mind in making your argument. First, it is usually more difficult to follow an oral argument than a written one. As a result, it is important to include sufficient roadmaps, signposts, and transitions. Make both the structure of your argument and the connections between ideas explicit.

Second, you need to manage your time. Do not spend so much time on one issue or argument that you do not have time for the other issues or other arguments. Because it is difficult to predict how many questions the court will ask, practice both a short version and a long version of each argument.

Finally, remember that your goal is to persuade the judge to rule in your client's favor. Consequently, do not avoid the "hard" arguments. If you think that the judge already agrees with you on a point, move to your next point.

§ 19.5.6 Answering Questions

You should welcome the court's questions. They tell you what the court is thinking about your case, what the judges understand, and what they still question. If you are not getting questions, it is usually a bad sign. The judges have either already made up their minds or are not listening.

Questions from the bench fall into several categories. Some are mere requests for information. The judge wants to clarify a fact or your position on an issue, or wants to know more about the rule or how you think it should be applied.

Other questions are designed to elicit a particular response from you. For example, at the appellate level, Judge A might agree with your position and want you to pursue a particular line of argument for the benefit of Judge B, who is not yet persuaded. Still other questions are designed to test the merits of your argument. These questions may have as their focus your case or, at the appellate level, future cases. If the court applies rule A to your case, what does that mean for cases X, Y, and Z?

Whatever the type of question, when the judge begins to speak, you must stop. Although judges can interrupt you, you should not interrupt them. As the judge speaks, listen—not only to the question that is being asked, but also for clues about how the judge is perceiving the case.

The hardest part comes next. Before answering the judge, think through your answer. Although the second or two of silence might make you uncomfortable, the penalty for answering too quickly can be severe. Although few cases are won at oral argument, some are lost, usually because in answering a question an attorney concedes or asserts too much. The second or two of silence is by far better than an unfavorable ruling.

When you know what you want to say, answer. In most instances, you will want to begin by giving the judge a one-, two-, or three-word answer. "Yes." "No." "Yes, but, . . ." "No, but, . . ." or "In some cases, ..." Then explain or support your answer. In doing so, try to integrate key points from your list of bullet points or from your outline. Instead of thinking of questions as interruptions, think of them as another vehicle for making your argument.

There are a number of things that you should not do in responding to a question. First, do not tell the judge that you will answer the question later. It is you, not the judge, who must be flexible.

Second, do not argue with the judge. Answer all questions calmly and thoughtfully. Do not raise your voice, and even if you are frustrated, do not let it show. If one line of argument is not working and the point is essential to your case, try another, and if that line does not work, try still another. When the point is not important or you have given all the answers you have, answer, and then, without pausing, move as smoothly as you can into the next part of your argument.

Third, after answering the question, do not stop and wait for the judge's approval or permission to continue. Answer the question, and then, unless asked another question, move to the next part of your argument.

Finally, do not answer by asking the judge a question. In oral argument, it is inappropriate to question a judge.

§ 19.5.7 The Closing

The closing is as important as the opening. Because it is a position of emphasis, you want to end on a favorable point.

One way of doing this is to end with a summary of your arguments, reminding the court of your strongest points and requesting the appropriate relief. Although this is often effective, it can also be ineffective. Many judges stop listening when they hear the phrase "In conclusion" or "In summary." Consequently, when using a summary, avoid stock openers. Catch the court's attention by repeating a key phrase, weaving the pieces together, or returning to the points made in your opening.

Another way is to end on a strong point. If you are running out of time, it might be better to stop at the end of an argument or after answering a question than to rush through a prepared closing. Like a good comedian, a good advocate knows when to sit down.

§ 19.5.8 Rebuttal

Perhaps the hardest part of the oral argument is rebuttal. In one or two minutes you must identify the crucial issues and make your strongest argument or response.

If you try to make too many points in rebuttal, you dilute the power of each. Therefore, as a general rule, do not try to make more than one or two points. The points should be selected because of their importance to your case: Do not merely repeat what you said in the main portion of your argument or respond to trivial points made by opposing counsel. Instead, make your rebuttal a true rebuttal by responding to significant points made by opposing counsel or questions or concerns raised by the court during opposing counsel's argument.

Because time is so limited, most advocates begin their rebuttal by telling the court how many points they plan to make: "I would like to make two points." This introduction tells the court what to expect. The advocate then makes his or her first point and supports it and, unless interrupted by a question, moves to the second point. Most advocates close by quickly repeating their request for relief.

§ 19.6 Delivering the Argument

Every advocate has his or her own style. While some are soft-spoken, others are more theatrical; while some are plain-speaking, others strive for eloquence. As an advocate, you will need to develop your own style, building on your strengths and minimizing your weaknesses. Whatever your style, there are certain "rules" that you should follow.

§ 19.6.1 Breathe

Before you start speaking, take a deep breath. The breath will allow you to clear your mind, focus, and control your nerves. In addition, if at some point during your argument you lose your place or become flustered, look down at the podium and breathe.

§ 19.6.2 Do Not Read Your Argument

The first, and perhaps most important, rule is not to read your argument. Similarly, do not try to deliver a memorized speech. Know what you want to say and then talk to the court. You are a teacher, sharing information and answering the court's questions.

§ 19.6.3 Maintain Eye Contact

If you do not read, you will be able to maintain eye contact with the judge. This is important for several reasons. First, it helps you keep the judge's attention. It is very difficult not to listen to a person who is looking you in the eye. Second, it helps you "read" the court. By studying the judges, you can often determine (1) whether they already agree with you on a point and you can move to the next part of your argument, (2) whether they are confused, or (3) whether you have not yet persuaded them. Finally, eye contact is important because of what it says about you and your argument. An advocate who looks the judge in the eye is perceived as being more confident and more competent than one who does not.

> **PRACTICE POINTER** When you are arguing to an appellate court, maintain eye contact with all of the judges, even when you are answering a specific judge's question.

§ 19.6.4 Do Not Slouch, Rock, or Put Your Hands in Your Pockets

In delivering an oral argument to the court, stand erect, but not stiffly, behind the podium. Do not rock from foot to foot, and do not put your hands in your pockets.

Although it might be appropriate to move around the courtroom when arguing to a jury, you should not do so when arguing to the court.

§ 19.6.5 Limit Your Gestures and Avoid Distracting Mannerisms

Gestures are appropriate in an oral argument. They should, however, be natural and relatively constrained. If you talk with your hands, mentally put yourself inside a small telephone booth.

You also want to avoid distracting mannerisms. Do not play with a pen, the edge of your notes, or the keys in your pocket. In addition, do not repeatedly move hair out of your eyes or push your glasses back up on your nose.

§ 19.6.6 Speak So That You Can Be Easily Understood

In delivering your oral argument, speak loudly and clearly enough that you can be easily heard by the judges.

Also try to modulate your voice, varying both the pace and volume of your speech. If you want to emphasize a point, speak more slowly and either more softly or more loudly.

§ 19.7 Making Your Argument Persuasive

In delivering your oral argument, you will want to use many of the same techniques that you used in writing your brief. In stating the issue, frame the question so that it suggests the answer favorable to your client and, in presenting the facts, emphasize the favorable facts by placing them in positions of emphasis and by using detail and sentence structure to your advantage. Also, present the law in the light most favorable to your client. State favorable rules broadly, use cases to your advantage, and emphasize the policies that support your client's position.

You should also pick your words carefully. Select words both for their denotation and their connotation, and avoid words and phrases that undermine the persuasiveness of your argument. If you represent the defendant, do not say, "It is the defendant's position that the officers violated the defendant's Fourth Amendment rights when they searched his car." Instead, say, "The officers violated the defendant's Fourth Amendment rights when they searched his car." Similarly, do not say, "We feel that the State engaged in purposeful discrimination when it used its peremptory challenges to excuse the only two Native Americans in the jury pool." Instead, say, "The State engaged in purposeful discrimination when it used its peremptory challenges to excuse the only two Native Americans in the jury pool."

§ 19.8 Handling the Problems

Because an oral argument is not scripted, you need to prepare for the unexpected and decide in advance how you will handle the problems that might arise.

§ 19.8.1 Counsel Has Misstated Facts or Law

If opposing counsel misstates an important fact or the governing law, you will usually want to bring the error to the attention of the court. You should, however, use care in correcting opposing counsel.

First, make sure you are right. If there is time, double-check the record, the statute, or the case. Second, make sure you are correcting a misstatement of fact or law, not the opposing party's interpretation of a fact, statute, or case. Third, correct the mistake, not opposing counsel. Instead of criticizing or attacking opposing counsel, simply provide the court with the correct information and, if possible, the citation to the record or the language of the statute or case.

EXAMPLE   **CORRECTING A STATEMENT MADE BY OPPOSING COUNSEL**

"Ms. Martinez did not see the assailant three times. She testified that she saw him twice: once when he drove by slowly and then when he pulled in front of her."

Finally, correct only those errors that are significant.

§ 19.8.2 You Make a Mistake

If you make a significant mistake, correct it as soon as you can.

§ 19.8.3 You Do Not Have Enough Time

Despite the best planning, you will sometimes run out of time. You might have gotten more questions than you expected, leaving you little or no remaining time for your last issue or your final points. When this happens, you have two options. You can either quickly summarize the points that you would have made, or you can tell the court that, because you are out of time, you will rely on your brief for the issues and arguments that you did not cover.

What you do not want to do is exceed the time that you have been allotted. Unless the court gives you permission to continue, you must stop when your time is up.

§ 19.8.4 You Have Too Much Time

Having too much time is not a problem. You do not need to use all of your allotted time. When you have said what you need to say, thank the court and sit down.

§ 19.8.5 You Do Not Know the Answer to a Question

Occasionally, you will be asked a question that you cannot answer. If it is a question about the facts of your case or about the law, do not try to bluff. Instead, do one of the following: (1) if you can do so in a few seconds, look up the answer; (2) tell the judge that at this point you cannot answer the question but that you will be glad to provide the information after oral argument; or (3) give the best answer you can.

EXAMPLE   **STATEMENTS THAT YOU CAN MAKE WHEN YOU DO NOT KNOW THE ANSWER**

"So that I can answer correctly, let me quickly check the record."

"I'm not sure what the actual words were. I will check and provide you with that information after oral argument."

"As I recall, the police officer testified that he asked the question twice."

If the question raises an issue that you have not considered, the options are slightly different. You can either trust yourself and, on the spot, give your best answer or you can tell the court that you need to give the question some thought.

§ 19.8.6 You Do Not Understand a Question

If you do not understand a question, tell the judge and either ask him or her to repeat the question, or repeat the question in your own words, asking the judge whether you understood correctly: "I'm sorry, I'm not sure that I understand your question. Could you please rephrase it?" "If I am correct, you are asking whether . . . ."

§ 19.8.7 You Become Flustered or Draw a Blank

It happens, at some time or another, to almost everyone. You become flustered or draw a blank. When this happens, "buy" a few seconds by either taking a drink of water or taking a deep breath and looking down at your notes. If you still cannot continue with the point you were making, move to another one.

§ 19.8.8 You Are Asked to Concede a Point

Concessions can work both to your advantage and to your disadvantage. You will win points by conceding points that you cannot win or that are not important to your argument. You can, however, lose your case if you concede too much. Therefore, before you walk into court, decide what you can and cannot concede, concede when appropriate, and otherwise politely but firmly stand your ground. If the court presses for a concession, you can try to move the court past the issue: "Assuming, *arguendo,* that this Court decides that the trial court erred, the error was harmless because . . . ."

§ 19.9 A Final Note

No matter how much they dread it initially, most individuals end up enjoy-ing oral argument for what it is, a stimulating dialogue among intelligent people.

§ 19.10 Checklist for Critiquing the Oral Argument

I. *Preparation*

- The advocate has anticipated and prepared rebuttals for the arguments the other side is likely to make.
- The advocate has anticipated and prepared responses to the questions the court is likely to ask.
- The advocate knows the law and the facts of the case.
- The advocate has determined what arguments he or she needs to make to win.
- The advocate has determined what points he or she can, or can-not, concede.
- The advocate has prepared two outlines: a long outline, which can be used if the court asks only a few questions, and a short outline, which can be used in case the court asks more questions.

II. *Content and Organization*

A. *Introduction*

- The advocate identifies himself or herself and the client.
- When appropriate, the advocate requests rebuttal time.

B. *Opening and Statement of Issues or Position*

- The advocate begins the argument with a sentence or phrase that catches the attention of the court and establishes the cli-ent's theory of the case.
- The advocate then presents the question or states his or her position.
- The question or statement of position is framed so that it sup-ports the advocate's theory of the case and suggests an answer favorable to the client.
- The question or statement of position is presented using lan-guage that is easily understood.

C. *Summary of Facts*

- When appropriate, the advocate includes a short summary of the facts in which he or she explains the case and establishes an appropriate context. When a separate summary of the facts is not appropriate, the advocate weaves the facts into the argument.
- The facts are presented accurately but in the light most favorable to the client. The positions of emphasis and detail are used effectively, and words have been selected for both their denotation and their connotation.

D. *Argument*

- The advocate discusses the issues and makes the arguments needed to win.
- The argument is structured in such a way that it is easy to follow: (1) issues and arguments are discussed in a logical order; and (2) sufficient roadmaps, signposts, and transitions are used.
- The arguments are supported. The advocate uses the law, analogous cases, policy, and the facts to support each of his or her assertions.
- The law, analogous cases, policies, and facts are presented accurately.
- The law, analogous cases, policies, and facts are presented in the light most favorable to the client.

E. *Questions from the Bench*

- When a judge asks a question, the advocate immediately stops talking and listens to the question.
- The advocate thinks before answering.
- As a general rule, the advocate begins his or her answer with a short response ("Yes," "No," "In this case") and then supports that answer.
- After answering the question, the advocate moves back into his or her argument without pausing or waiting for the judge to give permission to continue.
- The advocate sees questions not as an interruption, but as another opportunity to get his or her argument before the court.
- As he or she listens to the questions, the advocate adjusts the argument to match the concerns and interests of the court.

F. *Closing*

- The advocate ends the argument by summarizing the main points or on a strong point.
- When appropriate, the advocate includes a request for relief.

G. *Rebuttal*

- The advocate uses rebuttal to respond to the one or two most important points raised by opposing counsel or the court.

III. *Delivery*

- The advocate treats the argument as a dialogue; he or she does not read or recite the argument.
- The advocate maintains eye contact with all of the judges.
- The advocate has good posture, uses gestures effectively, and speaks so that he or she can be easily understood.
- The advocate does not use phrases like "I think," "We maintain," or "It is our position that . . . ."
- The advocate is composed and treats the court and opposing counsel with respect.

Glossary of Terms

Active voice. Active voice is the quality of certain verbs in which the subject performs the action of the verb: "Judges decide cases." (Compare with **Passive voice**.)

Analogous case. An analogous case is a case that is factually similar to the client's case. An argument based on an analogous case is an argument in which the attorney compares or contrasts the facts in a factually similar case with the facts in the client's case.

Analysis. When you analyze something, you examine it closely, identifying each part and determining how the parts are related. In law, there are two types of analysis: statutory analysis, which involves the close examination of a statute, regulation or rule and case analysis, which involves the close examination of a case. (Compare with **Synthesis**.)

Background fact. A background fact, while not necessary to decide the legal issue, is a fact that helps put the legally significant facts in context. (Compare with **Emotionally significant fact** and **Legally significant fact**.)

Case briefing. Case briefing is a technique used to analyze a court's written opinion. A case brief usually contains a summary of the facts, a statement of the issue(s), the court's holding, and the court's reasoning.

Case law. Although the term "case law" is often used to refer to common law, in fact its meaning is broader. It refers to all court decisions including those interpreting or applying enacted law.

Chronological organization. A writer using chronological organization for the facts in a brief sets the facts out in the order in which the related events occurred. (Compare with **Topical organization**.)

Citation (also **Cite**). A citation is a reference to a legal authority. Because different courts use different citation systems, always check the court rules to see which citation system is used by the court to which you are submitting your brief.

Cite checking. Cite checking is the process used to determine the current status of an authority and to locate sources that have cited that authority. The two most common systems for cite checking an authority are *Shepard's®,* which is available both in print and on Lexis, and KeyCite, an online service available on Westlaw.

Common law. The common law is a system of law created by the judicial branch. For example, much of tort law is common law: the causes of action and rules were created by the courts rather than by the legislature.

Concluding sentence. A concluding sentence in a paragraph is the sentence that sums up the main point of the paragraph. Although not every paragraph will have a concluding sentence, in those that do the concluding sentence is invariably the last sentence in the paragraph.

Confirmation bias. Confirmation bias is the tendency to process information by looking for information that reinforces one's existing beliefs.

Connotation. The connotation of a word is all the associations the word carries with it. For example, the word "lawyer" may have positive connotations for individuals who respect lawyers or who aspire to be lawyers, but it may have negative connotations for people who have had bad experiences with lawyers. (Compare with **Denotation**.)

Denotation. The denotation of a word is its dictionary definition. (Compare with **Connotation**.)

Dicta. Comments made by a court that are not directly related to the issue before it or that are not necessary to its holding are dicta. Such comments are often preceded by the word "if." For example, "If the evidence had established. . . ." Although in some cases dicta are easily identifiable, in other cases they may not be. If the issue is broadly defined, the statement may be part of the court's holding; if the issue is narrowly defined, the statement is dicta. (Compare with **Holding**.)

Dovetailing. Dovetailing is the overlap of language between two sentences that creates a bridge between those two sentences. Dovetails are often created by moving the connecting idea to the end of the first sentence and the beginning of the second sentence, repeating key words, using pronouns to refer back to nouns in an earlier sentence, and using "hook words" ("this," "that," "these," "such") and a summarizing noun. (Compare with **Substantive transitions**.)

Elements analysis. When you do an elements analysis, you systematically analyze a set of requirements set out either in a statute or as part of a common law doctrine by determining whether, given a particular set of facts, each requirement is met.

Emotionally significant fact. An emotionally significant fact is a fact that, while not necessary to decide the legal issue, may have an emotional impact. For example, emotionally significant facts may lead a jury to feel more favorably towards a plaintiff or a defendant. (Compare with **Background fact** and **Legally significant fact**.)

Ethos. Ethos refers to the reputation or character of the speaker or writer.

Finding. A finding is a decision on a question of fact. For example, a jury may find that the defendant was driving over the speed limit or trial court judge may find that a police officer read the defendant his Miranda rights. (Compare with **Holding**.)

Gender-neutral language. Gender-neutral language is language that treats males and females as having equal value. It does not assume being male is the norm or that certain jobs or positions are primarily filled by males or females.

Generic transitions. Generic transitions are those transitions that are commonly used in writing to describe standard mental moves, such as "consequently" to show cause/effect or "however" to show contrast. (Compare with **Dovetailing** and **Substantive transitions**.)

Harmless error. An error is harmless when an appellate court determines that an error occurred at trial but the error does not require reversal because the outcome would likely have been the same absent the error. The test the court applies in deciding if reversal is required turns on whether the error was a constitutional or a nonconstitutional error. (Compare with **Reversible error**.)

Headnote. A headnote is a one-sentence summary of a rule of law and is found at the beginning of a court's opinion. Because headnotes are written by an attorney employed by the company publishing the reporter in which the opinion appears and not the court, they cannot be cited as authority.

Holding. A holding is the court's decision in a particular case—often stated as follows: "When the court applied the rule to the facts of the case, it held that. . . ." Thus a holding has two components: a reference to the applicable rule of law and a reference to the specific facts to which that rule was applied. Because the holding is the answer to the legal question, it can be formulated by turning the issue (a question) into a statement. (Compare with **Dicta**.)

Kairos. Kairos refers to the making an argument at an opportune time.

Legalese. Legalese is a broad term used to describe several common features of legal writing such as the use of archaic language, Latin terms, boilerplate language, and long and convoluted sentences. "Legalese" is usually a pejorative term.

Legally significant fact. A legally significant fact is a fact that a court would consider to be significant, either in deciding that a statute or rule is applicable or in applying that statute or rule. (Compare with **Background fact** and **Emotionally significant fact**.)

Legislative intent. Legislative intent is what a legislative body intended when it enacted a particular statute. Attorneys and courts use legislative histories to determine what a state legislature or Congress intended in enacting a statute. In addition, some statutes include a purpose section, which sets out the underlying purpose of the statute.

Logos. Logos is an appeal to logic.

Main clause. A clause is a group of related words that has both a subject and a verb. A main clause is a clause that can stand alone as a sentence. (Compare with **Subordinate clause**.)

Mandatory authority. Mandatory authority is law that a court must apply in deciding the case before it.

Metaphor. Metaphor is figurative language that creates a comparison. For example, a journey is often a metaphor for life.

Negativity bias. Studies indicate that our brains are more apt to process, and retain, negative information as opposed to positive information.

Nominalization. Nominalization is the process of converting verbs into nouns (determine → determination).

Orienting transitions. Orienting transitions are transitions that provide a context for the information that follows. They locate the reader physically, logically, or chronologically. (Compare with **Generic transitions** and **Substantive transitions**.)

Paragraph block. A paragraph block is a group of two or more paragraphs that together develop a point within a larger document.

Paragraph coherence. A paragraph has coherence when the various points raised in the paragraph are connected to each other. Common connecting devices include repetition of key words, transitional phrases, parallelism, and pronouns.

Paragraph unity. A paragraph has unity when all the points raised in the paragraph are related to one larger point, the paragraph's topic.

Parallel citation. A parallel citation is a citation to another source that contains a copy of a case. Many state decisions are published in a state reporter as well as a regional reporter. The two citations for the same case are considered "parallel." Some decisions (such as those of the United States Supreme Court) have more than one parallel citation. Other decisions have no parallel citation.

Parallel construction. Parallel construction is the use of the same part of speech or similar grammatical structures in a pair or series of related words, phrases, or clauses. In other words, a noun is matched to a noun, a verb is matched to a verb, a phrase to a phrase, etc. Parallel construction is also required with correlative conjunctions such as *either/or, neither/nor,* and *not only/but also.*

Parenthetical case description. A parenthetical case description can be used when a full description of the case is not required—for example, when the case is being used to illustrate a specific point, or when one or two cases have already been described in full in the text and the writer simply wants to alert the reader to additional case law.

Passive voice. Passive voice is the quality of certain verbs in which the subject receives, rather than performs, the action of the verb: for example, "Cases are decided by judges." (Compare with **Active voice**.)

Pathos. Pathos is an appeal to emotion.

Persuasive authority. Persuasive authority is law or commentary that a court may consider in deciding the case before it.

Plain language. Plain language is the term used to describe a movement to encourage the use of simple, straightforward language in specialized professions (such as law) so that written documents are readily understandable by lay people.

Policy argument. A policy argument is one in which the attorney argues that a particular interpretation of a constitutional provision, statute, regulation, or common law rule is (or is not) consistent with current public policy—that is, the objective underlying a particular law. For example, child custody laws usually seek to provide stability for children; environmental laws seek to balance the interest of developers and preservationists.

Primary authority. A primary authority is a source that sets out the law. Sources of primary authority include codes and reporters. (Compare with **Secondary authority**.)

Priming. Priming is a technique in which the introduction of one piece of information influences how an individual perceives or processes subsequent pieces of information.

Published case. A published case is a case that the court determines is part of the legal precedent in a jurisdiction. While the highest court in each jurisdiction publishes all of its opinions, intermediate courts of appeal (and district courts in the federal system) look to specified criteria to determine whether a case should be published based on whether it adds to the body of law.

Purple prose. Purple prose is the overuse of flowery language that draws attention to itself.

Raise and dismiss. You can raise and dismiss issues, elements, and arguments. Because both sides will agree on the point, extensive analysis is not necessary.

Record. An appeal is based on the record created in the trial court. The record generally consists of documents filed, exhibits admitted, and transcripts of testimony.

Reversible error. Reversible error occurs when an appellate court determines that an error occurred at trial and the error affected the outcome of the trial. The test the court applies in deciding if reversal is required turns on whether the error was a constitutional error or a nonconstitutional error. (Compare with **Harmless error**.)

Rhetoric: Rhetoric is the art of persuasion.

Roadmap. Roadmaps are introductory paragraphs that give readers an overview of an entire document or a section of a document.

Rule. The rule is the legal standard that the court applies in deciding the issue before it. In some cases, the rule will be enacted law (a constitutional provision, statute, or regulation); in other cases, it will be a court rule (for example, one of the Federal Rules of Civil Procedure); and in still other cases, it will be a common law rule or doctrine. Although in the latter case the rule may be announced in the context of a particular case, rules are not case-specific. They are the general standards that are applied in all cases. (Compare with **Test**.)

Secondary authority. A secondary authority is a source that describes or comments on the law. Sources of secondary authority include treatises, law review articles, legal encyclopedias, and restatements. Secondary authority never has binding effect, but it can be used as persuasive authority based on its reasoning or the eminence of its author. (Compare with **Primary authority**.)

Shepardizing. Shepardizing is the process used to determine the current status of an authority and to locate sources that have cited that authority. For example, an attorney would *Shepardize* a court's opinion to determine whether it had been reversed, overruled, questioned, or followed and to locate other, more recent authorities that have cited the case as authority.

Signposts. Signposts are words and phrases that keep readers oriented as they move through a document. Transitional phrases, particularly ones like "first," "second," and "third," are the most common signposts. Topic sentences can also be considered a type of signpost.

Standard of review. Standard of review refers to the level of scrutiny an appellate court will use to review a trial court's decision. For example, in *de novo* review the appellate court does not give any deference to the decision of the trial court; it decides the issue independently. In contrast, when the standard of review is abuse of discretion, the appellate court defers to the trial court, reversing its decision only when there is no evidence to support it or the decision is manifestly unreasonable.

Subordinate clause. A clause is a group of related words that has both a subject and a verb. A subordinate clause cannot stand alone as a sentence because it is introduced by a subordinating conjunction (for example, "although") or relative pronoun (for example, "which"). (Compare with **Main clause**.)

Substantive transitions. Substantive transitions are connecting words and phrases that also add content. Unlike generic transitions, which signal standard mental moves, substantive transitions tend to be document-specific. (Compare with **Dovetailing** and **Generic transition**.)

Syllogism. A syllogism is a logical deduction from two premises.

Synthesis. When you synthesize, you bring the pieces together into a coherent whole. For example, when you synthesize a series of cases, you identify the unifying principle or principles. (Compare with **Analysis**.)

Term of art. Although sometimes used to describe any word or phrase that has a "legal ring" to it, term of art means a technical word or phrase with a specific meaning. For example, "negligence" and "mens rea" are terms of art.

Test. Although the words "rule" and "test" are sometimes used interchangeably, they are not the same. A test is used to determine whether a rule has been met. (Compare with **Rule**.)

Theory of the case. The theory of the case is the "theme" created for the case. A good theory of the case appeals both to the head and to the heart; it combines the law and the facts in a way that is legally sound and that produces a result the court sees as just.

Topic sentence. A topic sentence is the sentence in a paragraph that introduces the key point in the paragraph or that states the topic of the paragraph. Topic sentences are often the first sentence in a paragraph.

Topical organization. A writer using topical organization groups facts by topics. Topical organization generally works best when there are a number of facts not related by dates (for example, the description of several pieces of property), or a number of related events that occurred during the same time period (for example, four unrelated crimes committed by the same defendant over the same time period). (Compare with **Chronological organization**.)

Unpublished case. An unpublished case is a case filed for public record that the issuing court has determined has no precedential value. An unpublished case decides the issue for the parties involved, but does not become part of the body of law in a jurisdiction. While the opinions in unpublished cases are not included in reporters, they are often available on electronic databases. Some jurisdictions prohibit citations to unpublished cases.

Voice. Voice is the active or passive quality of a transitive verb.

Index

Abstract of the record, 144–145
Active voice, 34, 183–184
Addressing the court in oral
    argument, 291
"Airtime"
    appellate brief, 171, 176–177, 182,
      197, 214, 221, 222
    motion brief, 28, 30–31, 33, 61, 66,
      67–68
American Bar Association (ABA)
    Model Rules of Professional Conduct,
      12–13
    Standing Committee on Ethics and
      Professional Responsibility, 13
Anadiplosis, 6
Anaphora, 6
Antistrophe, 6–7
Antithesis, 5
Appeal as of right, 122, 123
Appellate briefs, 119–283. *See also*
      Argument in appellate brief
    appellant's sample brief, 236–263
    appellate review, 122–123
    appellee's sample brief, 264–283
    appendix, 232
    argument, 201–229
    argumentative headings, 191–199
    assignments of error, 131, 190
    audience, 127–128
    common problems in, 225–228
    conclusion, 231–232
    content of brief, federal rule on, 190–191
    court rules governing, 121, 129–133
    cover, 157
    editing, 233
    ends-means analysis, 147–150
    facts, use of, 163–164, 169–170
    format of, 129–133
    issues (questions presented), 159–165
    jurisdictional statement, 158–159

notice for discretionary review, 123
notice of appeal, 123
number of issues and headings,
    153–154
ordering issues and arguments,
    154–155
organizational scheme, 153–155
organizing the argument, 154–155
prayer for relief, 231–232
preparing to write, 138–146
proofreading, 233
purpose, 128–129
questions presented, 153–155
quotations, 220–222
record on appeal, 124–125, 145
researching issues on appeal, 146
responding to other side's argument,
    222–225
reviewing record for error, 138–139
revising, editing, and
    proofreading, 233
sample briefs, 235–283
scope of review, 124
selecting and ordering arguments,
    153–155
selecting issues on appeal, 139–144
signature, 232
statement of the case, 167–187. *See
    also* Statement of facts in
    appellate brief
statement of the issues, 159–165
subheadings, 153, 154
summary of the argument, 189–191
supplemental, 289
table of authorities, 158
table of contents, 157–158
taking copy to oral argument, 290
theory of the case, 150–153
types of, 125
types of appellate review, 122–123

Appellate review, 122–123
Appendix in appellate brief, 232
"Applied legal storytelling," 8–9
Argumentative headings
    checklist, 52–53
    conventional formats, 198–199
    functions, 47–48, 191–192
    length and readability of, 50–51,
        196–197
    number, placement, and typefaces,
        51–52
    persuasive techniques, 49–50,
        185–187, 191–198
    placement, 51
    positive assertion, 49, 192–193
    readability, 50–51, 196–197
    specificity, 195
    subheadings, 51–52, 198
    support for assertions, 194–195
    typefaces, 51–52
Argument in appellate brief, 201–229
    cases, presentation of, 210–217
    checklist, 69–70
    common problems, 225–228
    constructing and presenting
        arguments, 217–220
    example, 247–261, 272–283
    organizational scheme, 202–207
    persuasive techniques. *See* Persuasive
        writing and techniques
    preparation for writing, 201
    presenting arguments, 217–220
    presenting cases, 210–217
    presenting rules, 207–209
    quotations, use of, 220–222
    responding to other side's argument,
        222–225
    rules, presentation of, 207–209
Argument in motion brief, 53–68
    airtime, 67–68
    assertions and support for assertions,
        54–56
    cases, presentation of, 64–65
    checklist, 69–70
    deductive reasoning, 56–57
    example in defendant's brief, 80–87,
        102–107
    example in prosecutor's brief, 90–97,
        113–117
    inductive reasoning, 56–58
    language to use and to avoid, 68
    organizational scheme, 56–60
    persuasive techniques. *See* Persuasive
        writing and techniques

    presentation of arguments, 66–68
    presentation of cases, 64–65
    presentation of rules, 60–64
    reasoning, types of, 56–57
    rules, presentation of, 60–64
Aristotle, 4–5, 7
Art of advocacy, 1–14, 54
Assertions, 54–56, 192–195
Assignments of error in appellate brief,
    131, 190
Audience considerations, 17–18,
    127–128, 287–288

Background facts, 26, 170
Ball, David, 8
Bench memo, 128
Bias, 9–14
    confirmation, 10
    ethics of using implicit biases to
        support position, 12–14
    explicit, 11
    gender, 11
    implicit, 11, 12–14
    of judges, 11–12
    negativity, 9–10
    racial, 11–12
Briefs. *See* Appellate briefs; Motion briefs
Burden of proof, 61, 63, 161, 164,
    207–208

Canons of rhetoric from the Romans, 7
Cases, persuasive presentation of, 55–56,
    64–65, 210–217
Checklists
    argumentative headings in briefs,
        52–53
    argument section in briefs, 69–70
    issue statements, 43–44
    oral argument, 302–304
    statement of facts, 36–37
Chestek, Kenneth D., 9–10
Cicero, 7
Conclusion in appellate brief,
        231–232
    example, 262, 283
Connotation, 14, 27, 35, 68, 184–185,
        214, 299. *See also* Word choice
Constructing arguments, 53–56
"Court," capitalization of, 24
Courtroom procedures and etiquette for
        oral argument, 290–291
Court rules. *See also* Local rules of court
    governing appellate briefs, 121,
        129–133, 190–191

Deductive reasoning, 56–57
Denotation, 14, 27, 35, 68, 185, 214, 299.
    See also Word choice
Dependent clauses, 34, 182–184, 209,
    216, 217
Detail, effective use of in persuasive
    writing, 31–32, 177–179
Determining issues on appeal, 139–144
    abstract of the record, 144–145
    harmless error, 140, 143–1144
    preserving errors, 140–141
    reviewing the record, 139–144
    standard of review, 140, 141–142
Discretionary review, 122
Dovetailing, 6, 192
Dress, appropriate for oral argument, 291

Electronic filing, 23
Emotionally significant facts, 26–27,
    169–170
Emphasis, positions of, 32–33, 179–181
Ends-means analysis, 147–150
Enthymeme, 5
Error
    constitutional, 143–144
    determining presence of, 140
    harmless, 143–144
    nonconstitutional, 143
    preservation of, 140–141
    reviewing record for, 138–139
    selecting issues on appeal, 139–144
    standard of review, 141–142
Ethics
    disclosure of controlling cases, 222
    implicit biases used to support
        position, 12–14
    zealous representation, 12–13
Ethos, 4–5, 27
Explicit bias, 11. *See also* Bias

Facts. *See* Statement of facts in appellate
    brief; Statement of facts in
    motion brief
Findings of fact, 142, 145, 169, 217
Frivolous appeals, 140

Gender bias, 11. *See also* Bias
The Greeks and rhetoric, history of, 4–7
    anadiplosis, 6
    anaphora, 6
    antistrophe, 6–7
    antithesis, 5
    Aristotle, 4–5, 7
    enthymeme, 5

    ethos, 4–5
    kairos, 5
    logos, 4–5
    "modes for persuasion," 4–5
    pathos, 4–5
    Plato, 4
    Protagoras, 4
    "rhetorical appeals," 4–5
    Sophists, 4–5
    syllogism, 5
Gorgias, 3

Harmless error, 143–144
Humanists, 8

Implicit Association Test (IAT), 11
Implicit bias, 11, 12–14
Inductive reasoning, 56–58
Introductory section/paragraph
    in appellate brief, 190, 203. *See also*
        Summary of the argument
    in motion brief, 23–24
Issues on appeal, 124, 139–144, 146
Issue statements in briefs
    checklist, 43–44
    example in defendant's brief, 80,
        101–102
    example in prosecutor's brief, 90, 112
    format of, 40–41, 160–161
    lens through which judge views case,
        39–40
    ordering issues and arguments, 44–45
    persuasiveness of, 41–43

Jurisdictional statement, 131, 158–159
    example, 241, 267

Kairos, 5

Legally significant facts, 26, 27, 169
Legal storytelling, 8–9
Local rules of court, 18, 23, 51, 73–74,
    121, 125, 131, 165, 232
Logos, 4–5, 22
"Logos brief," 9

Middle Ages, rhetoric during, 7
Model Rules of Professional Conduct,
    12–13
Modes for persuasion, 4–5
Motion briefs, 1
    argumentative headings, 47–52
    arguments, 53–70
    audience, 17–18

Motion briefs (*continued*)
    caption, 23
    conventions, 18
    defendant's brief in support of motion
        for partial summary judgment
        (sample), 98–107
    defendant's brief in support of motion
        to suppress (sample), 75–87
    introductory paragraph, 23–24
    issue statements, 39–44
    ordering the issues and arguments,
        44–45, 56–60
    plaintiff's brief in opposition to motion
        for partial summary judgment
        (sample), 108–118
    prayer for relief, 24, 71–72
    preliminary statement, 23–24
    purpose, 18
    sample briefs, 73–118
    signing the brief, 72
    statement of facts, 25–37
    state's brief in opposition to motion to
        suppress (sample), 88–97
    theory of the case, 21–23

Nance, Jason P., 11
Narrative, 8–9, 26
Negativity bias, 9–10
Notice for discretionary review, 123, 124
Notice of appeal, 123, 124

Oral argument, 285–304
    answering questions, 295–296,
        300–301
    argument, 294–295
    audience, 287–288
    canons from early Romans, 7
    checklist, 302–304
    closing, 296
    concessions, 301
    correcting opposing counsel, 299–300
    correcting your own mistake, 300
    courtroom procedures and etiquette,
        290–291
    deciding what to argue, 288
    delivery, 297–299, 304
    dress, 291
    elements of, 292, 302–304
    excess time, 300
    eye contact, 298
    facts, summary of, 293–294
    gestures, 298
    introductions, 292
    notes, organization of, 290

    opening, 292
    organizing materials, 290
    outline of, 289, 290
    persuasiveness, 299
    posture, 298
    practicing, 289
    preparation for, 288–290, 302
    problems, 299–301
    purpose, 288
    rebuttal, 292, 297
    references to the record, 290, 294
    running out of time, 300
    seating, 290
    statement of issues, 293
Outline of oral argument, 289, 290

Parties
    terms to refer to parties to appeals,
        123, 165
    using personal names of, 35
Passive voice, 34, 183–184
Pathos, 4–5, 22
Personal names, use of, 35
Persuasive writing and techniques
    active and passive voice, 34,
        183–184
    airtime, 30–31, 67–68, 176–177,
        197, 214
    anadiplosis, 6
    anaphora, 6
    antistrophe, 6–7
    antithesis, 5
    arguments, presentation of, 66–68,
        217–220
    cases, presentation of, 55–56, 64–65,
        210–217
    checklist, 36–37
    confirmation bias, 10
    context, creating, 171–172
    dependent and main clauses, 34
    detail, 31–32, 177–179
    enthymeme, 5
    favorable context, creation of, 28–29,
        171–172
    identifying persuasive techniques,
        186–187
    negativity bias, 9–10
    organizational scheme, 56–60, 170
    point of view, 29–30, 174–175
    positions of emphasis, 32–33, 45, 68,
        179–181, 183, 197, 214,
        294, 299
    positive assertions and support,
        192–195

presenting arguments, 66–68,
    217–220
presenting cases, 55–56, 64–65,
    210–217
presenting rules, 60–64, 207–210
priming, 9, 14, 23, 27, 28, 169, 171,
    172, 190
readability, 50–51, 165, 196–197
rules, presentation of, 60–64, 207–210
sentence construction, 34, 165
sentence length, 33, 181–182
specificity, 195
storytelling, 8–9
syllogism, 5
word choice, 27, 35–36, 64, 68,
    161–163, 184–185, 214
Plato, 3, 4
Point of view, 27, 29–30, 174–175,
    197, 294
Positions of emphasis, 32–33, 45, 68,
    179–181, 183, 197, 214,
    294, 299
Prayer for relief
    appellate brief, 231–232
    example in defendant's brief, 87, 107
    example in prosecutor's brief, 97, 118
    motion brief, 24, 71–72, 87, 97,
        107, 118
Prehearing memo, 128
Priming, 9, 14, 23, 27, 28, 169, 171,
    172, 190
Protagoras, 4
Public policy as support, 55–56, 219

Quotations in appellate brief, 179–180,
    220–222, 295

Rachlinski, Jeffrey J., 11
Racial bias, 11–12
Rebuttal in oral argument, 292, 297
Record on appeal, 124–125, 145,
    290, 294
References to the record
    in appellate briefs, 174
    in oral argument, 290, 294
Renaissance, rhetoric during, 8
Researching issues on appeal, 146
Reviewing the record for error, 138–139
Rhetoric, 3–14
    anadiplosis, 6
    antistrophe, 6
    antithesis, 5
    arrangement, 7
    bias, 3, 9–14

canons from the Romans, 7
confirmation bias, 10
defined, 3
delivery, 7
enthymeme, 5
ethics of using implicit biases to
    support position, 12–14
gender bias, 11
Greek, 4–7. *See also* The Greeks and
    rhetoric, history of
history of study of, 4–8
invention, 7
Middle Ages, 7
memory, 7
modern use of, 8–12
narrative, 8–9
negativity bias, 9–10
"pagan art of rhetoric," 7
priming, 9, 10, 14
racial bias, 11–12
Renaissance, 8
The Romans, 7. *See also* The Romans
    and rhetoric, history of
storytelling, 8–9, 14, 25
style, 7
syllogism, 5
Rhetorical appeals, 4–5
The Romans and rhetoric, history of, 7
    arrangement, 7
    canons, 7
    Cicero, 7
    delivery, 7
    invention, 7
    memory, 7
    oral arguments, 7
    Quintilian, 7
    style, 7

Sample briefs
    appellate briefs, 235–283
    motion briefs, 73–118
Science of advocacy, 1–14, 54
Scope of review, 124
Seating at oral argument, 290
Sentences
    active and passive voice, 34,
        183–184
    persuasive writing, 33–34, 165,
        181–182
Signing the brief, 72, 232
    example, 87, 97, 107, 118, 262, 283
Sophists, 4–5
St. Augustine, 7
Stanchi, Kathryn M., 9

Standard of review, 128, 140, 141–142, 164, 203
  abuse of discretion, 129, 141
  clear error, 142
  de novo, 128, 141, 144
  substantial evidence, 141–142
Statement of facts in appellate brief, 167–187
  active and passive voice, 183–184
  airtime, 176–177
  background facts, 170
  detail, 177–179
  drafting the statement, 169–186
  emotionally significant facts, 169–170
  emphasis, 176–184
  example, 242–246, 267–271
  favorable context, 171–174
  legally significant facts, 169
  organizational scheme, 170
  paragraph length, 181–182
  passive voice, 183–184
  persuasive writing, 171–187
  point of view, 174–175
  positions of emphasis, 179–181
  priming, 169, 171, 172, 190
  procedural history, 168
  references to the record, 174
  rules governing, 167–168
  selection of facts, 169–170
  selection of organizational scheme, 170
  sentence and paragraph length, 181–182
  sentence construction, 182–183
  storytelling, use of, 9, 174–175
  subtle persuasion, 185–186
  word choice, 184–185
Statement of facts in motion brief, 25–37
  active and passive voice, 34
  airtime, 30–31
  background facts, 26
  checklist, 36–37
  dependent and main clauses, 34
  detail, 31–32
  emotionally significant facts, 26–27
  example in defendant's brief, 76–79, 99–101
  example in prosecutor's brief, 88–90, 109–112
  favorable context, creation of, 28–29
  legally significant facts, 26
  organizational scheme, 27
  point of view, 29–30
  positions of emphasis, 32–33

  selecting organizational scheme, 27
  selecting the facts, 26–27
  sentence length, 33
  storytelling, use of, 9, 25
  word choice, 35–36
Statement of issues in appellate brief, 159–165
  drafting the statement, 159–160
  example, 241, 267
  format, selection of, 160–161
  at oral argument, 293
  persuasiveness, 161–165
  readability, 165
  sentence construction, 165
  word choice, 161–163
Statement of the case, 167–187, 190
  drafting the statement, 168
  example, 242, 267
"Story brief," 9
Storytelling, 8–9, 14
Subheadings
  appellate brief, 153, 154, 192–194, 196–199
  motion brief, 27, 48–49, 51–52, 57
  typefaces, 193
Summary of argument in appellate brief, 189–191
  example, 246–247, 271–272
  length, 190
Supplemental briefs, 289
Syllogism, 5

Table of authorities for appellate brief, 158
  example, 239–240, 166
Table of contents for appellate brief, 157–158
  example, 237–238, 265
Theory of the case,
  appellate brief, 150–153, 159–160, 161, 163–164, 176, 206, 208
  motion brief, 21–23, 27–28, 30
  storytelling, 9
Time limits for filing notice of appeal, 123
Trial briefs. *See* Motion briefs

Venter, Christine M., 10

Word choice, 27, 35–36, 64, 68, 161–163, 184–185, 214
Writ of certiorari, 122–124

Zealous advocacy, 12–13